P9-ELT-264

# PARENTS AFTER THIRTY

Books by Murray M. Kappelman and Paul R. Ackerman

BETWEEN PARENT AND SCHOOL
SIGNALS: What Your Child Is Really Telling You
PARENTS AFTER THIRTY


Books by Murray M. Kappelman

The Child Healers (novel)
What Your Child Is All About
Raising the Only Child
Sex and the American Teenager

MURRAY M. KAPPELMAN M.D.
PAUL R. ACKERMAN PH.D.

# PARENTS AFTER THIRTY

*A Guide to
Making the Right Decision,
Having a Healthy Pregnancy,
and Normal Baby, and
Raising a Well-Adjusted Child
When You Are Over
Thirty Years Old*

Rawson, Wade Publishers, Inc.
New York

Copyright © 1980 by Murray M. Kappelman and
Paul R. Ackerman

All rights reserved.

Library of Congress Cataloging in Publication Data
Kappelman, Murray, 1931–
Parents after thirty.

Bibliography: p.
Includes index.
1. Parenting—United States. 2. Pregnancy in middle
age. 3. Childbirth in middle age. I. Ackerman,
Paul R., 1934–      joint author. II. Title.
HQ755.8.K357      649'.1      80-5485
ISBN 0-89256-748-3

Published simultaneously in Canada by McClelland
and Stewart, Ltd.

Composition by American–Stratford Graphic Services
Brattleboro, Vermont

Printed and bound by Fairfield Graphics
Fairfield, Pennsylvania

Designed by Francesca Belanger

First Edition

*To James Wade, an editor and friend
who continues to believe in what we believe.*

Grateful acknowledgment is made to M. Gregory Tompkins, Jr., M.D., and to Harper & Row, Publishers, Inc., for permission to reprint a chart (Incidence of Selected Major Birth Defects by Maternal Age) from "Maternal Mortality in Remote Areas" in *Clinical Obstetrics and Gynecology* (1963), 6(4): 910; and to the Center for Disease Control, Public Health Service, Department of Health, Education, and Welfare, for permission to reprint a chart (Comparative Decline in Maternal Death Rate at Each Age). The authors would also like to thank Dr. Philip Goldstein, Chief of Obstetrics and Gynecology, Sinai Hospital of Baltimore, Maryland, for his assistance in researching Chapter 5.

# Contents

Introduction: The After-Thirty Parent: Who Are You
and Why Are You?                                      3

## I. *Preparation*

Chapter 1:  Making the Decision: A Readiness Profile
            for the After-Thirty Parent                9
Chapter 2:  The Decision Is Made: Preparing for Par-
            enthood After Thirty                      30
Chapter 3:  Adoption and the After-Thirty Parent      49
Chapter 4:  Will My Baby Be Normal?                   60
Chapter 5:  Nurturing Your Body and Your Baby
            Through the Pregnancy                      81
Chapter 6:  How Many and How Far Apart?               99

## II. *Changing Lifestyles*

Chapter 7:  The Two-Career Family                     115
Chapter 8:  The Male Dilemma: What Inside Me
            Needs to Change?                           133
Chapter 9:  Being a Woman and a Mother After Thirty   146
Chapter 10: The Economics of After-Thirty Parenthood  159

### III. *Parenting from Birth Through Adolescence*

Chapter 11:   Preventive Parenting                                   173
Chapter 12:   Maintaining Healthy Children                           185
Chapter 13:   What Your Child Is Really Telling You   196
Chapter 14:   The After-Thirty Parent and the Only
              Child                                                  208
Chapter 15:   How Do I Parent Infants and Preschool-
              ers?                                                   225
Chapter 16:   How Do I Raise My School-Age Child?    241
Chapter 17:   Adolescence—Realistic Roles for the Ma-
              ture Parent                                            253
Chapter 18:   Preparing Your Adolescent for Life        265

### IV. *Special Problems of After-Thirty Parents*

Chapter 19:   Parenting Alone After Thirty                    279
Chapter 20:   Previous Families                                    288
Chapter 21:   Separation or Divorce of After-Thirty Par-
              ents                                                   304

### V. *Conclusion*

Chapter 22:   The Advantages and Joys of Mature Par-
              enting                                                 319

# PARENTS AFTER THIRTY

·

# The After-Thirty Parent: Who Are You and Why Are You?

Frightening, isn't it? Or perhaps others have told you it is.

You feel bewildered and confused. Or you don't feel certain about the decision you've made or are about to make.

You are acutely aware that you face a major decision when you consider having a child (or another child) when you are over thirty years of age. Undoubtedly you have heard all the myths and rumors, as well as the facts, that accompany this decision, but you probably have not been able to sort them out in your head. You think you want a baby, but you worry:

"Won't I appear ridiculous as an older mother or father?"

"Will the baby be retarded or have a birth defect?"

"How can I give a teenager the energy he'll demand, if I'm over fifty at the time?"

"Won't a child be embarrassed by having older parents when all his friends' parents are younger?"

"Am I too set in my ways to let a child intrude into my life?"

"How do I keep my friends when I change my life to one that is more child-centered?"

One final and major question: "Am I very different from younger parents because I'm over thirty?"

We think you are—in very positive ways.

   This book will try to answer these and many other questions about being a parent after thirty. The myths will be separated from realities. The options open to you as a parent will be explained, and you can see if they fit your ideals of parenthood. You will see how others carefully reached a mutual decision to become parents after thirty—and solved some concerns similar to yours. In this book you will find that the people in the examples have usually coped with parenting challenges better than their younger counterparts.
   Why? The answer is simple. Maturity.
   As a mature individual you have a chance to plan. You can think through problems and devise solutions; you have been doing that for some time in your work and in your personal life. You also, as a mature individual, know that you do not *have* to have that child. Conceiving a child or carrying a child is *your* choice. If you do become a parent, therefore, you will *want* and thus love that child, which gives the child a better than average chance of success.
   One of your immediate concerns will be whether you will find others of your age and interests who can join your circle of friends when you become an after-thirty parent. You will not have to look too far to find them, because the number of people facing the same situation grows each year. In 1977, for instance, there were 593,301 births to mothers over thirty; one out of every six births occurred to an over-thirty woman; and one out of every three new fathers was over thirty. This number of births to mature parents was 5½ percent greater in 1977 than in 1976. The figure is significant because birth rates have been decreasing steadily since 1970. The first sign of an increasing trend in births occurred in 1977, and was noted specifically in the 30–35-year-old parent group.
   But are after-thirty parents *your* kind of people? How do they compare to you and the way you live? Let us look at what the census has to say about a typical after-thirty parent. (Each of these examples is documented in or interpreted from scientific population reports issued by the National Bureau of the Census.)

   *Chances are that you married later than your parents did. The average age of marriage in 1978 was 24.2 for men and 21.8 for women; this is almost exactly one year later for marriage than in

1970. But these figures do not tell the whole story. If you tally the number of single persons between the ages of twenty and thirty, you discover some startling facts. The number of single persons between twenty and thirty has increased about 10 percent between 1970 and 1977, but the married rate after thirty years is about the same. *This indicates that marriage is being deferred as a growing social trend.* Many hundreds of thousands of people are waiting to a later age to get married and start a family.

*You probably have more education than the average member of the population. Many of you waited to put that task behind you before you started a family. In 1977, the figures show that almost 43 percent of all those new mothers over thirty had more than a high-school education, and 25 percent of them had a minimum of a college degree. The number of advanced college degrees among mature mothers is on the rise. The after-thirty fathers had even more advanced educational credentials. Add wisdom to the potential maturity you can offer a child.

*Both of you are probably working. You waited to start a career. The 1977 data show that the husband is the family's sole earner in only 26 percent of married couple families. In fact, when both spouses are earners, the median age for wives is thirty-seven years of age and for husbands forty. Of these couples, 22 percent have one child and another 21 percent have two children. Only 42 percent have no children.

*You probably live in a metropolitan area—at least that is what the statistics say.

*As a couple, your salaries are comparable, suggesting a mutual concern for career and financial security. One of your motivations for waiting was that you wanted to be able to afford a child.

*You make a substantial family income. Now you can add to your nuclear family without a great deal of personal sacrifice.

*You have seriously considered divorce at some time or another. If you actually went through the process of a previous divorce, you remarried in your early thirties. A new marriage . . . a new child.

This typical picture is, of course, only a statistical composite, not the *real* you or your mate. There is no need to find your counterpart within these numbers, which represent a whole spectrum of people, nor is there a safe haven in merely knowing that you are not very different from other after-thirty potential parents.

What can you learn from these statistics? Literally millions of people have decided to become parents after thirty, people who are well educated, secure, and wise. They have adjusted well to children—so well in fact that many of them have had several children as after-thirty parents. Some of you readers are considering parenthood for the first time; many other after-thirty readers have older children and are now pausing and wondering about the pros and cons of having another as mature people. Children of after-thirty parents thrive because they are wanted and loved; they are not pawns in a marriage. The youngsters are planned and they are needed. Whole patterns of living are altered in order to make room for the new members of the family, but without interrupting careers or life goals.

In other words, this book should show you that you *can* do an excellent job of parenting after thirty, probably even better than when you were younger. And this book should help you determine *how* to be that excellent parent. You have the motivation, the capacity, and the qualities of maturity, wisdom, and forethought. If you have the wish to be a parent, you will find some guidance in making the decision, experiencing the pregnancy, and rearing the child in the following chapters. You *are* different as an after-thirty parent. But read on. Find out how positive that can be!

# I

## *Preparation*

·

# CHAPTER ONE

# Making the Decision:
# A Readiness Profile
# for the After-Thirty Parent

You have made the decision. You want to have a child, to experience the new challenge of motherhood or fatherhood. Not an
easy or simple decision, you have found. However, whether the
thought spontaneously became a conscious desire in your minds
one night or was labored over during weeks of painstaking discussion, you have now arrived at the vital point of saying, "Yes. We
are ready to have a child . . ."; you hesitate to say aloud the rest
of the sentence, so you think it to yourself, ". . . even though
we're over thirty."

Often the decision to have children, particularly among
younger married couples, is far less complex or far reaching in personal significance. Fewer years together have not yet given you the
opportunity to build up the elaborate structure of responsibilities,
activities, and established routines of the after-thirty prospective
parent. Parenting frequently "just happens" to the younger couple. But to the after-thirty couple who have been married awhile
(or delayed marriage for career or personal reasons), the obvious
decision not to have children has been up until this time carefully
acted upon.

Now the moment has arrived to reverse the prevention of
parenthood and look into the future: a future that must be ex-

panded, modified, and reconstructed to accept and nurture a child. But there is a normal worry that keeps surfacing in both of your minds. A nagging doubt that is a healthy, natural response to this life-changing decision: "Even though we are over thirty years of age, are we ready at this point in our lives and in our relationship to have a child?"

In our opinion, you have one major factor going for you even before you consider your individual situations: your ages. Mature people are more likely to make mature decisions, decisions that have been considered, debated, researched, and finally resolved. Though we hate to admit it, we do lose small bits of our previous spontaneity as we grow older each year. This is a plus when it comes to making decisions about having children. Spontaneous parenthood is a very risky business for the child as well as the parents. Far too many young couples leap before they look into parenthood, with tragic results for the kids and the parents. Taking your time . . . resisting the pressures to reproduce, debating the problem repeatedly, possibly even holding off marriage until other important life processes have been settled . . . all of these things make you much better candidates for accurate decision making about your readiness for parenthood.

But maturity, of course, is not enough. Each couple is unique. There are no two mature people who are contemplating bringing a child into this world who carry the exact same baggage—have the same lifestyle or share identical emotional, financial, or social situations. So each couple must look within themselves and their own marriage to find out if their readiness-for-parenting light is glowing green, telling them to GO AHEAD AND HAVE THE CHILD. How do you know that you are ready? This is the key question, and only you can answer it about yourselves. But there are some obvious indicators that do suggest which couples over thirty years old are still not ready for parenting.

Certainly those of you who are contemplating parenthood for the first time will find the need to ascertain your readiness as an essential background to your decision making in this important area. However, those of you who have one or more children born during your twenties may be questioning whether to venture again into parenthood after thirty. Some of the readiness questions may not apply; but most of them are quite pertinent to your personal dilemma. You are very different people today from what you were when you had your earlier family. Take the time to reconsider yourselves through the use of these readiness exercises. You may learn a great deal about your ability to become an after-thirty parent with an already established family.

Try to answer this parenting readiness profile carefully. Consider each statement thoroughly and answer as honestly as you can. Then make your own decisions at the end of the exercise as to whether you are ready for the experience of parenthood. This series of questions is specifically designed for the person over thirty years of age who stands on the threshold of that major decision: to be or not to be a parent.

*Emotional Readiness:*

**1.** I can view myself comfortably in the role of mother or father.
Yes        No

**2.** I am ready to accept the dependency of a small child.
Yes        No

**3.** My emotional being is prepared for the added responsibility.
Yes        No

**4.** There is sufficient emotional room in my busy life for a new person.        Yes        No

**5.** I still have sufficient flexibility to manage child rearing.
Yes        No

**6.** Having a child is another of life's successes and accomplishments.        Yes        No

**7.** This is the time in my relationship with my mate when we need a child.        Yes        No

**8.** Having a child is necessary for a full, complete life.
Yes        No

**9.** An intuitive mothering/fathering instinct will get me through the early years.        Yes        No

**10.** I look toward getting older and being childless as a lonely and frightening time.        Yes        No

Together we will look at these ten crucial emotional factors and discuss each one as you review your personal responses. Analyze carefully the thoughts and feelings that went into that selection of a simple Yes or No answer.

You have reached, by this time of life, the position in both career and personal life where a number of "roles" are being played by you and expected by others. Within your career, you may be moving upward from one role toward another with increasing status and salary, an essential for career success. If you are a professional—doctor, lawyer, dentist, social worker, teacher, etc.— you spend your days performing the tasks expected of the professional role in which you have been trained. The older we become, the more responsibility becomes our role as "son" or "daughter" as our parents age and the dependency shifts in our direction. So it is clear that we become the players of more diverse but also increasingly significant roles when we cross the age marker after thirty.

Before you can comfortably answer Yes to the first, main question above, there are three important preliminary questions that must be looked at.

*First preliminary or subquestion:* Can I perceive myself as a mother? As a father?

This is the crucial subquestion. Some men and women find it perfectly natural and normal not to perceive themselves as mothers or fathers at any time in their lives. There is not the real inclination, desire, temperament, love of children, need, or willingness. The fact is that certain of us do *not* truly want to play the role of parent ever. This is natural, normal, and acceptable in modern society. However, if there is a nagging doubt about this fact, if there is subtle coercion either from spouse, or family, or society for you somewhat reluctantly to play this role, then stop here and say No. You are not ready and never will be. Reluctant parents rear troubled children and exist in chaotic and disrupted marriages. Careers are also affected. There is no gain in assuming a role to please someone else—a role you cannot see yourself fulfilling happily.

However, if you are able to answer Yes to this subquestion, you are ready to move on to the next.

*Second question:* How many other new roles am I trying to assume at the same time?

This is a period in many of your lives when you are faced with the opportunity to move in new directions in both your career and your social life. Are you considering switching jobs to one with a new role and new responsibilities? Are you thinking about going back to school for that advanced degree so you can be more competitive in the job market? Are you about to start practicing your profession? Have illnesses in your parents suddenly created added dimensions to your role as their "child"? There are key times in your lives when you must be available to grab hold of the career opportunities that swing by you only sporadically. This crossroads would not be the most propitious time to consider your first child. And there will be crucial periods in your life where others' needs come to the forefront, especially that of a spouse or parent; again, this is a poor time to add the role of parent to the other serious roles being played out in your life.

If you can count up and assess the roles in your life and find the available emotional time and space for that child you are planning, then move on to the next question.

*Third question:* Do I know what is in store for me when I play that role?

Nothing as serious as parenthood should ever be entered into with a lack of understanding of the meaning of the role about to be assumed. You may object and say, "But we're older, more mature. Of course we know." We must ask: "There are few courses in parenting. Where did you learn? When have you had the time in your busy lives to stop and consider? Are you aware of the day-to-day crises and demands and heartaches that go along with the many joys?" This is not an easy role to play—that of parent. It may be the hardest and most strenuous task in your life, as well as the most rewarding. But that fact is one which you after-thirty parents have already learned—anything worth having always costs. Parenting is exactly that type of transaction. It is essential that you have not dwelled solely on the pleasurable parts of being a mother or father—the cuddling of a cooing infant, the dressing up, the showing off, the companionship, the Little League ball games, the birthday parties, and so on. You should know that there are also many moments that are *not* joyous—not storybook happiness . . . days and weeks of worry and effort and anger that are part of parenting. Are you ready to assume this multifaceted role—a role that combines the bad times with the good?

Most of you probably are. And we can leave the first main question behind us with satisfaction. Now we face the second response you made to the emotional readiness profile, question 2, which asked about your ability to accept a small child's dependency.

You have stated that you are ready to accept the dependency of a small child. Do you know what that means? Both of you, for instance, may have had long, hard hours at work and when you return home, the baby is cranky—maybe ill—and needs your time. Or the baby wakes frequently during the night because he turns over on his back and can't get back on his tummy. Or your three-year-old has a nightmare, your nine-year-old needs help with her homework, your ten-year-old needs rides around the city to go to the library. Or your thirteen-year-old is in the school play and you are expected to attend. All of these things happen, and they will happen to you. The child will not sympathize with your long, hard day. *You* are depended upon to be ready and willing to be a parent in each of these situations. We are not trying to paint a bleak or frightening picture of parenthood, but merely attempting to point out that a child's continuing dependency requires an emotional adjustment from all parents. For you, who are prospective parents over thirty years of age, this emotional adjustment could be more difficult. Why? Because many more people may also be dependent on you in your daily professional existence, draining some of your emotional reserves. And in your private life, your marital relationship is one of mutual sharing and dependency that can shift as the balance of need changes. But your child cannot shift. His or her dependency is complete, and it is largely directed unquestioningly at you.

If you are prepared for this dependency, if you can give it a special, loving perspective and can make room in your emotional life for a tiny hand clinging tightly to yours in ultimate trust, then you have accurately answered Yes to the second main question in the emotional readiness profile.

As you consider your response to the third question about your own emotional readiness for the responsibility of an infant in your life, remember that there cannot be parenting without the assumption of responsibility. Responsibility comes in different forms, as does the style of parenting. But you cannot absolve yourself completely from the issue of responsibility. You can get all of the outside support help (nurses, maids, day care centers) but none of these external persons or groups can ever replace you in your responsible role as parent. We are not overly concerned about the quantity of time you have to spend with your child. Working parents can be dynamically effectvie as child rearers. We are extremely interested, however, in the *quality* of time that you are able to share with your child. The prime responsibility of after-thirties parents who have reached the stage of additional responsibilities in careers, education, or social life is their willingness to give "quality time" to the child on a regular basis. What is "quality time"? We will go into this in greater detail in a subsequent chapter, but a brief description is appropriate here. It means time spent with your child during which your child knows you are there, is aware that you know that he or she is there, is able to communicate and share with you, and has the sense of being the most important person in your life at that very moment. For your child, only five minutes of such experience can be very important.

Are you ready to give that kind of experience to a child? We are certain most of you are more than willing and ready, and have only waited this long so that such "quality time" would be available in your own lives. If we are right, then move on to the fourth readiness question.

In your answer to question 4, you have indicated that there is sufficient emotional room in your busy life for a new person—a child. Are you sure? How much emotional investment have you made in your career? When you have the time to allow your mind to relax—if you relax—what crowds your thoughts? Do you still think about the next move at the job, the people with whom you work, where you want to go next, and what you want to do next in your career? Bringing a child into your emotional life will not get rid of these obsessive thoughts. You must be able to reduce such demands on your consciousness in order to make room for the child—before the child arrives. How much of your emotional time is spent nurturing your marriage? If you realize that a great deal of your daily planning and contemplating is directly related to your spouse and your marriage, then you should seriously consider how a child will significantly cut into the amount of that time. Is there an adequate amount of emotional room in your marriage and in your career for this child? For most of us who have reached the age of thirty or older, there should be . . . in fact there must be. If there is not, you are on a collision course with physical and emotional overwork and illness. No marriage can survive a hot-house intensity of concentration that does not permit anything or anyone else to enter. No life can survive the same career or marriage intensity year after year.

Mental health specialists strongly advise that you readjust your life so that there is enough emotional room within it for new people and new experiences at all times, whether or not your readiness profile comes out in favor of children after thirty.

Thirty is not old; that is obvious. But the ten years between twenty and thirty are vital and creative years, during which you have discovered what works for you and what does not. They are years when certain schedules have been developed that allow you to do most of the important things you have crowded into your busy life. You are beginning to become a highly organized person. This is natural. It comes with age and responsibility, and a mild inflexibility somehow helps us to survive and to succeed.

But now imagine an unpredictable child's effect on that organized lifestyle. All those carefully ordered schedules are disrupted, possibly not continuously but frequently and without any warning beforehand. Do you have the emotional flexibility to manage that kind of chaotic change in your well-run life? Are you depending on the other person in your marriage to make all the adjustments of schedule, time, plans, and career while you continue along your predestined plan undaunted? If this is your vision, forget it. Not only will you have a child who does not know you but you may also lose a mate along the way. When you answer Yes to the question of flexibility readiness, be prepared to share equally in the calendar changes and demands made by a new person in *both* of your lives.

You have looked carefully at the first five questions on the emotional readiness profile scale. For your future child's sake, we hope you have been able to answer Yes honestly to all of the first five. Now how about the final five questions? Check your responses. Here the tide turns, for these are questions that needed negative answers. Let us explain why.

There is no question that having a child is a major step in the overall pattern of one's life. If the child was desired, its birth is the first step on a successful route that leads to the parenting of a happy, well-adjusted adult. But having a child is not like getting a promotion at work or winning second prize at the art show or finally getting that degree. Having a child is the desired extension and expansion of your nuclear family relationship. You and your spouse decided to add parenting to the other positive qualities in your marriage and succeeded in doing this. Sharing in making this decision is your initial area of success and accomplishment at this point. After that, the real job begins—and the successes and accomplishments in parenting are progressively harder to attain. Birth is but the beginning of a continuum of challenges that leads from infancy through adolescence to the adulthood of your child. Then and only then can you honestly measure the quality of your success and accomplishment as a parent.

Children will not bring two drifting people closer together in marriage. Children will not give life to a listless marriage. It is not only unfair but also unhealthy to expect the birth of a child to save a failing marriage. We are not certain that there is ever a time in a couple's relationship when the marriage *needs* the birth of a child. There may well be a point in the marriage when the birth of a wanted child is most timely for many reasons. But if you answered Yes to the fact that your marriage needed a child at this point, it is our advice to ask yourself why? If there are flaws in your relationship, work on these and correct them *before* you decide to bring a child into the family. There are far too many unhappy children of divorce who were conceived as a means of cementing a shaky, disintegrating marriage.

We will not deny that children add a richness to your life that is unique. Each of the authors has children and recognizes the added joy they have brought to our lives. But we are certain that had we chosen not to have children, each of us still could have experienced a full and complete life. You should not bring children into the world to complete some mythical circle or to fill in the missing pieces of your life. If you do, the child will be a constant source of disappointment during those many days when things are not going well and life seems neither full nor complete. Also this is an unnatural burden to place on any child. ("Come into the world and fulfill and complete my life.") We doubt that any child can live up to such grandiose and unrealistic standards. When one reaches thirty and takes stock of the situation, if it is obvious that your career is spinning along satisfactorily, that the marriage is a happy and mutually rewarding one (or that a delayed marriage is working), and that you and your partner are comfortably aware of your roles in society, then there is a natural tendency to ask: "What comes next? What is missing?"

"Why, of course. A child. That will make my life, my marriage complete."

Because parenthood should be a "next step" is a very poor reason to decide to become an after-thirty parent.

The adjustment to this new role of a parent can take an enormous amount of your energy—and commitment. Your relationships with each other will change. Nobody is a "born mother" or a "born father." So many mothers become panicky when the baby is first placed in their arms immediately after birth and no instant lightning flash of maternal instinct courses through their minds and bodies. We learn to love our children as they learn to love us—with growing intensity as the years pass. There are few courses in parenting, but even if there were such preparatory sessions, we could not be programmed to feel such an intense response as mothering or fathering. There is nothing intuitive about the skill of parenting; it is learned through watching, doing, reading, experiencing, living side by side with your child. Do not expect those difficult early years to become easy because some deeply hidden well of parenting skills gushes forth when you have that baby. Don't worry that it is too deep, too dormant, because you have waited too long—until you were over thirty years old to become a parent. Relax! That stored-up parenting intuition was most likely never there and you, like all the rest of us, are going to have to work, struggle, experience, and then slowly realize the skills of parenting. Please don't expect the unknown to get you through the early years of being a mother or father. Be prepared for a whole new life full of some of the most fascinating lessons you will ever learn: on how to parent effectively. So be sure to take a realistic view of the future and answer No to the ninth question (the intuition question) on the parenting readiness profile scale.

We are certain that many of us who reach the age of thirty and beyond have begun to consider the fact that we are moving toward middle age. And that middle age is but one quick step before old age. This thought sometimes scares us as we look around at older people and try to imagine ourselves as they appear to be. Few people look forward to growing old. Certainly few people over thirty do when they are at the prime of their social, career, and sexual lives. Having children will not halt the passage of time. Kids will not keep us young. That is a fallacy. There are days when each of us feels ten years older because of something our own children did or said or neglected to do. We snap back, but not into a state of being younger—perhaps with a new wrinkle, or gray hair, or ache. That is not you, just the normal aging process that goes along with being parents. We watched our parents age and our children will do the same with us. They may not accelerate the process but they are certainly not going to delay it either. "Staying young" is neither a valid nor a rational reason to have a child.

You may have an elderly aunt who was childless and who now lives alone. She seems so very lonely. You shudder as you put yourself in her place, imagine yourself without the emotional support of children during your older years. Be careful. There are two major points to remember before you decide to have children after thirty to prevent yourself from being that elderly woman who sits alone in her small apartment. First, are you so very sure that she is lonely and unhappy? We know a number of childless elderly people whose lives are as full and active as they wish them to be, and as full of the people they want to see and have around them as they desire. Secondly, what guarantees do you have that your child will eliminate the loneliness of your twilight years? You have no such assurances. In today's society, many parents and children live continents apart and visit in person only occasionally. The phone lines connect their detached existences.

It is highly unlikely that you have answered Yes to the last question. But even if the thought has run through your mind as a potential reason for becoming a parent after thirty, look at it carefully. You are fooling yourself. And you are giving a long-range responsibility to an unborn child that will be impossible to fulfill.

Now that you have considered the emotional readiness factors for parenting after thirty, you are ready to consider the social factors that also play an important role in your decision-making process. Here are the key statements. Think very carefully about your own innermost thoughts before you answer each one.

*Social Readiness:*

**1.** I am a highly organized person. I will be able to restructure my life so that little social activity will be lost as I make room for my child.       Yes       No

**2.** I plan to fit the baby into many of my social activities.
Yes       No

**3.** Almost all of my over-thirty friends are thinking about having children. This will make my social life more congruent with theirs.
Yes       No

**4.** I realize that I will have to give up some of my social activities. I am ready to do this for my child.       Yes       No

**5.** My spouse and I have had the opportunity to do many things. Now we are ready to do less and be more selective.       Yes       No

**6.** I am accepting of the fact that a significant portion of my social life may be child-oriented for a long period of time.       Yes       No

Read these social readiness statements again very carefully before you analyze your answers. There is a subtle deceptiveness to the areas being questioned. Think through your answers.

*So you are a highly organized person.* Most successful people over thirty years of age are. You very likely have been able to juggle your job, your marriage, your personal friends, and your social life by ordering the priorities in your life. Restructuring your life for one small seven-pound baby seems like child's play for an organizer like you. But wait! Let us introduce you to that new person in your life. That seven pounder is totally and thoroughly *disorganized*; cries as a response to hunger, wet diapers, or loud noises; is completely unpredictable; and will have your organized schedule hanging on the ropes within two days. Well, you say, I'll just wait a few months and then . . . Forget it! That infant is going to grow up into an adorable but equally unpredictable child, who will skitter through the school years and then explode through adolescence carrying you along as a reluctant but dedicated passenger on this developmental roller coaster. The truth is that you will not be able to be the same social being you were before the baby was born. That is a given fact. In no way will your social life fade entirely but it will, by necessity, have to be less predictable and more selective. If for one moment you believe that you can mold the wishes and whims of a new baby into the structure of your present social life, forget it . . . and think twice about your readiness to parent after thirty.

Statement 2 suggests that you can fit the baby into most of your social activities. You can't. Not only is it unfair to the baby and to you, it is also extremely unfair to the other people with whom you are involved. Let us take an extreme. Are you going to take the new baby into the theater with you? Of course not. But do you remember that last movie when a screaming baby annoyed an entire audience, causing the grumbling mob to stare angrily at mother and innocent child? Someone was trying to fit his/her child into a social life. Think about the time when your friend with the two year old dragged him over for the afternoon bridge game or the evening pinochle. The youngster got into everything, including the other people's hair. He was an innocent nuisance, placed in that inevitable position by an unrealistic parent trying to fit him into adult social life. Sometimes this situaton will work with family and a few very close and understanding friends—but usually your child and your sophisticated social life mix like oil and water.

The third statement needs a resounding No. The social pressures to belong to the peer group should be greatest during adolescence and fade rapidly after that. You are over thirty. Doing what everyone else is doing should be part of your past, not your present. At this stage of maturity, you cherish and nourish your individuality. Therefore, having a child so that you can be like all of your other friends or people on the same rung of your career ladder is regressive . . . you are thinking about peers like an adolescent. Social pressures should not be a major reason for considering parenthood after thirty.

If you answered Yes to statement 4, you are moving in a positive direction on your social readiness scale. You will have to give up some of your social activities for your child. This is much harder for you because you are older and more mature; your tastes are more refined. You have more money to explore more things. You have developed rather distinct and pervasive social habits. But there must be a readjustment. You know that. And you have said that you are ready. Yes was an important answer to this question.

Again, a Yes to the fifth statement indicates a sensitivity and perceptivity to the importance of making the decision for parenthood later in life. You have had the freedom to do many things that having children at an earlier age could have hindered or delayed. You recognize the benefits of this deferral of parenthood but also know that, after the arrival of your child, you will have to be more selective in what you do socially so that you can have a private, individual life apart from your child at the same time that you integrate part of your life into your child's existence.

It is not uncommon to hear the over-thirty prospective mother or father exclaim to friends: "I refuse to have my whole life become child-oriented." We agree with this. It is very unhealthy for any parent as well as any child to have the mother's or father's entire life oriented toward the child. However, the hidden message in that statement sometimes is: Not a single aspect of my life will become child-oriented or -dominated. This is impossible. The only way to eliminate a *partial* child orientation from one's social life as a parent is to deprive your own child. Visits to the zoo, watching Little League baseball games, PTA meetings, school plays, taking turns in the under-five play group, even going back and forth to pick up babysitters and having to come home at an hour demanded by the sitter—all these are but a few of the child-oriented aspects of a normal parent's social life. Knowing this, preparing for this, accepting this, especially after many years of total personal social freedom, is essential for honest readiness to have a child after thirty.

People by thirty and beyond have often developed a highly structured network of social persons and activities that has been accumulated, assessed, selected carefully, and set into place within their lives. You are probably both very social beings, on the job and within your social network. Before you make the decision to have a child and, as a result, "unsettle" this social structure, the two of you must sit down and think through these six statements again—very carefully. You owe it to your prospective child and to yourselves.

You are beginning to develop your own after-thirty parenting profile, which fits only you. It is your image, reflected back to you from these questions and discussions. This exercise may be an important step in your own personal decision as to whether it is time, whether you are ready, whether it is wise for you now to become a parent.

Careers are a very common reason to postpone parenthood. In today's difficult world, the availability of good jobs for high school graduates is dwindling. The ordinary college degree guarantees little in the way of a job with prospects of advancement and security. Young people are frequently forced to seek advanced degrees in order to compete in the job market. Often those who find a promising job after a lesser degree will work assiduously for years to prove that they are equal or superior to the more educated competition. What does this mean? It clearly indicates that there is little time or room in such upwardly mobile lives for children. In fact, delayed marriage often comes first in these situations, followed by delayed parenthood. As a result, we are seeing the rising prevalence of after-thirties parents in the two-career marriage.

Career readiness questions, therefore, would be important as part of the decision-making process. These statements should be answered by both husband and wife:

*Career Readiness:*
1. I still have two more years of graduate school, but I'm not getting any younger. I don't want to be an old parent. So we'll try now.      Yes      No
2. We both have very good jobs. But I guess I have to take the time off now even though I'm in high gear; after all, I'm the woman.      Yes      No

**3.** Having a child is almost necessary for the job. All the other men in the office have kids; they are beginning to regard me as irresponsible.     Yes     No
**4.** My job situation is unsteady now; I might move or I might stay. But I can't let my job situation affect my decision to have a child.     Yes     No
**5.** Having a child now won't affect my job performance. How could it?     Yes     No

Loaded questions? Rather obvious meanings? We suspect that they are, but we wonder as you reread them if any of these thoughts have already crossed your minds yet remained unspoken. Look at the statements one at a time and identify the problems within each of them. If you are over thirty and have a career, you are caught somewhere within the web of these simplistic and seemingly obvious pointers. It is important for both husband and wife to answer these questions and share their answers. Some insight into the feelings of the other person about career versus parenthood may emerge from this mutual discussion. These are the unspoken rationalizations that require clarification through open discussion in order to detect any erroneous or dangerous ideas about parenting in couples who are over thirty and deeply involved in their careers.

Whether you are potential mother or father, attempting to have a child during the stressful period of graduate education is not always the wisest decision. It is a rare woman who can handle pregnancy, childbearing, and infant care while also coping with the time and work required to earn a graduate degree. What usually suffers is the education, with the ultimate surrender by the woman of her right to the degree or deferral until much later, which can entail years of resentment. In the future father's case, he may suffer the stress of nurturing his wife during her pregnancy, the potential loss of income during the last months, the sleepless nights with a new baby, the worry over feedings, illnesses, and finances. Put these extracurricular distractions together and they often result in failure for the new father still in school. We have seen this happen repeatedly in graduate education. Sometimes it is wise to wait until the degrees have been conferred. Then start graduation with a new beginning, a new career, and a new baby.

In a two-career family, it is essential for both people to analyze as carefully as possible the best time for the pregnancy. When
the couple is over thirty years of age, both careers are often in
high gear. But they may not be harmonious. The wife's career may
be zooming ahead at one time while the husband's stands still,
awaiting the next opportunity. Then, within a year, the tables may
have turned. It is wisest to wait until a quiet period in a career pattern before planning a pregnancy. There is absolutely no reason to
jeopardize a woman's career accomplishments in order to hurry an
over-thirty pregnancy. One or two years more will not prove a
major problem for a couple who have delayed parenthood for
sensible career reasons.

We would hope that, in today's enlightened society, men and
women do not marry because people in the office are wondering
about their private sex lives. Similarly, it is foolish to consider having a child because it will make the man into a "family man" who
better fits the corporate image. Any business that equates the size
of your family with the quality of your work is not worth your
time and energy as an employee. The "responsibility" of parenthood comes in the careful planning and decision making you are
now doing. Waiting or even deciding to be childless can be far
more responsible than having children before you are emotionally
or financially ready and able to care for them.

It is vital that you *do* let your job situation affect your decision
to become an after-thirty parent. The more stable the job situation, the less tense the pregnancy and the better prepared emotionally and financially you both will be to receive your new baby.
Wait until you can predict some stability in your careers before
you decide to become parents. A new child in an over-thirties
household is sufficiently chaotic and unsettling to the usual routine. Don't add a new job, or a new city, or the sudden crisis of
unemployment to the task of over-thirty parenting. You need a
fair share of both of your energies for adaptation.

Of course, having a child when you are over thirty is going to
affect your job performance in some way. It has to. If you are the
woman, you might well be working during your pregnancy, endur-
ing the queasy first three months and lumbering through those

heavy last three months while trying, at the same time, to maintain the quality of your work. Then there is the time off for childbearing. After you return, there will be calls from the person you
hire to care for your child while you work, calls that interrupt
the normal work flow. Or you may not go back to work right
away. And when you do, it will mean a prolonged period of readjustment. As the potential mother, you must be prepared to
adapt to these personal inconveniences at your place of work. Does
your job permit this? Is there sufficient flexibility? Will your career
suffer at this point from these adaptations? These critical questions
must be admitted to your career readiness profile when contemplating pregnancy.

We'll bet that a lot of the men answered Yes to the fifth
statement. How could their wife's pregnancy and the new baby
affect their job performance? Well, let us tell you how this will
occur from several personal experiences. You are punched in the
ribs at three o'clock in the morning—it is your turn to feed the
baby. Afterwards, you can't fall right back to sleep and the next
morning you walk into work yawning. Melissa is two years old and
she has a cold and fever and develops a tightness in her throat
known as croup. The doctor tells you to take turns steaming her
in the bathroom. Another lost night of sleep. Your wife calls to
tell you that Billy fell down at school and might have broken his
arm. She's taking him to the doctor. You sit at your desk unable
to work, worrying about your son. Today's father is not merely an
onlooker while the mother does the work and the worrying. The
after-thirty father of the 1980s plays a significant role as househusband and housefather. You are thinking about becoming a
father after thirty? Be prepared to stay home on occasion when
your child is ill and your wife has important meetings at her job.
Stand ready to go to school for meetings during the day. Having a
child at this point in your life will certainly affect your job performance. For the most part, it will be for the better. A happy
father makes an ambitious, dedicated employee. But there will be
times when your child comes before your job. Consider this carefully before you make the decision whether or not you should become a father after thirty.

Finally, we urge you to take a very hard look at your finances.

The economic topic will be handled in greater detail in Chapter 10; for now, do a rough estimate. Not only must you be ready emotionally and socially, and able to balance career and parenting, but you must also be in a financial position to afford becoming a parent. Just because you are over thirty years of age does not mean that you are fiscally secure and sound. As you have moved up in your career and social standing, the cars have gotten bigger, the clothes better, the apartments or houses somewhat more elaborate. Possibly your education has drained some of your earnings. And inflation has speeded well ahead of many of your career jumps. So despite your ages, the two of you must consider carefully the following statements to ascertain your financial readiness profile:

*Financial Readiness:*
1. We want this baby. We'll find a way to afford it whatever the cost.      Yes      No
2. I want to stay with the baby for at least six months after it is born, but we won't be able to afford that. I'll go right back to work.      Yes      No
3. What's the big deal? Children are little; they can't cost so much.      Yes      No
4. We'll have to move—but housing is so expensive. We'll just stay in this one-bedroom flat for a year or so.                          Yes      No
5. We've been saving a little bit each week. We'll keep that up and try to predict what's coming so we'll be ready.      Yes      No

We sympathize with the first statement. There is a strong temptation to say Yes to that. If you want a child badly enough, you probably can do whatever is necessary to afford it—an extra job, overtime. But suppose you can't. Suppose this is a time in your lives when you are just not financially prepared for that child. Why not wait and save money until you can afford the child, or stick to an effective savings plan during pregnancy? It is so much saner to bring a baby into a financially stable home than struggle to pay bills with the infant in your arms. Your parenting skills and attitudes will be far better for your child without the financial worries on your minds even if you're a few years older. A thirty-five-year-old parent can give just as much love and affection as a thirty-year-old parent (particularly if there's enough food in the refrigerator and money in the bank).

The second question does not have a clear-cut Yes or No. The responses are so private, so very personal. The correct answer for you is up to you. If you are the woman in the family, then this question most likely touches you the most. How did you respond? If you answered Yes, then you are willing to give up those first months of intense mothering so that there will be financial stability in the home. If you give your baby "quality time," it is unlikely that the infant will be any the worse for your decision. But will you? That is the big question. Are you giving up too much? How much loss, how much resentment, how much bitterness will you feel day after day at the job if you truly wanted that very intense six-month mothering experience and had to forgo it for financial reasons? Would it not have been wiser to have worked and saved for one or two years and earned the time for those first six months? Many women are very comfortable leaving the young infant and returning to their careers within weeks of delivery. These women schedule their evenings to be child-oriented and share child-rearing responsibilities with their husbands. The careful selection of the person responsible for child care during the days alleviates much of their concern. These mothers experience no guilt; nor should they. They have made the decision that satisfies their needs without harming their infants. It is the mother who unwillingly rips herself away from her baby to return to her work who is suffering and who may adopt mothering patterns that are over-compensations due to the guilt and concern felt during the working day.

"Children are little; they can't cost so much." Wow, somebody's in for a very big surprise. And the surprise grows bigger as the child grows bigger. It costs one helluva lot of money to feed, clothe, educate, doctor, and babysit childern today, just to name a few of the major expenses. Never enter parenthood with blinkers like that over your eyes. You are over thirty years old; you know by now that there are no "free lunches," and having children requires money and love. Do not be discouraged, but be prepared. Children are worth a sacrifice, and that sacrifice hurts you less if you anticipate it.

Children need space in which to grow. It is unfair to the developing child to be cooped up in a small apartment sleeping in the living room while the parents save for that big house in the suburbs. Every youngster should have a bedroom, whether it is shared with a sibling or his or her own. When parents and child fall over each other in cramped quarters, the result is bickering rather than intimacy. Try to wait until you have the space before you have the child, but if this is not possible, try not to keep the child in that alcove more than one year. Look for that larger apartment within the foreseeable future. Say No to the fourth statement after you've thought it over and discussed it with your spouse.

Can you say Yes to the fifth? If you can, then you have spent the years before your thirtieth birthday doing a sane and sensible thing—saving for parenthood after thirty. You can bring your child into a financially stable home. There are no guarantees that it will always be so; we all know that. But none of us are born with guarantees. What we hope for our children is reasonable stability. After thirty, we can be wise enough and flexible enough to adapt if the situation suddenly changes. If you have said Yes to question 5, your readiness profile rating is highly positive.


You have just finished looking at yourself realistically from the standpoint of your readiness to become a parent after thirty years of age. Often you answered hesitantly, knowing that you felt more than one way about a particular question or statement. Nothing in our lives is so simple, so right or wrong, so easy to answer. And yet you should have a sense of how well you can make a sane and rational decision to become a parent after waiting until you were over thirty years old. You should now feel rather comfortable. You took the readiness test, accepted the challenges, and came through with the feeling that you are ready to become an after-thirty parent.

CHAPTER TWO

•

# The Decision Is Made;
# Preparing for Parenthood
# After Thirty

The two of you decided that you were ready to become parents. One of you stopped using contraception. And you waited each month for the first indication of pregnancy. Or perhaps you are over thirty and did not have the opportunity to plan, to decide the state of your readiness for parenting. One month was suddenly different from the ones proceding it and you found yourselves unexpectedly expecting.

Whether it was a conscious or accidental decision, and no matter how carefully you anticipate the actual event, it is not until you must live through the pregnancy and the imminent arrival of a new person in your family that you are faced with the stark realities of the parenting situation. This is the time to begin preparing for the months and years ahead, adjusting your world to the dramatic changes about to occur with the birth of a child. You are over thirty years old and you have developed within your life, marirage, relationships, and career certain routines that succeed. Now *all* of that is going to change. Preparing for this change as early as possible with as much insight and care as you can find within yourself may save you hours and days of difficulty during the pregnancy and after your baby has been born.

What are the major areas that need your attention early in
30

the pregnancy so that the alterations in your future life can be accepted comfortably? What must be prepared for in advance so both of you are ready for the arrival of the child?

*Preparing:*
1. Your marriage
2. Your relatives
3. Your friends
4. Your colleagues at work
5. Yourself

There are key areas of preparation in any pregnancy; and they are particularly meaningful in the after-thirties marital situation. Let us consider each one and attempt to resolve the problems before they begin.

## Preparing Your Marriage

*The Husband–Wife Relationship*—Mature men and women whether married for long or short periods of time frequently have the wisdom, built on past experience and age, to create a mutually sharing relationship in marriage. A carefully constructed balance is developed so that each of the two members of the marriage feels there is sufficient attention being paid to his or her individual needs. If during one week the husband is going through a worrisome job evaluation by his boss, his wife focuses upon his needs. The next week, the male's crisis having passed, the wife may take center stage in the marriage with personal or career problems of her own to occupy their collective thoughts. Thus a marital balance has been established. Enter pregnancy, which may change and shift this balance dramatically.

For the first time in the marriage, one of the two members has the main focus within the marriage. The woman is pregnant. She carries within her the potential future family of the childless couple. Attention will be paid to her every symptom. The first three months when she has morning sickness, the doctor's visits, the growing bulge in her abdomen, the first flutterings of life, the

heaviness of the final months, the sleep problems, the swollen legs
. . . all of these plus many more events which mark a normal
pregnancy cause the woman to become much more self-centered
than she has ever been before in her life. This is both natural and
understandable. Will this one-sided focus cause problems? Yes.
There will be problems unless some preparation for this change
in marital relations is recognized *and accepted* as temporary and
normal.

Let us not forget that while the after-thirty woman is feeling
strange and unusual things from the beginnings of her pregnancy,
her husband is not, except as he hears about them. He cannot
feel them. This shifts the focus of the pregnancy in her direction.
If all he hears about are pregnancy symptoms when he has been
accustomed to a more interesting, varied conversation, he will tire
quickly of the subject. In addition, just because his wife has become pregnant, the husband has not stopped having his own job
and personal problems, or other incidents that require discussion
and advice. The shift of the balance of attention toward the wife
may, if excessive, shut off the husband's willingness to share his
own needs and feelings.

There must be space and time for the husband during this
nine-month experience. Also the husband must understand that
what is happenig to his wife's body, after the many years of personal care and exercise, is at the same time both frightening and
fascinating to her. She must talk about it, muse over it, complain
a bit and worry some. It lightens the load to share it.

Once the baby is born, there should be a gradual realignment
of the couple's balance, with a return to mutual sharing. But both
husband and wife must also be prepared for the fact that a new
person has entered that balanced marriage and will occupy some
of their precious sharing time. Preparing for these changes, recog-
nizing that they will occur and are natural and normal, avoiding
the extremes, talking about the shifts openly with each other—
these preparations will strengthen a marriage and help to develop
a readiness for parenthood.

*Getting Ready for the Baby*—You both are very busy people, over
thirty; moving upward in your careers; adding new social contacts

every year; beginning to think about caring for your own parents as they grow older; filling your days and nights with friends, parties, work, books, plays, activities—a full and exciting life. And now you are a pregnant couple preparing to have a child. Do you have the time to get ready to have this baby?

*You must find the time*, and you must find the time in your busy schedules to prepare for this coming baby *together*. Locate classes for expectant parents and attend them. Learn about pregnancy and delivery *together*. Make sure that the husband can be present in the delivery room and that both of you can touch your baby as soon after birth as possible. Find out about labor and prepare to experience it *together*. Meet your pediatrician before your baby is born so that both of you will greet a familiar face when he or she walks into your room to tell you the state of your baby's health. Do all of these things together.

The baby will have to sleep somewhere, probably in a room selected in your home. You may have to move to larger quarters or maybe one of you will relinquish a den, music room, or writing room to create a nursery. In either case, there will be an element of sacrifice and sharing. Make these decisions together and then, as a couple, begin to buy the furniture, wallpaper, diapers, and many other new and exciting things that must be ready for that day when you bring the new baby home. No matter how crowded your calendar, cancel something so you can do these things as a couple. Begin sharing your baby before the baby is born.

*Sexual Understanding and Trust*—Sexual issues during pregnancy usually are *not* a problem, but occasionally can create unnecessary tension in the after-thirties marriage. As the woman grows larger and more conscious of her distorted figure, her sexual drive may diminish to the point that she asks for a temporary postponement until after the birth of the baby. This usually will not be because of a medical suggestion but more than likely will be a personal wish on the wife's part. The husband should try to understand that it is her body that has changed so dramatically and that, even though he still finds her sexually attractive and loves her more than ever, she herself may have problems with her sexual image and want a "time out" from sex. The maturity of the after-thirty husband should enable him to understand and accept this request without rancor or resentment.

"I'm fat. I'm unattractive. Having sex with me must be a duty. Especially when he has all of those beautiful secretaries at the office." As a pregnant after-thirty wife, will you ever think this? Probably. But as the thought crosses your mind, also remember that you have trusted that man for all the months and years prior to the pregnancy. Why the sudden loss of faith? Men who cheat on their wives usually do not begin during the women's pregnancies. That only happens in novels and films. In real life, these men started long before the pregnancy. A faithful, trusted husband does not change his colors during those few months before his baby is born. He may be thirty-two, handsome, successful, sexually exciting, but he's yours. You are carrying his baby. You want this pregnancy. And he loves you, so relax and trust him. He's got a major important job lying ahead of him, and he may need your trust and your help—for the first time in his mature life, he is going to be a father.

*The Nights Alone*—During the latter part of the pregnancy, there will be many nights when important career activities in the husband's life are taking place. There may also be ritual social events in both of your lives, such as weekly bridge games, poker games, parties, etc. which you are expected to attend. Having nights alone is strictly up to you as the pregnant wife. If you wish to hide what is a normal and thrilling change in your body from the outside world, then you will be sending him out to these affairs alone as you sit waiting for him to come home. You will be feeling sorry for yourself unnecessarily. Each time you turn down an invitation for yourself, ask whether it is your *body* or your *state of mind* that rejects the invitation. We suspect your husband knows that it is vanity. Pregnancy is not an illness; it is not a cosmetic disfigurement; it is a joy to be shared. Be careful. Don't damage your marriage by preparing for pregnancy behind closed doors. "Confinement" died out with Queen Victoria.

*Sharing Responsibilities*—In the two-career family with husband and wife over thirty, it is often essential for responsibilities to be shared or the jobs simply would not get done within the home. However, there are frequent situations where the sharing of responsibilities is *not* balanced; one member, most often the wife, assumes a much greater share of the household burdens. This may work when there are only two of you who require care. Some women actually convince themselves that it is easier to "do it myself" than have to walk behind a husband cleaning up the mess made while he was cleaning up the house. Or the woman will consider the hours put in by each of them and decide that she has more time. With the arrival of a child, all of these considerations go out the window. Two active mature people, busy in their daily lives, *must* share the responsibilities of the house and the child if everything is to be accomplished that has to be done.

The time to start this shared responsibility is during pregnancy. This is the perfect time for learning "who can do what" best (or at the least, adequately). Do not wait until you come home from the hospital and then expect your husband to "pitch in." The poor fellow won't have the foggiest notion what he is to pitch and he will be "all thumbs" and discouraged from taking an active role in child care. Give your husband a break. Educate him before the baby comes so he can share the responsibility of being a parent with a less exhausted you.

## Preparing Your Relatives

Do you realize how long both of your parents have waited for that moment when you would announce that you were going to have a baby? Picture the slow shaking of heads as they sat in their living room thinking about their private deprivation, the lack of grandparenthood. They tried valiantly to understand why two sensible, healthy, mature people actually delayed having a child until they had reached the antique age of thirty or more. In their day . . . enough already. You have the picture. But you should also realize that with the declaration of the news must come the subtle but progressive education for grandparenting so necessary because they have been waiting for so long.

Prepare them for the fact that this is a perfectly normal pregnancy. Just because you are over thirty, you do not need to be carried bodily from place to place. You go out. You can dance, swim, run, jog, play tennis, live a perfectly normal life . . . just like those young twenty-four year olds.

Prepare them for the reality that you are financially able to travel this journey into parenthood without outside assistance. It is unwise for prospective parents over thirty to seek support or help from parents. This lessens the autonomy of the mature couple in their parents' eyes and opens the door to more and more interference with your parenting.

Help them to understand that you will not be focusing on your health every minute of the day during the pregnancy and you sincerely would appreciate that mutual conversations linger as briefly as possible on your nausea, your belly, and your weight.

Last and most important, clearly demonstrate that the two of you are prepared to play the complete role of parents without any outside help and advice. When you wait for something, it seems somewhat more precious when it arrives. Your parents will naturally feel this way about this grandchild. But so will you—and you are the child's parents. You will discipline, love, and reward. There is a role, a very important role, for grandparents to play: the warm, comforting, loving older person who has few of the responsibilities of child rearing and many of the joys. Help your parents to assume that role, which they may have been waiting for silently much longer than either of you realized.

The same is true for all other relatives—aunts, uncles, sisters. Just because you waited until you were over thirty to have this child does not mean that your baby is any different from or more special than any other in the family. This is essential for you and particularly for your child . . . "specialness" can create problems that you will have to deal with for many years afterward.


## Preparing Your Friends

Many of you who have waited until after thirty for parenthood have friends who have also decided to wait or who have resolved to remain childless. This is to be expected since you move in career circles where such decisions are commonly made. In addition, your freedom to move about socially at your whim would limit the available contact with the couples with children. Therefore, it may be true that a significant number of your friends are at the same stage as you are.

Now you are going to have a baby. You have become different. Think back over the years to when other couples in your social lives had children. Did you maintain the same relationship? Or was there a conscious or subconscious sense that they had crossed the line into another country, foreign, different, and therefore not as comfortable as before? Did you slowly widen the times between visits? Did you call less frequently? When something exciting came to mind, did you dismiss them immediately because they would have to get a babysitter? Were you bored with the constant talk about children in your childless world?

Let's be honest. Couples with children are not as accessible. Their concerns shift perceptibly. Money is not as freely spent; spontaneous social life is dampened. When you have a six-month-old, can you look at the evening paper at seven-thirty and decide that a great new film is in town and you'll go? No, of course not. You are on the verge of becoming a couple who plans the future. Your times away from the baby must be worked out in advance.

What can you do to maintain these valuable and important friendships with childless couples? Prepare them for what you will be facing once the baby has been born. Begin having intimate dinners at each other's homes. You will be able to manage this type of social activity with a baby and a Porta-Crib. Suggest that you buy a subscription to the theater, symphony, or opera. You will get your tickets in advance and can plan well ahead. Work hard at keeping up the phone calls. Spare your friends every detail of your new parenthood. Their childlessness should signal your tactful omission of too much child-oriented detail; try to remember shared interests.

Let these friends know that you do not intend to allow them to drift away merely because you have become a couple with a child. Devotion and dedication to their friendship should weather the changes, the differences, and the reminders of their childlessness, which could be a source of silent concern in their lives. Prepare your friends for the fact that there will be a change in the flow of your relationship with the birth of your child, but that you are going to make every effort to keep the friendship alive and well.

## PREPARING YOUR COLLEAGUES AT WORK

For the career woman who is pregnant, understandings must be reached with co-workers and superiors. During the early months there may be mornings when less work can be accomplished due to mild morning sickness. During the latter months some help in moving around on the job will be deeply appreciated. The ability to rest during the day may make you more productive and less tired. An understanding as to when you will stop work before delivery and when you will return after the baby is born must be negotiated during the middle months. This will prevent the career woman from finding herself with a long-range project thrust upon her without the time to complete it adequately.

Later on there will be days for both the mother and father when childhood illness, school demands, or important appointments will necessitate one or the other staying home from the office. Some of these absences are predictable and can be planned. Many are not. For the dedicated, over-conscientious career person reaching for that important after-thirty promotion, this could pose a real threat to his or her security. But if the future parenting is discussed clearly and dispassionately in advance with those in command, work expectations usually can be realistically modified when necessary. Remember there are other parents working in the same organization, getting promotions, moving ahead, even though an occasional unanticipated day is lost as a result of child-related problems.

The key to blending career and parenthood successfully is the realization that they complement each other. When you are at work, you must be involved with your career. When you are at home, your child and husband or wife are your central concerns. If work encroaches on home, it would be better to be where your thoughts are, rather than to perform poorly. If your child needs you, stay home. If work presents unexpected problems, get child care and spend that extra morning at the office. Be fair to both aspects of your life so you can succeed at both.

## Preparing Yourself

There are three basic areas in which each of you must invest some thought and preparation before the baby arrives so that you will be ready to assume the new responsibility in the healthiest, most sensible way.

We will call them the three areas of care:

1. Child Care
2. Husband/Wife Care
3. Self Care

*Child Care*—A decision must be made early in the pregnancy about when the mother in the two-career family is going to return to work. As mentioned earlier, each woman has the right and privilege to make this personal decision. Some after-thirties career mothers will take prolonged leaves of absence so that they can spend the early nurturing years wholly immersed in motherhood. Others return to important careers as early as six weeks after the birth of the child. Both can be excellent parents. What is important, however, for both (particularly the working mother) is the quality of care given to the infant by the selected caretaker. This person must be carefully screened (see Chapters 14 and 15). Letters of recommendation should be carefully analyzed. Performance on the job must be assessed before you return to work. Whether the caretaker is with your child only sporadically to give you a breather or stays every working day, you are entrusting your baby to a virtual stranger, at least in the beginning. So start as early as possible investigating prospective caretakers. Do not stint on the salary; you will get the quality you pay for. And make certain that the care includes not only feeding, diapering, and cleansing but affection and proper language surrounding your child. This caretaker will not, and should not, ever replace you in the child's life.

But there is no doubt that she will be an important element in your child's upbringing. Be certain that the influence is a healthy, loving, positive one.

Selecting your child's doctor is as important as selecting the surrogate caretaker (see also Chapter 15). When your child becomes ill, you want a physician with whom you can communicate, someone whose competence is unquestioned and whose child-rearing practices and advice are in agreement with your own. You have far too much experience in the outside world to accept the casual "He'll outgrow it," when you question the doctor about a significant behavioral symptom in your child. As an older parent, you will resent being shielded from information about your child's illness. Therefore, the second selection process you should go through during your pregnancy is the careful search for the best physician to help you care for your child in health and in illness. Ask friends whose judgment you trust. Talk to your obstetrician. Call the local medical school for the recommendations of the department of pediatrics. Visit several offices to meet the doctors. Select a pediatrician who will regard you as an adult, an intelligent, mature individual who can understand complete and uncensored information about your child. You aren't looking for a substitute father, or an older, supportive husband, or a nanny who will guide you every step of the way in rearing your child. You are looking for a competent, available doctor, nothing less and nothing more. Remember these things when you interview your pediatrician candidate before your baby is born. Then make your choice. Don't wait until after the baby is born to meet the baby's doctor. Again, you are putting your child into someone else's hands. Be sure you are comfortable with those hands.

It is never too early to think of time—child care time. Both of you are active, occupied people. Where on your busy schedules is that extra hour that you will need to rock and cuddle and nurture your infant, play blocks with your eighteen-month-old, hide and seek with your three-year-old, and so on? All during those many years you must be able to find the necessary hours to be with your child. This must be child-oriented time—"quality time"—not time spent wordlessly staring at a television set, but interactive, communicative, touching, caring, discussing, debating time.

Check those daily schedules now. What has to go? Maybe the weekly bridge game, or the tennis game, or a reshuffling of appointments, or coming home from the job earlier without that big attaché case full of work. Something has to give so that there will be the time both of you must devote to the new member of your family. Find those hours before the baby is born. The time to find time is *now*.

*Husband/Wife Care*—Let us share an example of the possible "you" who has to make decisions about the care of your husband at this important crossroads.

You are a thirty-four-year-old woman. You and your husband live in a major city in a moderately large apartment. He is a junior partner in a solid law firm and you are a buyer for a merchandising company. Together you share the pleasures of the theater, long camping trips, European vacations, football games, and frequent small dinner parties with friends. You dress well but not extravagantly. The two of you have saved, but have found putting money away more and more difficult. Now you are pregnant and it is time to prepare for "husband care." What are some of the areas to look into?

Can you entertain and be entertained by his work associates? These evenings could be crucial to your husband's career.

Answer: Why not? Pregnancy is not a disease. Certainly the conditon is not contagious. Unless you are very unusual, your first few months will be tolerable. Any trouble, if it occurs, will usually be in the mornings. As you grow larger, your body will adapt and your ability and agility will not diminish enough to hold you down, unless you allow it to, so you should have the capacity to continue this social pace. Yes, you might tire a bit more. You are a bit older (sorry, but it's true). So leave a little earlier or take a short nap before dressing to go. Maternity clothes today can be very attractive, and the sight of a pregnant woman is not an oddity, even in the least child-oriented social groups. Many women take on a glow of unquestionable beauty during the latter six months of a pregnancy.

How about after the baby is born? Of course you can be social. There may have to be a degree of selectivity because of the cost of babysitters and the age of the infant but, in general, the important events can be attended. Early on, family, or close friends may stay with the very young infant. You may find, or start a babysitting pool. Later, older teenagers, known to be trustworthy, can be hired. It is not unreasonable when invited for dinner at the home of a close friend to ask that the baby be brought in a Porta-Crib and allowed to sleep in an adjoining bedroom and breast or bottle fed at some point in the evening. You should worry about your friendship if your friends hesitate even slightly in responding to your request.

Next problem: You are carrying the baby; you are giving birth; you are mothering. How do you keep your husband from feeling shoved aside in the mature marriage in which the two of you were so close in the past?

The answer is contained in two words: *shared responsibility*. Even during the pregnancy, your husband should be asked to assume some of the chores that you took care of before. As the pregnancy proceeds, he may have to do more than his normal amount of sharing responsibility so that you can keep the frequent doctor's appointments, get the proper rest, and prepare yourself at work to leave either for a short or a prolonged period.

After the baby is born, there is again a great deal of room for shared responsibility. Night feedings, changing diapers, making the formula, walking the baby in the good weather, even visits to the doctor can and should be a shared responsibility with two mature, career-oriented individuals. A new element undoubtedly has entered the lives of two people used to a freer routine—an element that can be divisive if viewed as a deterrent to enriching the lives and marriage of the two people. Or the child can become another memorable experience to be shared in a firmly cemented relationship.

One last word: some women have an unconscious tendency to shift attention and physical love subtly away from the husband and toward the newly born baby. This can result from the natural tendency to see the infant as helpless, vulnerable, and demanding of physical attention and love. To a husband accustomed to the mutual expressions of both of these positive elements in the marriage, any significant lessening can cause hurt and anger. Often the husband feels guilty and confused as to why he is suddenly resentful of his baby, unaware that he is experiencing a deep wound of rejection. There is no reason why this should ever occur. Preparing each other for the expansion of your expressions of affection to include the coming child is the first important step. Remember, there are untapped rivers of potential love in all of us. We need not divert the stream from one person in our lives toward another.

Another issue to be faced: pregnancies cost money. New babies cost money. There could be a temporary drop in income. A move to a larger apartment or home may be essential. There is baby furniture, baby equipment, doctor's bills, etc. Prepare your husband for the change in the personal spending style that both of you must attempt as a sensible aftermath of the new baby. Dreams need not be buried, merely deferred. Nights out should not be discontinued, probably only decreased, with a careful selection of top priorities. Impulse buying of clothes will have to become a memory until later. It is essential to prepare each other for this because if one of you recognizes the need for financial readjustment and the other doesn't, the tension of the unpaid bills will create waves of anxiety and throw the marriage and parenting process into chaos.

There are many more potential crises faced by the over-thirty father coping with the first pregnancy and moving into mature fatherhood. We will deal with these at length in a future chapter.

Here's another "you" to ponder:

You are a thirty-six-year-old man. Your wife, who is thirty-one, has just told you that after six years of marriage, the two of you are expecting a child. You recently received your Ph.D. after many years of combining work, research, and study. Having taught at a major university for four years, you are now trying desperately to get a stable tenured teaching position. Your wife is also a teacher. She has her master's degree in special education and has been teaching a group of severely retarded children in the public school system. Her salary has been essential to your financial balance through the past years. But you both agreed that if you did not experience parenthood at this time in your lives, the two of you might postpone it indefinitely. You agreed that the options were parenthood or some luxuries and you chose parenthood. But you know that your wife must return to work within six weeks so that the family can survive the strain of low academic salaries. How can you pick out key areas to give sensitive "wife care" before and after the baby is born?

Stop for a moment and select three issues that should be worked on by you as the husband during the next nine months.

We see the first major issue as a shift in emphasis. Your career goals have been in high gear for the past years; so much has been deferred or sacrificed so that you could obtain your degree. That degree will benefit the family. But the focus in your marriage has been on you for a long time. Now your degree is official and your wife is pregnant. Isn't it her turn? She has waited and she has worked, and together you have decided to forego some of the postponed pleasures for one that you don't want to put off any longer—parenthood. What is her unspoken need at this point? Not an overt coddling or pampering, to be sure. She is a mature woman capable of success and independent in her own right. What she needs is the subtle shift of the marital focus in her direction, interest in each aspect of the pregnancy, concern over her job adjustments, patient listening to her fears and concerns. You did all of this before, but so did she during your dissertation struggle. Now give her center stage. It is the right moment.

The second area of wife care at this time stems from your wife's need to go back to work so quickly after the baby is born. Help her to adjust to any negative feelings or concerns about this issue. Accept her need to negotiate a contract with you that gives her permission to take time off if and when the baby needs her. Recognize that the child care that will satisfy you both may be costly. But also understand that she and you are right in carefully screening and paying more for your infant's daytime caretaker. Accept in advance the "quality time" mothering that she will want to do during the weekends and plan to share with her during those times. Reassure her that she has the flexibility to assume simultaneously both important roles in her future life: mother and career woman.

Older women becoming mothers for the first time usually experience a gnawing concern that has been fostered by the popular media: they fear that their baby has a high risk of serious abnormalities. We will deal with this concern in a subsequent chapter. But as her husband, sensitively consider her anxieties. Every day she cares for damaged children and now she carries within her a child about whom she knows nothing, but fears the worst. The daily exposure to the tragedies of conception makes her all the more sensitive to the risk of handicapped children. Your wife shares this feeling with other people who work in the medical, nursing, special education, physical therapy, and related professions that deal with birth defects on a regular basis. She is not unusual or alone in her fears. It becomes your task in "wife care" to help her feel that your baby will be normal. Fetal monitoring is part of the answer. You must also constantly reassure her that she is dealing in her job with a highly unrepresentative population and that there is a world of normal children born to older parents. Don't underestimate her unspoken concern. If necessary, bring the subject up yourself and deal with it.

Again, the dilemmas of mature motherhood are wide-ranging and will be discussed at length later. These are but three examples of "wife care." The male in the case history could be anyone with a new job, a new promotion, a new degree—anything that has consumed the energy of the couple over a long time.

*Self Care*—If you are a woman over thirty who has been told that you are pregnant for the first time, you must give yourself a number of "permissions" that allow you to take care of yourself and prepare you for motherhood. We are going to ask you a list of "permission questions." Answer each one honestly and develop your own sense of whether you are caring enough about yourself.

1. Have you selected an obstetrician with whom you can communicate and in whom you have confidence?      Yes      No
2. Have you met his or her associates who could be on call the night you deliver? Are they equally acceptable?      Yes      No
3. Have you selected a hospital that will allow rooming-in with the baby?      Yes      No
4. Have you asked every important question during your OB visits?      Yes      No
5. Have you notified your employer and/or co-workers about your

pregnancy so that more job flexibility will be acceptable during these nine months? Yes No

6. Have you discussed diet with your doctor and your husband so that you will not gain excessively, have a high risk pregnancy, and be faced with the problem of losing the weight after the baby is born? Yes No

7. Are you aware of the dangers of smoking, drinking, and taking any drugs or caffeine-laden substances during the pregnancy to you and your baby? Yes No

8. Are you willing to cut down or cut out any harmful habits? Yes No

9. Are you finding that rest and naps are not a sign of weakness but a sensible, rational aid to a healthy, happy pregnancy? Yes No

10. Are you doing exercises and taking classes (with your husband) to make the delivery and postpartum period safer and easier? Yes No

11. Are you looking as well groomed as you did before your pregnancy? Yes No

12. As your pregnancy grows, are you finding that you're asking your husband for more help with heavy chores? Yes No

13. Have you planned certain activities during the earlier months of the pregnancy that may become difficult toward the end and afterwards, such as camping and sports activities, long trips? Yes No

14. Have you arranged for proper help for the time when you bring the baby home from the hospital and when you decide to return to work? Yes No

15. Have you given yourself permission to become a mother without giving up the other important parts of your life as a wife, career person, friend, relative, community worker, etc.? Yes No

These fifteen permission questions are key self-care issues. You must be able to answer Yes to each and every one if you are to devote the proper quality of self care to becoming a mother.

Men over thirty sometimes approach fathering with a great deal of concern and trepidation. They feel the natural mature reservation about assuming such an awesome new responsibility. It is only the young who slip into parenthood as if it were merely a promotion into the next grade in high school. The mature person sees very clearly the long road ahead when a child is born into the family. Therefore, the over-thirty father also must take care of himself throughout the pregnancy to prepare himself for fatherhood. Here are some permission questions for the mature expectant father that are essential in helping him become a parent comfortably.

1. Have you met the doctor who is caring for your wife during her pregnancy and who will deliver your child?      Yes      No

2. Are you participating jointly in classes on pregnancy, delivery, and child care?      Yes      No

3. Are you preparing yourself and your marriage for the added financial responsibility of a child?      Yes      No

4. Have you looked at your time commitments and figured out the priority of your various activities so that you can give quality time to yourself, as well as to your wife and child?      Yes      No

5. Have you checked on your overall health recently?
Yes      No

6. Have you reassessed your current insurance coverage, as well as your wife's, from the perspective of increased family size and commitment?      Yes      No

7. Have you reached an agreement with your wife as to how you will share child care?      Yes      No

8. Have you analyzed your current career situation to make sure that major shifts in location or salary will not occur during the crucial period of pregnancy and early infancy?      Yes      No

9. Are you prepared for less spontaneity in your social and career life during the coming years?      Yes      No

10. Are you prepared to share your wife with another person, very small but very powerful in the emotional influence he or she will have in your lives?      Yes      No

It should be obvious that these ten permission questions cover a broad range of your concerns. We are asking you to answer Yes to all ten and to take full responsibility for the care of your physical, emotional, social, career, and marital health. This is a lot to ask. But unless you spend the necessary time attending to the changes precipitated in your marriage and your life, you will *not* be prepared for fatherhood.

Are you prepared? Are you ready to become an after-thirty parent? If not, make a list of things that must be done before that first labor pain, and take the time now to get yourself ready for your new life.

·

# CHAPTER THREE

# Adoption and
# the After-Thirty Parent

The decision to adopt a child—one of the most important decisions in your entire life—is rarely made unemotionally. Many months if not years precede such a decision, with endless talks, consultations with other adoptive parents, tentative conversations about the subject with your own parents, and, perhaps, tense and emotional talks with a physician. But you finally get close to the decision and give yourself permission to hope, to fantasize about a baby entering your life, and you are at the stage of wanting to know what your chances will be with an adoption agency. Now that you have clearly made up your mind, you wonder how likely you are to get that child *soon*.

Several factors will determine your chances for adopting a baby through a legitimate agency. Age, unfortunately, is one of the major factors. Adoption agencies, faced with a declining number of babies available for adoption, are also faced with an ever-increasing number of prospective parents. The social workers must decide the characteristics of the persons with whom they will place these precious adoptable children. They often choose the younger parents. They reason that younger parents are closer to the statistical "norm" of parenthood. It is the contention of agency philosophy that younger parents have higher energy levels and that younger people are more flexible in adopting new lifestyles to meet child-rearing needs.

Factors that will help you adopt a child, like a desire to adopt a child who is handicapped or of a different race, or of an older child, will still be influenced to some degree by your age. You will find, in fact, that each year you wait before starting an adopted family will make adoption that much harder. Some agencies even have ceilings for prospective adoptive parents—they may not take your application at all if you are over thirty-five years old!

If you are ready to adopt and you meet this resistance, what will be your reaction? Will you believe the arguments of the child placement specialists, as many do? Will you resign yourself to an attempt at a happy, but childless life? Will you seek the "black market baby"? Before you decide on any one of these options, let us look at the facts of after-thirty parent adoptions.

The facts are quite different. Parents after thirty are just as able to adopt a child *of any age* and raise it successfully as any younger parents—better, we think. After-thirty parents usually offer a child more economic stability, maturity, and experience. Through attention to the quality of time spent with a child, they can offer an adopted child as much energy and attention as that child will need during the passage from infancy through adolescence. The fact that after-thirty parents are discriminated against in the adoption process is an *injustice*—an inequity in our social and legal systems that may be well on its way to extinction given recent civil rights legislation prohibiting age discrimination.

Parents who are older often must become militant to adopt a child. They must sometimes crusade against bigotry, and they may have to take legal action in order to adopt. But they deserve to adopt and, more importantly, parentless children deserve after-thirty parents. You can become more than adequate parents of children, be they adopted or biological. This chapter gives the prospective adoptive parents "inside" information about what will be asked by the agencies and professionals who make the final decisions. It will help those parents prepare for the process of adoption planning and counselling. But the information offered here will not be that much different from that which would be offered to a younger counterpart, because *you have as much right to an adopted child as a younger parent*. This chapter will help you in the pursuit of both justice and parenthood.

Mature couples arrive at the decision to adopt from many perspectives. Certain persons are motivated to adopt not because they cannot conceive but because adoption rather than natural birth fits a philosophy of living. Such parents may be concerned about overpopulation and decide that they can help by adopting a child already born rather than continuing the drive of general society toward procreating and depleting our earth. Others want to adopt a special child, such as a child with handicaps or one from a different racial background, in order to give that child a better chance in life than he/she could have expected. Still others may have a specific child in mind to adopt—a child of a widowed relative or an orphan within the friend or family sphere. These couples choose adoption because they want children and they want to further a philosophy of life at the same time. They will face the adoption process well prepared to defend their position. They usually have thought through the many ramifications of having this special new child in their lives. They have had sufficient time to observe others in the same situation. Time has been taken to consider and agree on this choice of adoption. This couple should have little trouble "selling" their unique philosophy to a child placement specialist.

A majority of other couples, however, face adoption as an unexpected alternative to their long-range plans for a natural family. Children have always figured prominently in the future of their marriage. Now, after a frustrating time, they find themselves unlikely to conceive. In order to have children, they must look beyond themselves, usually to adoption.

To these potential adoptive parents, the process of adoption may be an even more difficult decision for each than that of getting married. When you were married, both of you desired it; the tests you had to face were common and expected; and both of you had many friends and relatives working for a common goal—the development of your life together. Adoption is different in one major respect: *before* you can realize your dreams of an adopted family, and *before* you can receive the best wishes of others, you have to pass some very important, unusual, and unexpected hurdles—emotional hurdles within yourself and society.

The first hurdle to overcome is your own personal bias about the "natural order" of families.

Ted, an articulate, graying father of two healthy adopted children, likes to tell of his after-thirty adoptions, but his feelings were poignant when he described his family's reaction to his adoption. "There were so many times during that first year," he told us, "when a member of my family, or a friend, said wasn't it a pity that I couldn't have my own children." Tactless and crude, even stupid, this reaction nevertheless comes from innocent people who have spent their lives being drilled in the "natural order": birth, then marriage, then children. Anything other than biological children violates the "natural order."

The emotionally adjusted adoptive parent must believe that adoption offers parents the potential for a normal family in which all of the children can be first-rate. The reasons for wishing to adopt would be the same as those for a nonadopting family—a desire for children and a willingness to provide a nourishing environment for them.

A second hurdle encountered by the prospective adoptive parent is the ability to accept a condition of sterility if such is the case. You have to believe that you as a person, rather than you as a sperm or ovum, are far more important in your role as a future parent. If you feel that you are handicapped because you cannot conceive, then you should think twice about adopting. You will be considering both yourself and the child as second-choice actions; neither of you deserve that. Come to the point where you are ready to face the future as parents who have psychologically chosen rather than biologically conceived your child.

The last hurdle you will encounter in your search for an adoptive family is the barrier constructed by societal attitudes, that adoptive parenthood should first be offered to young parents. This counterproductive and unfair practice of the "youth cult" still exists in many adoption agencies. It is an insidious philosophy, and one with which the potential adoptive parent who is over thirty will have to cope. You may have to threaten legal action, or shop for an agency or a legitimate professional who knows the value of parenthood at any age. Age discrimination is not only unfair; it is now illegal. The defense in a discrimination suit would have to prove that older persons are unfit as parents; the defense counsel for the agency would have no research to verify such an argument. In fact, the judge may have had his or her own child(ren) after thirty years of age. This bigotry must be brought out into the open and changed. A precedent must be set, and *you* may have to help set it. You must feel good about yourself as parents to do this.

When you feel that you have overcome, or *can* overcome the obstacles of "natural order," "sterility," and the "youth cult," you can make a rational decision about whether you want to apply for adoption. If you have talked to anyone who has gone through the adoptive process, you will find that adoption is almost always preceded by conversations with doctors, social workers, or other child placement workers. The purpose of these conversations is to try to help the agency or the doctor make sure that you are ready for adoptive parenthood.

Many of the same questions that these specialists ask will be put to you in this chapter. The purpose of asking these questions is not only to help you decide some of the more crucial issues surrounding adoption but to help you with your answers to those placement specialists. We suggest that you discuss these questions together with your spouse and possibly your parents. Take notes. Then compare the notes to the comments following the questions here. If your answers did not contain some of the essential elements described in the comments, consider the question a second time to discover new meanings within yourself. Be totally honest, however, or you will be hurting your cause by fooling yourself. It is unlikely you will fool the professionals. The possibility exists that you really do not want children. If so, it should be discovered now. The realization is not a feeling to be ignored or suppressed. Use these questions to uncover your own hidden attitudes about yourself and adoptive parenthood before you brave the blinding light of agency interrogation. There are no right or wrong answers, just answers that are appropriate for you.

## Questions

1. Why do you want to adopt a child?
2. What will you tell others who question you about having adopted children?
3. How do you feel about not being able to have biological children?
4. How and what do you intend to tell your child about his or her adoption?
5. How do you feel about accepting a child who might be different from a biological child?
6. How do you feel about adopting a child who is handicapped?
7. How do you feel about accepting an older child rather than a baby?
8. How much of a fight are you willing to wage to adopt a child?

## Comments

1. *Why do you want to adopt a child?* Answers to this question must be primarily child-oriented, for example, "We're stable people who can offer a consistent environment of love and discipline to a child." The answers should not be filled with the values which a child will bring to the mental health of either parent or to the health of the marriage. Does your answer suggest a personal religious conviction about the responsibilities of married people to have children? If so, reexamine your sincerity in wanting children for *you* as a person rather than as a means of satisfying your religious or societal value system. This issue becomes the first and probably most important question you will be asked by the professionals. Any social worker will take any statement you make and ask you, "How do you know that's true?", especially statements like, "I love children" or "I'd be a good parent." Think through these answers carefully. Be ready with a response that suggests that together you have weighed all of the options and have thought about and fully agreed on parenthood.

2. *What will you tell others who question you about having adopted children?* This question is geared, once again, to asking you about your attitudes toward having adopted children. If you harbor a sense of shame about the need for adoption or feel that adoption produces a second-class family, you likely will go to great

lengths to hide the fact that your child is adopted—even from the youngster. The parent who is proud of his or her child, however, is proud of adoption. Simulate meeting a stranger on the street who asks, "Gee, does the baby take after you or your wife/husband?" and answer spontaneously. You will gain some insight into how your attitudes toward adoption will be reflected in your everyday life.

3. *How do you feel about not being able to have biological children?* Many couples simply bury their feelings about their inability to conceive. They approach adoption as an alternative, become excited about the idea, and never really talk about their infertility. They may even deny that there is a problem. All of us grew up in a society that places value on reproduction. We may think we have accepted an inability to conceive or to carry a child full term; but when we adopt because biological conception is impossible, we inevitably face some kind of failure feeling, conscious or not. The adoption agency will want to know that you recognize that there *are* inherent problems associated with an inability to have children, and that you have sought help in resolving your feelings by talking them over with your spouse and with another reliable person such as your physician, priest, or a family member. Many couples have adjusted to the problem by talking it out extensively with each other. The adoption professionals want the problems of this sterility separated, as far as possible, from your motivation to adopt. Adoption should be attempted for positive reasons, not to cover a "failure."

4. *How and what do you intend to tell your child about her or his adoption?* Most adoption agencies will insist that you tell the child about his or her adoption at the earliest moment possible, often at the moment that you bring that child home. Ted was thirty-five when he and his wife adopted a little girl. He told us that he and his wife had a nightly ritual of putting the child into bed and, while kissing her goodnight, murmuring the sentence: "Goodnight, Terri; we love you and we're glad we adopted you." This sentence was repeated throughout all of her early years. It helped Ted and his wife to say the word "adopted" easily, and it helped Terri to understand the process as a loving gesture when she grew old enough to comprehend the meaning.

Television is filled with dramas of adopted children "search-ing" for their "real" parents, knowing that this discovery will somehow "fulfill" them, give them their roots, and solve all their personal problems. The absurdity of these plots should be appar-ent; but what motivates these adopted children who do search (a new and increasing phenomenon) is not so apparent. More than likely, some of the underlying motivation can be traced back to the manner in which these children learned about their adoption. If adoption was presented as a negative condition, or if it was pre-sented in such a way that the child felt important information had been withheld from him, a "search" idea to discover the mystery leaves fantasy and becomes reality. Ted's ritual of telling his child, every night, of his happiness at the adoption probably prevented the negative impact of the adoption on Terri. But what about the other information she might want to know? When she was seven years old, Terri asked for more information about her adoption. Ted then told her everything he knew about the physical attributes and health history of her biological parents. That satisfied Terri; she trusts her parents and has made no further inquiry. She prob-ably never will. That is all the adoption agency wants to know, just that you can be and will be happy and open about that very natural act: adoption.

5. *How do you feel about accepting a child who might be different from a biological child?* Often adopting couples feel that they have a right to expect a child who is healthy, cute, and bright. Do you think that? Or do you realize that adoption, like biological parenting, offers no guarantees? The adoption agency wants to know if you can accept the same parenting risks as other prospective parents. Obviously you know the answer the professionals are seek-ing. Is your answer an honest one? Can you reconcile yourself to a less than perfect baby? Think about it as you prepare for adoption. And think, too, about the possibility of taking a handicapped child or a child who obviously would not be part of your racial or religious heritage—possibly a child of a different race or ethnic background. These are serious questions you will be asked by the adoption agency. They do not have to be answered in the affirmative. But they should be answered by both of you beforehand—as another clue to yourselves as potential adoptive parents.

6. *How do you feel about adopting a child who is handicapped?* Many agencies have, as "unadoptable" children, those who have handicaps. The workers are often willing to place these special children in any good home situation. Parental age in this situation is frequently overlooked. Although many people feel that handicapped children pose an insurmountable problem to a family, there are other older couples who feel that they are uniquely suited to helping a child who has been disadvantaged by a mental or physical handicap. These people can indeed provide a loving and therapeutic home for *any* child, with or without problems. These people, usually mature and stable, provide wonderful homes for handicapped children or children disadvantaged by socially unaccepted racial mixtures or poor environments. Families in which handicapped or disadvantaged children are wanted are homes full of wellsprings of spontaneous love and joy and sharing, all of which far overshadow the problems of the handicapping condition. The parenting problems are, of course, different. Educational needs have to be met in special ways. Preparation for adulthood requires learning a set of skills often unusual to the experience of parents of nonhandicapped children. But for parents from a stable home that contains love and the financial resources to provide this special child with needed help and who know intrinsically that they share the flexibility to deal with new problems, for these parents, the addition of the adopted special child will provide them with a unique kind of love, the love developed from a family working together for the slow but steady progress of a handicapped or disadvantaged child. The rewards, though often slow and small, seem mammoth when they arrive. Ask any parent in a similar situation about that love. Like the late Senator Hubert Humphrey, he or she will tell you that it is a "unique, God-given love."

7. *How do you feel about accepting an older child rather than a baby?* This is one of the first challenges you will face from an adoption agency. Most parents have idealized images of a cherubic baby being handed to them by the social worker from the adoption agency; the rather rambunctious, sometimes unstable older child just doesn't fit the picture. But think about your life—your flexibilities or lack of them, your career patterns, your future

plans for retirement, your interests. Might these characteristics fit better into the pattern of raising an older child? Consider this option very carefully. There can be much joy in adopting an older child. It is a totally personal decision, but it will automatically be offered to you as people over thirty. Sometimes it will be offered as the *only* option (unless you decide to fight). Talk to others who have adopted older children if you are undecided. Most will tell you of the limitless pleasure following that decision.

8. *How much of a fight are you willing to wage to adopt a child?* This is not a question to consider for your interview with an agency. You are making this decision for *yourself*. Despite the fact that after-thirty parents are often better parents than younger persons, adoption agencies and professionals will frequently decide to place available children with younger parents. Their reasons are shallow, ranging from, "We're concerned with the energy levels of parents who have adolescent children when they are older," to, "We feel that younger parents offer a more natural setting for children because most biological parents are of a younger age." This type of reasoning is, of course, nonsense. Both statements reflect a bias on the part of agencies—a bias toward youth. This bias permeates all of modern society. The questions you must ask each other are these: Are we willing to be bypassed in favor of younger parents? Do we honestly believe that we have parenting skills superior to most younger parents? If the answer to the first is No, and to the second is Yes, the next question must be answered: How do we fight to adopt a child? First, try all possible agencies and professionals, asking about your chances for adopting a child. Keep records, shop for the "right agency." Then talk to an attorney about the civil rights issues involved and your willingness to fight for your right to adopt. Your attorney will advise you how to proceed from that point. You may be helping thousands of future after-thirty prospective parents by winning the battle for more mature parents adopting children.

If your answers to these questions and your inner struggles with personal insight still point you toward adoption, you will want to know what your chances are.

Chances vary from agency to agency and in different parts of the country. The supply of children becomes more limited each year, so agency priorities often become a battleground for after-thirty parents. But you can win.

Ted, now forty-five, has two adopted children. His children are as proud of their adoption as their parents are and talk about it freely with their friends and relatives. Ted has not forgotten the day ten years ago when he committed himself to being a father. He remembered it especially one evening when he was bending over to kiss his ten-year-old Terri goodnight. She looked up at him, smiled, and whispered: "Goodnight, Daddy. I love you and I'm glad you adopted me."

## Bibliography and Suggested Reading

Carson, Ruth. *So You Want to Adopt a Child*. Public Affairs Pamphlet No. 173-A (N.Y.).

Day, Dawn. *Adoption of Black Children*. Lexington Books, 1979.

Dyasuk, Colette T. *Adoption—Is It for You?* Harper and Row, 1973.

Jewett, Claudia. *Adopting the Older Child*. Harvard Common Press, 1978.

Kadushin, A. *Adopting Older Children*. Columbia University Press, 1970.

McNamarra, Joan. *Adoption Advisor*. Hawthorne, 1975.

Meezan, William and Katz, Sanford. *Adoptions Without Agencies: A Study of Independent Adoptions*. Child Welfare, 1978.

Rondel, F. and Michaels, R. *The Adopted Family* (2 vols.). Crown, 1965.

Shornack, Lawrence. *Adoptive Parent Study: A Report of Survey of Parents Raising Adopted Minority, Older and Handicapped Children*. Open Door Society, 1976.

Stein, Sara. *Adopted One* (Open Family Series). Walker and Co., 1979.

Wishard, Laurie and Wishard, William. *Adoption: The Grafted Tree*. Cragmont Publications, 1979.

.

# CHAPTER FOUR

# Will My Baby
# Be Normal?

For many years you've probably heard, repeatedly, that older women have a greater chance of having a baby who has serious problems. Each year that you've waited to have your first child has increased that unspoken anxiety that you are increasing your child's risk of an abnormality. We've known couples who have seriously considered remaining childless after 30 because of that fear. In the world of today's advanced scientific technology, such a decision is not very sensible unless the mother is over 45. And even then, there is reason to hope for a totally normal youngster. So, stop worrying needlessly! You have modern science on your side. Being over 30 does not mean you are at greater risk for an abnormal child, if you and your doctor work together.

We are going to present you with a lot of statistics and figures that make the point over and over again: you *can* have a normal baby if you use the results of certain scientific tests to make certain decisions. The decisions, however, are not simple. Fear and concern are natural bedfellows when you first learn that you are pregnant. You have heard that the older you are, the greater chance there is that you are carrying a defective fetus. Going through the procedure of tests will make you feel different from younger mothers who don't have that worry. And what will the doctors find? Will you be the one faced with the frightening choice of carrying a defective baby or terminating that long-awaited pregnancy? We are acutely aware that all of the data in the world can't remove even a trace of these monumental feelings you will face when the thought of your baby's possible normalcy becomes an issue in your mind during your pregnancy. We can, however, try to lessen some of your concerns. Your risks are probably not as great as you imagine. We *can* test for the most serious defects. And you will have the private and personal ability to choose whether or not to continue the pregnancy. Only if pregnancy termination is denied you through legislative fiat will you be forced to live with the inevitable; at present the decision remains with you and your husband. Certainly such decisions are tough and painful. But at least you are living in an era of medical science in which you have that opportunity.

There are several areas that we should look into:

1. The baby's position during delivery
2. The good outlook for premature babies
3. The small chance of fetal death
4. The possibility of birth defects:
   *chromosomal
   *structural
5. Early detection of defects
6. Making decisions

Many medical advances of the last few years have increased the chances for a healthy pregnancy and normal childbirth for mature mothers. An outline of the latest expert opinions and research in the field follows. You will find that many advances are accepted without debate by leading researchers while a few still cause controversy in the medical community. In an effort to eliminate medical jargon, we have taken the liberty of paraphrasing the studies, adding what we know to be true, and what we believe to be good sound advice.

## The Baby's Position During Delivery

The most significant work to emerge among many good studies was that of a special "Perinatal Study" by Dr. Sidney Kane, a leading biomedical researcher who looked at the deliveries of 36,452 women who had their first pregnancy at 25 or more years of age. Of this group, 11,508 women were over 30 years of age.

Usually, the baby's head emerges from the mother first and is followed by the shoulders; this is the *most easily deliverable* position. How did the position at delivery differ by the age of the mother in Dr. Kane's analysis? The 25–29-year-old mothers had this normal delivery position in 81.8 percent of the pregnancies. The 30–34-year-old women declined very slightly, with 79.2 percent, while the 35–39-year-old women dipped slightly more, with 75.5 percent. First-time mothers over 40 years of age had this normal presentation in 68.9 percent of all deliveries.

The feet-first or breech delivery statistics increased only slightly for births at older ages. The 25–30-year-old mothers had 5.2 percent breech babies compared to 6.0 percent in 30–34-year-old women; 6.9 percent of 35–39-year-old women had breech presentations; the figure jumped to 8.9 percent in the over-40-year-old mother.

We must remember that the feet first (breech) baby can be delivered quite easily by an obstetrician and is nothing to worry about. But you should know that your doctor will be facing a *slightly* higher chance of an unusual but manageable presentation of your baby for delivery.

Is there much increase in the rate of truly difficult births for older mothers in Dr. Kane's study? Make your own judgment. Here are the percentages of high risk deliveries by age of mother:

| | |
|---|---|
| 25–29: | 0.4% |
| 30–34: | 0.7 |
| 35–39: | 0.9 |
| 40–45: | 1.4 |

When we begin dealing with fractions of percentages, we're talking about individuals rather than trends. The figures suggest that *possibly*, but not probably, you will have a more complicated delivery when you are older. But the most significant differences are those that can be easily managed by a carefully chosen obstetrician.

*Type of Delivery*—Again using Dr. Kane's data, the percentage of Caesarean sections arises significantly as the first-time mother's age increases. Some doctors have linked this to the higher incidence of benign fibroid tumors in the older woman's uterus or womb, which would make a delivery somewhat more difficult. But remember that delivery by Caesarean section is quite safe for you and your baby. Your expert obstetrician can extract as healthy a baby by this procedure as by a forceps delivery. Study the figures. It is the older first-time mother who should consider Caesarean section as a real possibility.

| Age of Mother | % of Caesarean Sections in Dr. Kane's Study |
|---|---|
| 25–26 | 5% |
| 27–28 | 6 |
| 29–30 | 7 |
| 31–32 | 9 |
| 33–34 | 12 |
| 35–36 | 16 |
| 37–38 | 22 |
| 39–40 | 26 |
| 41–42 | 35 |

The possibility of a Caesarean section will probably *not* affect the health of your child. With the support of today's excellent obstetrical surgical technology, the risk to the infant (and the mother) during Caesarean section is not much different from the risk in a delivery by natural means.

## THE GOOD OUTLOOK FOR PREMATURE BABIES

There seems to be an increase in the percentage of premature births with the increasing age of the mother. For mothers between

25 and 28 years in Kane's study, the rate was approximately 8 percent while the rate moved up to 10 percent for women between 29 and 32 years old.

Eleven to 12 percent was the figure for the women in the 33–36 age range, and 14 percent in first-time mothers between 37 and 41 years of age. Thus, though the likelihood of your giving birth prematurely does increase with age, the percentage of increase is slight.

We must stress the more encouraging data from this study, which show that there is no difference in the *survival rate* of these infants. It would seem that an infant born prematurely to a first-time mother of older age has *no* greater risk of dying than does one born of a much younger mother. In addition, very recent work in pediatrics shows an increasingly good outlook for even the very tiny "preemies" (those weighing 2 pounds and less) because of new technological devices in special premature nurseries found throughout the nation and the world.

## THE SMALL CHANCE OF FETAL DEATH

Many older expectant mothers feel anxious about the survival of their child in the womb. Kane's report highlights some figures that suggest that by the late twenties the risk of fetal death begins to creep upward. There is a cluster in the 27–32 year group which then rises to another grouping in the 33–42 age range. How high is the risk? Not as high as you might imagine. There is a 10 per 1,000 risk if you are 25 years old that your infant will not be born alive. This rises to a mean of 15 per 1,000 from 27 through 32 years, and to a mean of 24 per 1,000 from 33 through 42 years of age. These are not high figures and should in no way dissuade anyone from attempting parenthood at a later age.

The encouraging news from the same study is that there is absolutely *no* difference in the mortality of infants born to mothers of any age (from 25 through 45). Present obstetric techniques, intrauterine diagnosis, and prenatal decision making (pregnancy termination), excellent nursery care, and good prenatal nutrition and monitoring have all resulted in making the situation of the newborn baby born to the older mother no more risky than that of the infant of the younger mother. So relax and enjoy your healthy newborn without concern.

## The Possibility of Birth Defects

Although we know that the risk of birth defects increases in older mothers, recent advances in fetal diagnoses coupled with your ability to elect termination of your pregnancy now offer you, as an older first parent, a very great opportunity to reduce the risk of birth defects. The graph below comes from *The Journal of the American Medical Association* (*November, 1979*). The rise in birth defects in this national study, conducted by the Birth Defects Branch of the Center for Disease Control in Atlanta, begins slowly at age 35, rises sharply at age 40, and peaks after maternal age 45. It is in the area of chromosomal defects that the greatest increase occurs after 30 years of age. However, it is interesting that after eliminating those birth defects that could be prevented or eliminated by detection techniques, it was discovered that for mothers from 35 to 44 years of age, the risk of bearing an infant with a severe birth defect was reduced to a level comparable to that for younger women. The 30–35-year-old age group appears to have very little greater risk than their 20-year-old counterparts if *mothers have good prenatal medical care and fetal detection.*

For the older mother, birth defects are often related to chromosomal abnormalities, many of which can be diagnosed prenatally. Others such as underdeveloped central nervous system (brain) tissues or deformities of the spinal column and cord show somewhat less relation to maternal age, but can also be diagnosed before birth.

The overall incidence of major birth defects for pregnant women younger than 35 years averaged 15 cases per 1,000 live births. The differences between the 20-year-old and the 34-year-old mother is not great. So having a baby before 35 appears to carry very little more danger of birth defects than for younger mothers.

However, after 35, the risks do rise. From 35 to 39 years of age, the overall incidence rose from 15 to 17 cases per 1,000 live births

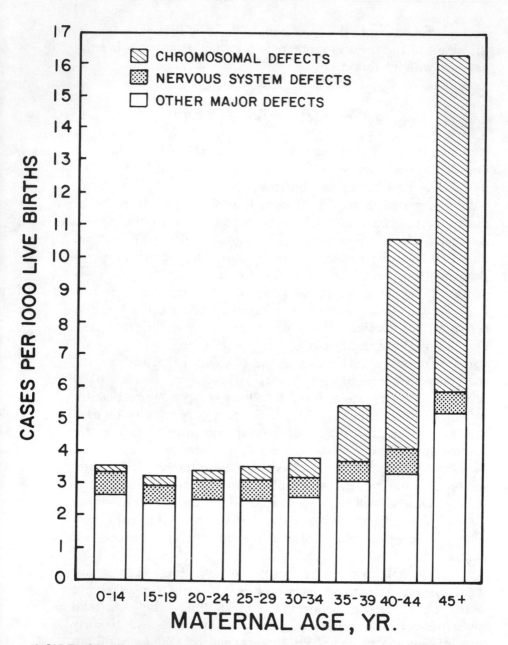

INCIDENCE OF SELECTED MAJOR BIRTH DEFECTS BY MATERNAL AGE, NATIONAL CENTER FOR HEALTH STATISTICS, 1973 TO 1975

(a small but perceptible increase). After 40, the figures escalate alarmingly. From 40 to 44 years of age, the overall incidence of major birth defects reaches 31 per 1,000 live births, and the 45 or older mother faces the danger of a potential 76 cases per 1,000 live births. In other words, for the after-45 mother, the risk of bearing a defective baby is over five times as great as it is for a 31-year-old mother.

These frightening figures *do not* take into consideration the important new techniques of fetal detection and monitoring, as well as the parents' right to choose whether they wish to rear a prenatally determined defective baby. The estimated effect of using prenatal diagnosis and elective abortion for severe chromosomal problems or nervous system defects is dramatically encouraging, to say the least. For pregnant women aged 35 to 39 years, the risk of bearing an infant with a severe birth defect is potentially reduced by 28 percent (16.7 to 12.0 per 1,000 live births). For women aged 40 to 44, the risk could be reduced by 56 percent, bringing the previously alarming rate of 30.8 down to 13.7 per 1,000 live births. Although admitting that their figures were based on smaller numbers of pregnant mothers over 45 years old, the researchers found this risk for older women could be reduced by 62 percent, bringing their rates down from 76.2 to 28.6 per 1,000 live births, through prenatal detection and intervention.

What does this mean to you? If you are under 45 years of age and pregnant and you have prenatal diagnosis by one of the many techniques we discuss later, and if you choose to terminate a defective fetus, your chance of having a baby with birth defects is *no different* from that for birth defects found among pregnant women under 35 years of age.

The over-45 mother is another story—still promising, but not quite as comfortable—which we'll talk more about later in the chapter.

What are these birth defects? Most commonly, they are *chromosomal* or *structural*. A chromosomal defect is a problem that arises from an abnormality in the structure or placement of the genes in the egg or sperm that combine in the initial process of creating the baby. Structural defects are abnormalities in the formation of organ systems, such as the central nervous system, that occur during the growth of the fetus inside the uterus.

*Chromosomal High Risk Defects*—The chromosomal abnormality that terrifies most older potential parents is Down's Syndrome, better known as Mongolism. These youngsters have low-set ears, full faces, slanted eyes, widened nasal bridges, short fat fingers with a deep linear palm crease, very lax muscles and joints, and loose skin particularly at the nape of the neck. In addition, they are prone to congenital heart disease, infections, intestinal obstructions, and leukemia. Probably most significant is that this group of children is mentally slow in varying but usually significant degrees.

Is it a myth that older mothers have a greater risk of bearing children with Down's Syndrome? No. It's true. Let's explore further to find how important an issue this syndrome is among older mothers.

Ernest Hook of the Birth Defects Institute of the New York State Department of Health analyzed the rates of Down's Syndrome reported on birth certificates in upstate New York (New York State exclusive of New York City) from 1963 to 1974 and corrected these figures to compensate for cases not reported to the Health Department:

| Age of Mother | Incidence of Down's Syndrome (*cases per 10,000*) |
|---|---|
| Under 20 | 6 cases per 10,000 |
| 20–24 | 6.3 |
| 25–29 | 9.2 |
| 30–34 | 13.1 |
| 35–39 | 40.3 |
| 40–44 | 126.8 |
| Over 45 | 415.5 |

Actually, the figures may be even more staggering. One clinician estimated that approximately 13.6 percent Down's fetuses spontaneously abort and 6.4 percent are stillborn; so only 4 out of 5 are born alive. Other work is even more alarming statistically, suggesting that of babies born to mothers in the 35–39 age group,

1 in 72 (139 cases per 10,000) and in the 40 plus age group 1 in 17 (588 cases per 10,000) are Down's Syndrome fetuses, many of which do not complete the nine-month pregnancy.

There is a fascinating controversy now brewing in the international medical community about the influence of paternal age on the occurrence of Down's Syndrome. A group at Johns Hopkins found no relationship between the father's age and the occurrence of Down's Syndrome, while a group of researchers in Denmark concluded that with advancing age, men carry an increasing risk that their newborn children will have Down's Syndrome. Above the age of 55 years, this increase appeared to the Danish doctors to be clearly significant. But an American study conducted at the Birth Defects Division in Atlanta suggests that the father's chromosomes *can* have an influence on the occurrence of Down's Syndrome, but a paternal age effect must be very modest indeed.

Are there risks for other chromosomal abnormalities as the maternal age rises? Yes. The 30–35-year-old age group appears to fall very close to their younger peers, thus making them a lower risk for chromosomal abnormalities in general. However, one scientist found gene defects in 1.6 percent of fetuses of 35–39-year-old women, 6.0 percent of 40–44-year-old women, and 25 percent in the 45–49-year-old group of pregnant women.

Another group phrased it in a different way, but the meaning was still very clear: the older you are when you conceive, the greater the danger you have of producing a fetus with chromosomal defects. This applies particularly if you are over 35. The second group of researchers concluded that the frequency of abnormal chromosomes in fetuses in different maternal age groups increased from 5.0 percent at 38–40 to 6.4 percent at 41–43, and finally to 22.0 percent in women of 44–46 years of age.

These figures could scare any over-35-year-old mother away from parenthood. But wait. Medicine has discovered techniques to diagnose most chromosomal defects early enough in your pregnancy to allow you the opportunity to terminate the pregnancy and try again. The chromosomal test may reveal a genetically *normal* infant during the second pregnancy. However, if abortion is not an option for you because of your religious or moral values, we suggest you study the above figures very closely, particularly if you are in your late thirties or forties and are thinking about that first child. There may be a risk involved that the two of you might not wish to take, considering your lifestyle and values.

*Structural High Risk Defects*—Work by two researchers (S. Hay and H. Barbano of the National Institute of Health) early in the 1970s strongly suggested that the number of structural abnormalities increased in the newborn as maternal age advanced. They noted a positive correlation between increasing maternal age and increasing incidence of cleft palates/lips.

Looking at the neurologic abnormalities, the more recent Atlanta study indicated that the rate for neurological abnormalities increased only in the baby of the over-45-year-old mother.

Hay has done subsequent work investigating 6,000 cases of cleft lip and palate. The incidence of cleft palate and of cleft lip/palate was found to increase among infants of older parents when the clefts were the only malformation noted. This relationship to parental age did not appear for cleft lip without involvement of the palate. The rise appears to begin at maternal age 35 and to rise dramatically when the mother's age reaches 40 years. At 35, we see 1.5 times the expected number of cleft cases as compared to the normal newborn population of younger parents. When the mother is over 40, cleft lip appears in twice the expected number of cases and cleft palate in four times the expected number.

It becomes apparent that the greatest risks occur when pregnancy begins after 40 years of age, and escalate dramatically at age 45. E. O. Horger 3d and his group of obstetricians in South Carolina looked at 440 pregnancies occurring in women over 40 and detected increasing frequency in complications for both the infant and the mother. The infant death rate in this study was three times greater than that of the general obstetric population. The risks after 40 increase appreciably. Although we can reduce the infant risks in women over 45 by detecting the majority of problems in the womb, we cannot eliminate all risks associated with this advanced maternal age.

*Genetic Counselling*—If you are aware of abnormal health conditions that tend to run in your family, such as diabetes, cystic fibrosis, sickle cell disease, cleft lip, and so on, it would be wise to consult a trained genetic counsellor before planning the pregnancy so that you will receive the facts as to your child's chances of inheriting the familial condition. If after amniocentesis or other prenatal detection procedures, you discover an abnormality in your unborn child, whatever your final choice of action, you should seek the genetic counsellor's advice about the likelihood of the abnormal fetal condition repeating during a subsequent pregnancy.

## Early Detection of Defects

We are in a new era in medicine in which most birth defects can be detected early in the pregnancy. This information allows the parents to make an intelligent and carefully considered decision about whether to have the baby or to terminate the pregnancy and perhaps try again. For each couple, this decision is a very personal and very difficult one, but offers a right to choose that which was not possible in past generations. For this enlarging group of after-30 parents, these new discoveries are particularly important and welcomed.

What are these tests? Are they more worry and danger to you and your baby than the defect? How successful are they? And exactly what will they tell you?

*Amniocentesis*—Amniocentesis is the relatively painless technique of inserting a very thin needle through the wall of the womb into the fluid-filled sac surrounding the fetus and withdrawing a small amount of the amniotic fluid for analysis. This procedure is usually done during the sixteenth or seventeenth week of pregnancy. Amniocentesis is also recommended during the last three months of pregnancy when testing the fluid is necessary to determine whether the baby's lungs are mature enough to function outside the womb or whether the level of infant jaundice in babies afflicted with Rh blood incompatibility has reached dangerous heights.

Since 1968, the use of this procedure has increased dramatically. In 1978, the National Institute of Child Health and Human

Development Task Force reported that 15,000 amniocentesis procedures had been performed in that single year. In more than 95 percent of cases, the analyses of this fluid surrounding the immature fetus indicated that the fetus was healthy. The procedure is now used routinely in pregnancies where there is any risk of hereditary diseases or congenital defects in the fetus. This certainly applies to the over-30 mother; the need increases as the mother's age advances.

At this time, two experiments can be done on the amniotic fluid. The fluid itself can be tested for specific chemicals; and the cells found within the fluid can be cultured and tested for chromosomal and structural contents. What can be found? Essentially *all* chromosomal abnormalities in the fetus. Astounding? Yes, but true. You can know if you are going to have a Down's Syndrome child when you are sixteen weeks pregnant, and thus make a personal decision at that time. Seventy-five percent of all serious congenital metabolism defects can be detected. In addition, the testing of a special chemical, alpha feto protein, will tell you in 80 percent of the cases whether your child has one of the nervous system defects such as an underdeveloped brain or a serious defect in the spinal cord and column.

An unexpected benefit of the testing is this: You can know the sex of your baby. This is important medically for sex-linked genetic diseases like hemophilia. It also gives you a jump on what color to paint the room and which names to fight over during the next five months.

The procedure is not dangerous to you or to your unborn infant. A good deal of research allows us to make this statement. During 1971 through 1974, the National Institute of Child Health and Human Development sponsored a study which showed that there were *no* statistically significant differences between the health of two groups of mothers and babies: those who did not have amniocentesis and those who did have the diagnostic procedure. Doctors at nine major medical centers looked for an increase in loss of fetus, problems in the newborn period, lower birth weights, birth defects, prematurity, and complications in the group who had amniocentesis. There were none. Similarly, no significant differences could be found in growth, development, behavior, or intellect in 1-year-old children from amniotic fluid-tested pregnancies and those in whom amniocentesis was not done. In summary, it would certainly appear from extensive study that not only is the procedure of amniocentesis a vitally important one for pregnant women over 30 years of age but it is safe as well.

*Ultrasound*—Ultrasound is the technique of using high-frequency sound waves to create diagnostic images by reflecting sound off the fetus in your womb just as sonar beams are used in submarines to scan the waters ahead to detect the structure of a hidden object. The major advantage of ultrasound is that it uses a different energy source than X-ray and gives a different image. Ultrasound has *never* been shown to harm or cause permanent damage to either the fetus or the mother. The experience with ultrasound diagnosis in pregnancy now runs into millions of tests, so we are dealing with a very safe and extremely informative technique of detection during pregnancy.

If your obstetrician suggests an ultrasound procedure during your pregnancy, what might he or she be searching for in your unborn child?

Examination of the central nervous system could detect an enlarged head, poorly developing brain, or serious defects in the spinal cord or canal. Doctors have diagnosed obstructions of the bowel and herniation of the bowel into the umbilical cord through the use of ultrasound. An enlarged kidney in the fetus can suggest blocked tubes leading from the kidneys, cysts, or tumors of the kidney.

When your doctor prepares to do the amniocentesis and insert the needle into your womb, he or she wants to be particularly careful not to pass the fine needle through the placenta attaching the baby to the wall of your womb. Ultrasound can help greatly in locating the placenta so that the needle can be inserted safely into the amniotic cavity. Ultrasound can determine precisely not only the position of the amniotic fluid and the placenta-free area of the wall of the womb but also the depth to which the needle must penetrate to aspirate fluid safely. This technique is safer and easier than the old fluoroscopic technique, and it also saves the fetus from the considerable radiation dose that used to be necessary before we had ultrasonic guidance.

Another use of ultrasound is to make sure that your baby is all right if movements become sluggish at any point in your pregnancy. The use of ultrasound to demonstrate fetal movements is extremely useful, indicating whether or not the fetus is alive and, if normal movements are noted, to reassure mother, father, and doctor alike that the fetus is well.

*Fetoscopy*—The fetoscope is a small instrument which is inserted into the womb and through which the obstetrician can observe the fetus, note defects, and remove potential materials for analysis. This procedure is still under investigation because of the undetermined risks to fetus and mother. There is no question that it is a valuable tool in direct visualization and instrumentation of the unborn fetus. What has not yet been sufficiently ascertained is whether the risks to the pregnancy justify the use of the fetoscope in any but few selected cases.

*Alpha Feto Protein Determination in Blood and Amniotic Fluid*—There is an elevation of this protein chemical in the blood and amniotic fluid of women whose fetuses have neural tube abnormalities which will result in serious central nervous system defects at birth. Many medical centers test the amniotic fluid of all over-30 mothers routinely for a possible elevation in this chemical. Studies have shown that the high risk individuals in this regard are those mothers who have had a previous child with a defect in this range or have a relative with such a congenital nervous system problem. There is no argument that these women need this analysis during pregnancy. Also the over-45 mother tends to have a higher risk for infants with this problem, as noted in the Atlanta study. These mothers should be tested. Whether other over-30 mothers need such analysis is highly controversial at this writing. Our feeling is that the high number of false positives and anticipatory worry may sway us to eliminate this prenatal defect determination in over-30 women unless they fall into the high risk categories.

## Making Decisions

There are three decisions to be made by the after-30 parent confronting the question: Will my baby be normal?

**1.** The first is whether or not to go through the tests necessary to determine the general chromosomal and structural health of your fetus. We strongly encourage you to assert your right to have these tests performed so that you can have an informed and, hopefully, worry-free pregnancy.
**2.** The second decision you must make is to believe the results of the tests once they have been reported to you. If you get a good report, then it is essential that you accept its validity, reduce your anxiety, and relax through the remainder of the pregnancy. The figures of accuracy are impressive: essentially complete reassurance against chromosomal aberrations and at least an 80 percent chance to rule out nervous system problems. Obviously not all congenital defects will be ruled out by these tests. However, with only a few exceptions, you, as over-30 parents, are at little greater risk for these than the rest of the parenting population. Just think of all the healthy, happy youngsters you have encouered in your life. You have, after a good report from the tests, a very fine chance of seeing the same normal, healthy youngster in your house.

If the tests return with the verdict that you have a fetus with a defect, we caution you to *accept* the results and not waste time in doctor-shopping to find someone to tell you that the tests were wrong. False positives in the testing for chromosomes or in using ultrasound are too infrequent to cause you to delay the inevitable.
**3.** The third decision-making crisis will apply only to a small percentage of over-30 parents. This is when a few of you receive a positive indication that you have a fetus with Down's Syndrome or a serious nervous system defect or any other debilitating congenital mental or physical birth defect. It is at this painful but critical moment that the two of you must decide whether to continue or terminate the pregnancy. We cannot help you through this very personal and individual decision; each of us knows what

we would do personally, but we are not the two of you. Seek out-side help from your obstetrician, your minister, priest or rabbi, your family, your close friends. If necessary, see a professional counsellor. But mainly talk to each other, over and over again until there is a mutual acceptance of the final decision. If you decide to continue the pregnancy, prepare for the battles of rearing an exceptional child. If the decision is termination (abortion), then go into the procedure willingly with the firm conviction that you will try again unless there are strong genetic reasons against such a decision.

For religious or personal reasons, there will be those among you who decide to continue the pregnancy and bring this special child with handicaps into your family. If you do, seek the right kind of help even before the birth of your child (or, without ques-tion, soon after the birth, if you have waited). Ask your pediatri-cian to refer you and your exceptional child to a special diagnostic and treatment center that deals with all of the problems faced by your family. Some of these centers are at universities and medical schools; others are housed within private institutions or founda-tions. Your pediatrician should know the location and capabilities of these centers.

If your doctor fails to give you thorough information and total guidance, you must assume an assertive role. Call your local chapter of the March of Dimes. This group deals with congenital defects and can assist you in finding help. Also communicate with the De-velopmental Disabilities Council, which can be found in your gov-ernor's office. This group has a complete list of the facilities available throughout the state that you and your child will need. In addition, you should ask the Council representative about groups of parents with similar children and similar interests who meet regularly; there will be no better support group for you. The Council staff can provide you with the names of the closest places to seek good medical, educational, social work, and counselling services for your child and your family, all of whom are involved in the handicapped condition of your youngster.

You will face one additional option if you choose to continue the pregnancy after learning that you are carrying a child handi-capped with a condition such as Down's Syndrome that will cause retardation of varying degrees. This option is the decision whether to rear the child within your home or to seek the help of an outside institution for day care or residential care. This decison again is a very personal and individual one. Most Down's children do much better physically, intellectually, and emotionally when raised within their own families. But not all families can adapt comfortably to the presence of a Down's child. This must be your decision, just as the decision to continue the pregnancy was yours, and yours alone.

Most occurrences of Down's Syndrome in women over 30 are random rather than genetic. That means that the lightning of chance error has struck only one egg, rather than having Down's Syndrome lying in wait within all or a certain predetermined percentage of unfertilized eggs in your ovary. However, to be certain that your chances for another Down's baby (or other chromosomal defects) are no greater than any other after-30 mother's, we suggest that you seek the genetic counselling of your obstetrician or the counselling clinic of any major teaching hospital. You will be referred to a laboratory where husband and wife will have the painless, simple test of chromosome counts in an effort to predict the possibility of a chromosomal defect occurring in your subsequent pregnancies. Knowing that the possibilities of birth defects are no greater than by chance alone when you become pregnant the next time can ease a great deal of the tension and indecision about that next pregnancy. If you are under 45 years of age and take advantage of the methods of prenatal diagnosis and pregnancy termination after positive reports, you have the *very same* chances for a normal, healthy baby as women of a younger age.

### BIBLIOGRAPHY AND SUGGESTED READING

Akesson, H. O. and Forssman, H. "A Study of Maternal Age in Down's Syndrome," *Ann. Hum. Genet.*, 29:3, 271–276, March 1966.

Alberman, E. "Main Causes of Major Mental Handicap: Prevalence and Epidemiology," *Ciba Found Symp.*, 59, 3–16, 1978.

"Aneuploidy and the Older Gravida. Which Risk to Quote" Letter, *The Lancet*, 1:8077, 1305–1307, June 17, 1978.

"Antenatal Diagnosis; Amniocentesis," NIH Consensus Development Conference—*Clin. Pediatr.* (*Phila.*), 18:8, 454–462, August 1979.

Ash P., Vennart, J. and Carter, C. O. "The Incidence of Hereditary Disease in Man," *The Lancet*, 1:8016, 849–851, April 16, 1977.

Biggs, J. S. "Pregnancy at 40 Years and Over," *Med. J. Aust.*, 1:11, 542–545, March 17, 1973.

Connon, A. F. "Congenital Malformations and Genetic Counseling," *Med. J. Aust.*, 2:24, 805–807, Dec .10, 1977.

Erickson, J. D. "Down Syndrome, Paternal Age, Maternal Age and Birth Order," *Ann. Hum. Genet.*, 41:3, 289–298, January 1978.

Geisler, C., Wulf, H. C., and Philip J. "Chromosome Abnormalities in Children of Mothers 40 Years of Age or More," A Retrospective Investigation, *Hum. Heredity*, 24:5–6, 449–453, 1974.

Goldberg, Marshall F., Edmonds, Larry D., and Oakley, Godfrey P. "Reducing Birth Defect Risk in Advanced Maternal Age," *J. of the Am. Med. Ass.*, 242:21, 2292–2294, Nov. 23, 1979.

Hay, S. "Incidence of Clefts and Parental Age," *Cleft Palate J.*, 4, 205–213, July, 1967.

Hay, S. and Barbano, H. "Mongols and Their Mothers," Independent Effects of Maternal Age and Birth Order on the Incidence of Selected Congenital Malformations, *Teratology*, 6:3, 271–279, December 1972.

Hook, E. B. "Estimates of Maternal Age—Specific Risks of Down's Syndrome Birth in Women Aged 34–41," *The Lancet*, 2:7975, 33–34, July 3, 1976.

Hook, E. B. and Chambers, G. M. "Estimated Rates of Down Syndrome in Live Births by One Year Maternal Age Intervals for Mothers Aged 20–49 in a New York State Study—Implications of the Risk Figures for Genetic Counselling and Cost-Benefit Analysis of Prenatal Diagnosis Programs," *Birth Defects*, 13:3A, 123–141, 1977.

Hook, E. B. and Fabia, J. J. "Frequency of Down's Syndrome in Live Births by Single-Year Maternal Age Interval: Results of a Massachusetts Study," *Teratology*, 17:3, 223–228, June 1978.

Hook, E. B. and Lindsjo A. "Down's Syndrome in Live Births by Single Year Maternal Age Interval in a Swedish Study: Comparison with Results from a New York State Study," *Am. J. Hum. Genet.*, 30:19, 1978.

Horger, E. O. 3d and Smythe A. R. 2d. "Pregnancy in Women Over Forty," *Obstet. Gynecol.*, 49:3, 257.261, March 1977.

James, W. H. "Central Nervous System Malformation Stillbirths, Maternal Age and Birth Order," *Ann. Hum. Genet.*, 32:3, 223–236, January 1969.

James, W. H. "Parental Age Differences," *J. Biosoc. Sci.*, 6:1, 93–106, 1974.

Kane, S. H. "Advancing Age and the Primigravida," *Obstet. Gynecol.*, 29:3, 409–414, March 1967.

Mariona, F. G. "Is Pregnancy a Risk in the Elderly Woman?" in E. S. Hafez, ed., *Aging and Reproductive Physiology*, Ann Arbor, Ann Arbor Science, 1976.

"Maternal Age and Down's Syndrome Editorial," *The Lancet*, 2:8079, 24–25, July 1, 1978.

Matsunaga E., Tonomura, A., Oishi, K., and Kikuchi, Y. "Reexamination of Paternal Age Effect in Down's Syndrome," *Hum. Genet.*, 40:3, 259–268.

Meredith, R., Taylor, A. I., and Ansi, F. M. "High Risk of Down's Syndrome at Advanced Maternal Age Letter," *The Lancet*, 1:8063, 564–565, March 11, 1978.

Minogue, M. "Childbearing at 45 and Over," *Ir. Med. J.*, 69:20, 526–528, December 1976.

Moran, P. A. "Are There Two Maternal Age Groups in Down's Syndrome?" *Br. J. Psychiatry*, 124:0, 453–455, May 1974.

Moric-Petrovic, S. and Kalicanin, P. "Mother's Age and Down's Syndrome," *J. Ment. Defic. Res.*, 12:2, 138–143, June 1968.

Morrison, I. "The Elderly Primigravida," *Am. J. Obstet. Gynecol.*, 121:4, 465–470, Feb. 15, 1975.

Mulcahy, M. T. "Down's Syndrome in Western Australia: Cytogenetics and Incidence," *Hum. Genet.*, 48:1, 67–72, April 17, 1979.

Mulcahy, R. "Effect of Age, Parity, and Cigarette Smoking on Outcome of Pregnancy," *Am. J. Obstet. Gynecol.*, 101:6, 844–889, July 15, 1968.

Murphy, J. F. and Mulcahy, R. "The Effects of Cigarette Smoking, Maternal Age and Parity on the Outcome of Pregnancy," *J. Ir. Med. Assoc.*, 67:11, 309–313, June 15, 1974.

Polani, P. E., Alberman, E. Berry, Blunt, S., and Singer, J. D. "Chromosome Abnormalities and Maternal Age Letter," *The Lancet*, 1:7984, 516–517, September 4, 1976.

Sachs, E. S., Jahoda, M. G., Niermeijer, M. F., and Galjaard, H. "An Unexpected High Frequency of Trisomic Fetuses in 220 Pregnancies Monitored for Advanced Maternal Age," *Hum. Genet.*, 36:1, 43–46, April 7, 1977.

Sigler, A. T., Lilienfeld, A. M., Cohen, B. H., and Westlake, J. E.

"Parental Age in Down's Syndrome (Mongolism)," *J. Pediatr.*, 67:4, 631–642.

Simmons, O. W. and Brown, W. E. "The Elderly Primipara," *J. Arkansas Med. Soc.*, 65:6, 217–222, November 1968.

Soumplis, A. C. and Lolis, D. E. "Elderly Primipara. Analysis of 1574 Cases," *Int. Surg.*, 52:4, 340–344, October 1969.

Stene, J., Fischer, G., Stene, E., Mikkelsen, M., and Petersen, E. "Paternal Age Effect in Down's Syndrome," *Ann. Hum. Genet.*, 40:3, 299–306, January 1977.

Stene, J. and Stene, E. "On Data and Methods in Investigations on Parental-Age Effects," Comments on a Paper by J. D. Erickson, *Ann. Hum. Genet.*, 41:4, 465–468, May 1978.

Sternlicht, M., Staaby, J., and Sullivan, I. "Birth Order, Maternal Age, and Mental Retardation," *Mental Retardation*, 13:6, 3–6, December 1975.

Tsuji, K. and Kakano, R. "Chromosome Studies of Embryos from Induced Abortions in Pregnant Women Age 35 and Over," *Obstet. Gynecol.*, 52:5, 542–544, November 1978.

·

# CHAPTER FIVE

# Nurturing Your Body and Your Baby Through the Pregnancy

You have been waiting over an hour in the obstetrician's office for your first appointment. Looking around, you notice the marked differences in ages of the women sitting in the office. Some seem like teenagers barely out of their childhood, while others appear in their mid-thirties. You are thirty-four years old and this is your first pregnancy.

The selection of this particular obstetrician took time and research on your part. You consulted friends with babies; you checked with your family physician and called several relatives; you wanted someone who was not only competent but also patient, willing to sit with you and answer your many questions. Several nurses live nearby in your neighborhood. You checked who they considered "thorough and thoughtful" obstetricians; you found out exactly who they used as an obstetrician when they had their own children and what they thought at the time. Your husband's secretary is married to a medical student; you asked him to inquire which obstetrician was being used by the medical students' and the doctors' wives. During the days and months when you were preventing pregnancy, you consulted the gynecologist at the local Planned Parenthood branch. She had been warm, understanding, and competent; you trusted her. So you called her also and asked her advice. One name kept cropping up over and over again. And now you are sitting in his office for your first appointment. But, you were warned, you might have to wait a long time in the outer office because he takes a lot of time with each patient. That's fine with you—you have a small notepad full of your own questions.

At last your name is called. You enter the examining room. In a quiet, efficient voice, the nurse tells you how to prepare for the examination and takes the preliminary history: your last menstrual period, your symptoms, your family history, any preceding illnesses or operations.

Climbing up onto the table and waiting, you lie there staring at the white ceiling hoping that the symptoms have not fooled you. You want to be pregnant. You and your husband have waited until now, and you feel that this would be the very best time for your first child. A small knot of anxiety is beginning to tighten in your abdomen as the door opens and the doctor enters the examining room.

After a thorough but gentle examination, during which the obstetrician quietly explains each maneuver and the nurse stands by the side of the examining table taking notes, accepting specimens, and occasionally touching you as a sign of support, you are invited to join the doctor in his office. He grins warmly at you and says with a noticeable overtone of enthusiasm and pleasure, "Well, I'm happy to tell you that you're about seven weeks pregnant."

Easing back into your chair, you let out a deep sigh of relief. "I'm glad," you reply. He smiles, his eyes wrinkling. "That's good," is his response. There is a momentary silence. Then he speaks again. "Do you have anything to ask me?" You cannot suppress a soft chuckle as you pull the pad out of your pocketbook. He joins your laughter. "I thought you might," he says easily as he watches you open the little book and begin to ask the most important questions for the next months of your life, the most important questions for your health and that of your unborn child (the following is taken from actual taped interviews):

Q: How long will I be able to work?
A: Unless there's some reason for your having a medical com-

plication in pregnancy, you can work up until the last week of your due date.

*Q*: I've got a pretty important career. Will I have to cut down on my job activities?

*A*: No, not unless your career involves heavy physical labor. As a matter of fact, I've not had any women who had executive positions or who were professionals themselves who found it necessary to stop working.

*Q*: How soon after the baby comes could I return to work if I wanted to?

*A*: I've had people return to work within three to four weeks at full capacity. A lot is going to depend on the type of delivery you have, and the quality of the labor you have. Labor is darned hard work and there's no way to prepare for it. It takes a long time to get your strength back. But if it becomes an absolute necessity, well, let me say that one woman I remember distinctly went back to work within two weeks.

*Q*: Is it going to knock me out more because I'm over thirty?

*A*: I don't think so, given adequate health prior to the initiation of your pregnancy.

*Q*: Because I'm older and don't have quite the muscle tone, would you recommend special exercises for me?

*A*: Yes, there are several exercises and exercise classes for pregnant women. Probably, though, the best exercise is swimming because it doesn't require the jarring of the body like jogging or bicycle riding. Any activity such as swimming or long walks would be very desirable.

*Q*: But you did mention jogging as a problem. I jog every morning with my husband.

*A*: If you've been jogging, continue. I don't like people to start doing something for which they have no preparation during a pregnancy. For instance, I've had women who were professional skiers. If they ski prior to the pregnancy, then I see no reason for them not to ski until they feel uncomfortable doing it. If they bowl, and many of my patients bowl, they can continue to bowl. I don't think they should *learn* to bowl, or *learn* to roller skate, or *learn* to ice skate during pregnancy. The change in the physical status, the change in equilibrium, the different posture, the hormone influence on the bones and on the ligaments all contribute to instability. So unless somebody has a clear, developed talent, they should not learn a new technique while they're pregnant.

Q: When would you think I should stop active sports?

A: Well, most people stop when they start to feel uncomfortable. I usually let the patient decide that.

Q: How can I be sure that my body is going to return to normal afterwards? I'm noticing some changes already, being a little older.

A: Well, your body is *not* going to return to normal afterwards. You will have, by a year, probably achieved equal tone to what you had prior to the pregnancy, given an adequate diet, exercise, and adequate vitamin supplementation. But you are *never* going to have the same body contour with respect to your breasts, for instance, or with respect to the muscles that are in front of your abdomen, called the recti; they will always have a separation between them. Primarily, the changes you may see will be stretch marks. They may be more cosmetically unpleasant than inhibitory as far as your physical structure is concerned. The color of your nipples will change. You may maintain a discoloration in the midline of your abdomen.

Q: Because of my age, am I going to be more prone to varicose veins?

A: Probably not. I think the most important determinant of that is whether your family is prone to varicose veins.

Q: Would I be more prone to hemorrhoids because I'm older?

A: I don't think so.

Q: What should I do to avoid complications like high blood pressure which, I understand, tends to be a bit more of a problem with older women?

A: It looks as though the most important thing to do is to maintain a normal nutritious and comprehensive diet. A high protein diet, with between 110 and 125 grams of protein, appears best, and we have some books and pamphlets to help you plan those diets. You do *not* have to have a high meat diet because protein is not necessarily contained in meat. You could be on a vegetarian diet. You need calcium because both you and the baby need calcium for bones and teeth. You are going to need some iron because the baby will essentially be borrowing and sharing *your* iron. Stay away from a high fat diet, because women who are pregnant are predisposed to gall bladder disease. The more fat you eat, the more use you have of the gall bladder; thus the more stones you may develop. A good diet is the most important factor in avoiding medical complication before delivery. The second most important factor is guaranteeing yourself enough rest. What we know about the high blood pressure pregnancy is that when socioeconomic conditions are good, people tend to have less high blood pressure problems. This fact seems to follow the thesis that diet and rest are very important for healthy lives.

Q: Speaking about diet, what else shouldn't I eat?

A: I think the initiation of new foods is not a good idea. There's a great deal of confusion about "junk foods." A good hamburger probably has all the nutrition in it that you need. On the other hand, a "junk food" like potato chips is useless. It contains a lot of fat, very little protein, it supplies you with calories that will make you gain weight, and it doesn't have any nutritive value as far as the rest of your body is concerned.

Q: I drink a lot of coffee. Is there any chance that this could be a problem?

A: Recent research suggests that too much caffeine can harm the fetus. Remember that caffeine is not just in coffee, but in soft drinks, tea, and hot chocolate as well. Drink your morning coffee if you will, but then switch to the decaffeinated brands for the rest of the day.

Q: Because of my age, should I be taking more in the way of vitamins or calcium or iron than other women?

A: One vitamin that you probably could benefit from is folic acid; if you have a diet that is high in leafy green vegetables, you probably will get enough folic acid. If not, then we recommend that you take some additives.

Q: Is this folic acid supplement necessary because I'm older?

A: No. It's simply because folic acid is a requirement for making blood, and it's a building block in human development. Since you have a very rapidly growing fetus inside of you, it makes sense to supply it with building nutrients.

*Q:* All of these things you are telling me—you would tell a younger woman as well?

*A:* Yes.

*Q:* How much weight can I gain?

*A:* Well, we try not to regulate it too much. We know that the complications that you may develop will start for sure at forty pounds weight gain. On the other hand, I don't want you to starve yourself when you're pregnant. Again, this would apply to you as well as to a younger woman. We also know that the complications that occur in pregnancy will occur if you gain less than ten pounds. So someplace in that range of twenty to twenty-five pounds tends to be a usual figure. Thirty pounds would be perfectly acceptable.

*Q:* You know, I've been noticing that I've really begun to spread a little bit as I've gotten older and I was thinking of trying to watch my weight. Is there a risk to dieting?

*A:* Yes. If you diet during pregnancy and the diet is effective, the object of all diets is to lose weight, that means to lose fat. When you lose fat, you excrete a product which we call ketones. Ketones seem to occur with high frequency in children who will develop some form of mental retardation. So we think that avoiding ketones in the urine and ketones in the blood is an insurance policy toward your child's nervous system development.

*Q:* I'm a social drinker. Being a career person, a woman who's out in the business world, I drink socially. Can I drink now that I'm pregnant?

*A:* Yes, I think you can drink, but moderately. There is a concern that people who take more than a couple of drinks a day may have a problem with the fetus. But it is very unclear in the research right now whether a little alcohol, one drink or a couple of glasses of wine, is going to have any detrimental effects on you or the baby.

*Q:* I'm a one-pack a day smoker, doctor. I guess it's the stress of my job. What effect is that going to have? Should I try to stop?

*A:* Yes, I'd like to see you stop smoking, and if you find that impossible to do, then at least cut down to the lowest concentration of tar and nicotine you can find. Or you can chew gum or find some other form of substitute. There's no question that cigarette smoking is associated not only with changes in the newborn baby, but with changes during uterine life.

*Q:* My husband and I are used to living a very hectic life. He's asked me how much rest I'm going to need.

*A:* I don't think we can answer that for any individual person. The pregnancy itself will force people to be much more at rest. The hormone that is produced in enormous amounts, progesterone, is a soporific. It's a kind of a biological sleeping pill, and many women who are pregnant commonly want to sleep, so we don't generally worry about that. On the other hand, forcing yourself to go to sleep or thinking that there's something wrong with you if you want to sleep is definitely wrong. There's nothing wrong with somebody who's tired when they're pregnant; they're carrying a tremendous load.

*Q:* The mornings have been pretty rough. Is it because I'm older? When is it going to stop?

*A:* If we treat you or if we don't treat you, it'll stop around twelve to fourteen weeks of pregnancy. The drugs that we have to stop this nausea and vomiting will provide you with some relief from the nausea. And they are safe. It's funny how people worry about the drugs that are used to treat medical problems, but don't consider that the problems, left untreated, may also in fact affect the fetus. Nausea and vomiting are a case in point, because severe and prolonged vomiting may have a very detrimental effect on the fetus.

*Q:* Since I'm older, do I have a higher risk of miscarriage?

*A:* Probably not at your age. If there is a risk of miscarriage, it's going to occur in an older woman.

*Q:* What do you mean by "older"?

*A:* I would say near forty, several years older than you are.

*Q:* My husband and I like to disco. We really like to go out. Would you say that I should slow down on that also?

*A:* No, I think that's okay. Again, you should let your own body be its guide. If you feel tired, then you should stop, that is, if you are having a perfectly uncomplicated pregnancy. There seems to be no question that increased activity will predispose you to increased uterine contractions. And increased uterine contractions contribute to premature labor. If you're having any of the complications of uterine contractions, then I wouldn't advise any kind of strenuous activity. In the absence of complications, it seems reasonable to go ahead.

*Q:* What breast care should I take to keep myself in shape?

*A:* We like to have our patients call the people at the Le-Leche League. We think that they have good information for patients. There are other women who have breast fed and they also have information about nutrition. Should people not want to avail themselves of that service, I usually have patients make sure that they have a good, wide-strapped bra so that they do not have shoulder pain. I suggest that they use plain baby oil or some other form of mild oil that can be rubbed into the nipple. If there's any colostrum or expression of milk (which can be washed off once or twice a day) they should use the oil. Also I suggest that they do use a pad in their bra so that if there is any excretion, they can throw the soft cotton pad away and the nipple won't be irritated. For those women who have inverted nipples, we have a little exercise to evert the nipples and again, with the use of lanolin-based oils, or with baby oil, or with mineral oil, the breasts become very supple and the nipple very capable of being utilized.

*Q:* Will I have problems with breast feeding because I'm older?

*A:* Oh, no.

*Q:* Are there special precautions that I should take during my pregnancy because I'm older?

*A:* Not really. Live your life as normally as possible. There will be a couple of lab tests that we will suggest because you are over thirty. One is the procedure of amniocentesis to test the fluid around the baby. The other is ultrasound—the use of high-speed but harmless sound waves that will outline the baby inside your womb. These tests will help us reassure you that the baby is okay (see Chapter 4).

*Q:* Could I have natural childbirth at my age?

*A:* Absolutely.

*Q:* Would you recommend it?

*A:* Sure. As long as you know that you're not committed to it. My only concern about natural childbirth is that people think that's the goal. It isn't a goal; it's an entry into being a mother. You don't fail at motherhood if you decide that you are either too uncomfortable or you're too anxious to attempt natural childbirth. It means different things to different people. I think that if you do not want to have drugs during your labor, I'm all for it. If you want to have drugs during your labor, then it becomes my job to make sure that they're not going to hurt you or your infant. We can decide that as your pregnancy progresses.

Q: How long can my husband and I still have sex?

A: I don't think anybody has ever answered that question satisfactorily, so I tell my patients that they can have sex up until the end of the pregnancy. Again, for the average couple sex is both anatomically and physiologically uncomfortable toward the end of the pregnancy. That doesn't mean that you won't need touching and caring from your husband. I'd like to see him sometime during the pregnancy so that I can talk to him about the changes that are going to occur to you. Similarly, what you two should know is that at the moment the baby is born, you will instantaneously become for each other the second most important person in the world, and you and your husband should discuss the fact that you will no longer be the most important people to each other. That's very important.

Q: Will I still desire sex until the very end?

A: Absolutely. You should know that if you have intercourse and your husband has an ejaculation, the products of his sperm contain a hormone that can make the uterus contract. This is nothing to make you terribly concerned about. Similarly, it appears that if you have an orgasm at the time of your sex, you will have increased uterine activity, and again this is usually nothing for you to be concerned about. Whether or not you can actually initiate labor in this way is a matter of pure conjecture. Women are also often worried about the possibility of an infection because of intercourse. The vagina, from a bacteriological point of view, is a wellspring of bacteria, so that we are not any longer terribly concerned about sex even if the cervix is apparently open. A recent study has suggested that sex during the final month could lead to infection of the infant in the birth sac. The study is quite controversial, but you should know that such a warning has been published in the medical literature. Now, we don't think that sex should be a vigorous and once or twice a day process, but certainly to fulfill certain interpersonal relationship expectations of each other, there's no problem with reasonable sexual activity.

Q: You mentioned my husband. What do you think I should do to help him through this pregnancy and delivery?

A: That's one of the advantages of suggesting that you go to natural childbirth classes. Again you must realize that going to a natural childbirth class does not commit you to practicing that routine. But the husband is an integral part of the birth coaching these days, and I think that in understanding the process that his wife goes through, he is no longer excluded from the process, that fatherhood is an active process and not a process by which you only watch your wife. By having him go to the classes, take a tour of the labor room with you, be aware of the changes in your body, and having a counseling session with me, he will contribute to the post-natal adjustment.

Q: Do I have a greater risk of having a premature baby because I'm older?

A: At your age, no, but in women just a little bit older that's probably true.

Q: Is there any way that I could prevent it?

A: No. Again, rest and a decent diet seem to be the most important positive things that one can do in a pregnancy.

Q: How can I prepare myself so that I'll have the easiest possible labor? Is that possible to do?

A: Yes. I think that the more you know about your labor and the more you know about your pregnancy, the easier the labor will be. The maintenance of exercise patterns and nurturing the development of your own body are crucial. Some women actually go through one of the courses dealing with vaginal stretching exercises. But I think that the psychology of the birthing process lends itself to a far more satisfactory labor than any physical act can do. We see a tremendous range of women's physiques, but there's one consistent patient who has an easy labor—that's the patient who is relaxed, who understands herself, and who understands what's going on about her.

Q: Therefore, it's really more in my mind than in my body?

A: I think so.

_Q_: What about baths?

A: Many women will take a bath even after they are in early labor. No problem there.

_Q_: How about keeping myself clean? Things like douches?

A: I am opposed to douching under any circumstances. I would prefer that you not douche at all. I'm also concerned about why you want to douche. If it's because of a vaginal discharge, you should see me as soon as possible.

_Q_: Now, I've got to travel a lot for business. Can I travel until I deliver, or should I begin to stay home and tell the boss I can't go out after a certain time?

A: Well, it makes sense to tell the boss that you can't go out after a certain time. The comfortable woman, the woman who understands what's going on and is in a familiar environment, is likely to have a much more uninvolved labor. If you're traveling and in a site which is unfamiliar to you and in which your physician or labor coach or husband are not around and you go into labor, you're simply not going to have the same amount of comfort or support during labor. You can travel, provided you understand the consequences. From a physical point of view, I don't see any reason not to travel.

_Q_: So what you're really saying is that if I _have to_ travel later in my pregnancy, to check with you and find out the name of a doctor in the area where I'll be?

A: That's correct.

_Q_: Should I be particularly careful about coming into contact with any illnesses?

A: Well, I think that any viral illness is potentially dangerous to you. Your lungs are different when you're pregnant. Your ability to deal with certain infections seems to be changed when you're pregnant. So avoidance of large crowds in which cold and flu symptoms are prevalent makes sense.

_Q_: But I'm a schoolteacher who is in constant contact with sick kids. What should I do?

A: Well, there are some vaccinations which would help you. Of course, the flu vaccine is one which we recommend. During your pregnancy, no matter how old you are, we are going to check you for rubella to make sure that even though you don't remember having the German measles, you might have had them, and we'll check your blood to see if you've already had the illnesses. This is not the time to be immunized, but on the other hand it's a time to make sure that if there's an outbreak in your school, you are not around.

*Q:* Tell me something, doctor. How would I know if something was not right with my pregnancy?

*A:* Well, our patients will commonly tell us when the baby is not moving well. That's just about the only way that you can detect any abnormality. Doctors use other characteristics of the pregnancy: the rate of the growth of the baby in the uterus, the quality of the way the baby feels when we examine you. As far as you yourself understanding whether or not there's anything abnormal about the pregnancy, about the only thing you could identify would be the absence of fetal movement. We want you to call us immediately if you think you haven't felt life.

*Q:* Is that a greater risk because I'm older?

*A:* Probably not. In the absence of any other systemic process such as high blood pressure, I don't think so.

*Q:* Because I'm older, would I be better off having a Caesarean section?

*A:* It's hard to say, but it certainly cannot be predicted. If you mean that from your point of view you are worried about a vaginal delivery because of the stress of having a baby that way, then it's my job to make you understand that having a Caesarean section is a terribly stressful procedure. It is not a substitute for a vaginal delivery. It is a major surgical procedure and has to be approached like that.

*Q:* So you think I can deliver from below just as easily?

*A:* Usually.

*Q:* What am I going to have to do during the six weeks after the baby is born to get back to normal? What should I look forward to?

*A:* Well, a lot of it depends on whether you're breast feeding or not. I recommend breast feeding for a variety of reasons, not the least of which is it will make the uterus smaller more quickly. It will stop the vaginal bleeding quicker. It will more quickly improve your pelvic reconstruction, so to speak. I start people doing some "push-aways" from the wall ten times twice daily within the first few days they are home. Then there are some straight leg lifts, just gently raising the feet up off the ground to a count of ten, ten times, a couple of times a day. This is so that there's some tone built up in the upper body as well as across the abdomen. I think a walk as soon as you have gotten yourself acclimated to being back home, especially when the weather's nice, is to your advantage. I usually see patients short of six weeks myself; most people are well enough to do just about anything they want to by three or four weeks. Since there's commonly a need, for instance, to reinstitute intercourse, this becomes an issue. Few people are interested in waiting until the doctor says that it's all right to have intercourse; they're going to initiate intercourse any time.

*Q:* And that's okay? That's safe?

*A:* Yes, I think it's safe. I don't know any reason why that could be dangerous. Again, what are you worried about? The only thing I would be worried about would be discomfort.

*Q:* Can I expect to have pain on intercourse either during pregnancy or afterwards? My husband asked me this question.

*A:* Women will commonly have pain from a mechanical point of view prior to having their child, and this is, as I say, almost purely mechanical. There is always a normal vaginal discharge. But sometimes, during pregnancy, the very high hormone levels in the body will produce such excessive stimulation of the vagina that there is a specific discharge which can cause irritation to both the husband and the wife that is not pleasant. There is not much you can do about that. The solution to the mechanical activity, of course, is simply to find a sexual position which is compatible for both partners; and commonly this is a "woman above" position, so that she can regulate the pressure on her abdomen.

From the post-delivery point of view, however, again if you're breast feeding, you should know that the vaginal wall takes a long time to get back to normal. If you are breast feeding, there's a possibility that you will not have enough stimulation from your ovaries to make the lining thick and healthy again. This will lead to decreased lubrication, increased discomfort, and, at times, intermittent vaginal infection. I see many women who think there's something wrong with them at that point because they have discomfort during intercourse and, therefore, it's much less pleasurable than it was prior to the pregnancy. All one has to do is use some standard lubricant or to be a little bit patient and understand the process, and everything will be back to normal within a few months.

Q: Wouldn't a lubricant that kills bacteria be the most sensible thing to use?

A: It makes a lot of sense. Different people react to these medications in different ways. Sometimes the lubricant itself is an irritant. Sometimes from a sexual point of view, there's an aesthetic liability because of the feel of the material, it's "gummy" a few minutes after application. As long as you understand that it's not a problem between the two of you, that it's a mechanical problem due to the pregnancy, your sex life can be manipulated to meet your needs at that point. The most important thing to understand is that this is always temporary, and with a little patience, things will be back to normal within several months.

Q: What about another pregnancy?

A: Well, another pregnancy is unlikely to occur at that time. Again, although breast feeding is not a pure contraceptive, it certainly seems to be protective up to about six or eight weeks. After that point, you will start to ovulate, even though you are breast feeding, and then it's no longer a satisfactory contraceptive.

Q: Suppose I wanted to go back to work? Could I stop breast feeding after about six weeks? Will it be okay for me and for the baby?

A: You can stop breast feeding, but don't expect to stop lactating. It's very important for you to understand that. Once lactation is initiated, nothing medical science can do is going to stop it. We certainly would never supply you with hormones at that time. What we would like you to do at that point is to take a very tight bra, perhaps one that is a pre-pregnant bra, strap it on, take aspirin, grit your teeth, use ice packs, and within thirty-six hours, lactation will be severely inhibited.

Q: Could I tolerate going a full day without feeding the baby if I fed the baby at night, when I came home, and in the morning before I went to work?

A: It's a terribly individual thing. Chances are you could tolerate it, but what I would prefer to see you do would be to use some form of mechanical milk pump.

Q: This question is probably the most important to me. What can I do to assure that I'm going to have the healthiest baby possible?

A: Well, I think we've covered a lot of that. First of all, be immunized against the standard infections that people usually have, especially rubella. Second, put yourself on a decent diet, that you have taken the time to understand. Third, have some kind of an exercise pattern that allows you to keep your muscle tone and body tone in good shape. Fourth, you find some classes or counselling which allow you to understand the changes that are going on in your body; preferably doing that in a group setting. You're in a very large sorority with other people who have the same fears, the same anxieties, and the same questions you have. Lastly, make sure that you and your husband *want* the child, that you can *plan* the pregnancy rather than have it appear as an interruption in the relationship between the two of you. Then, given a little luck, you're going to have a very healthy and happy baby. That's what I wish for you.

Q: Thank you. Speaking of embarrassing questions, I guess I really have to ask this embarrassing question and that is the thing that probably worries me most. Being thirty-four, is there a greater risk that something serious could happen to me? Do I have a greater risk of dying than a younger woman?

A: Probably you do. But the chances are so remote that I would strongly support people who wanted to get pregnant getting pregnant up until age forty. At your age, I would not be worried at all.

At this point the doctor pauses, reaches behind him, and pulls a thin orange textbook off his shelf. The words *Clinical Obstetrics and Gynecology* flash by your eyes. He leafs through the pages slowly. Your eyes follow his fingers as your mind digests his response to your last fearful question. He finds the page and points to the following graph.

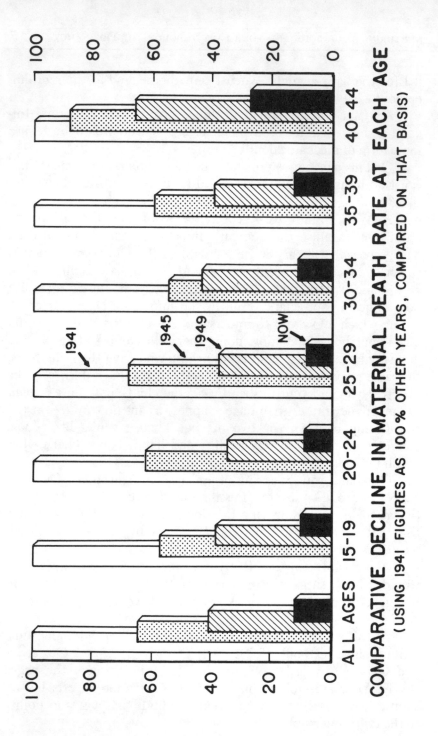

COMPARATIVE DECLINE IN MATERNAL DEATH RATE AT EACH AGE
(USING 1941 FIGURES AS 100% OTHER YEARS, COMPARED ON THAT BASIS)

Q: What does that mean?

A: This Canadian study was extensive and important. You can see that, in this day and age, the risk of maternal death during pregnancy is not very great. Your risk may be just a shade greater than for a woman in her twenties. Even those women over forty, where the last bar rises, are not at great risk. Look at the figures. Look at how the risk of pregnancy has fallen over the years. Don't worry. Together we're going to make sure you are as healthy after your pregnancy as you are right now.

Q: Will I have to see you more frequently?

A: No. Not unless problems arise. And I don't expect any. So we will visit on a monthly basis for awhile. But don't hesitate to call me if any questions or problems arise.

Q: Thank you. You've made me feel much more relaxed.

A: It really makes things much easier for me as well as for you in the long run, so I'm equally glad we had this chat. There is one more thing, however.

Q: What is that?

A: I think your husband should join you during a few of your visits. I would like to meet him before the baby is born. And I think he should be as involved with your pregnancy as he will be with the baby after it arrives. Tell him he has the same freedom to call me. I look forward to hearing from him and seeing him.


You leave the office. Most of your questions have been very well answered. But you will have many more as the specific daily minor problems and concerns of a normal pregnancy happen to you and your body. This is just the beginning of a close and trusting relationship among you, your husband, and your obstetrician. You have made a wise selection. You have picked the right doctor for you and your baby. Now you are a team working to produce the best baby in the world.

## BIBLIOGRAPHY AND SUGGESTED READING

Bean, Constance. *Methods of Childbirth*. Doubleday, 1972.
Berrill, N. J. *The Person in the Womb*. Dodd, 1968.

Cherry, Sheldon H. *Understanding Pregnancy and Child Birth*. Bobbs-Merrill, 1974.

Kippley, Sheila. *Breast Feeding and Natural Child Spacing*. Penguin, 1975.

Lamaze, Fernand. *Painless Childbirth: The Lamaze Method*. Pocket Books, 1972.

Leboyer, Frederick. *Birth Without Violence*. Knopf, 1975.

Nilsson, L. and Ingelman-Sunberg, A. *A Child Is Born: The Drama of Life Before Birth*. Dell, 1971.

Salk, Lee. *Preparing for Parenthood*. McKay, 1974.

Sasmor, Jeanette. *What Every Husband Should Know About Having a Baby*. Nelson-Hall, 1972.

·

# CHAPTER SIX

# How Many
# and How Far Apart?

The February 1978 U.S. Bureau of the Census Report noted that during the 1970s American women married later, waited longer to have their first child, and allowed more time between births than did comparable women in previous decades. The report stated: "The ability to limit fertility effectively and the intention of having relatively few children have likely led many couples to a more deliberate and careful spacing of the children they do have."

How many children do you want and how far apart should they be?

With age comes responsibility; you now know that you no longer have the privilege or flexibility for totally spontaneous sexual behavior. The "Oh, well, if it happens, it will just happen" attitude is not healthy for couples of *any* age, but is particularly unsettling to the after-thirties husband and wife. There are far too many factors that should be considered in decisions about children. Possibly you have come from very large families and felt a lack of individuality, or one or both of you were only children and regretted or loved the feeling of being center stage at all times. This will play a role in your decision. Perhaps both of you are concerned about population control and have determined to do your part in maintaining a population equilibrium. Your finances, your job situation, your own parental responsibilties, your emotional frame of mind, your health, etc., all are potential reasons. In each individual situation, these factors are unique. Each of you is different; your lives together are different; and your outside influences distinctive and not like any other after-thirty couples. So the decisions must be yours. You'll want to look at some of the important considerations, realities, and myths about numbers and spacing of children, particularly as these factors apply to after-thirty parents.

## Interrupting a Career

Having children results in some degree of career interference, particularly for women. A pause in the momentum of their careers is almost always experienced by new mothers. In addition, the after-work demands of the baby, the doctor's visits, the illnesses, the night feedings, the dependency, and the nurturing needs are greatest for parents right after the birth of their child. It is difficult, therefore, to resume a career in high gear quickly after the birth of the child. The duration of this slower phase of career development depends on the individual parent and varies markedly with child care arrangements and temperaments.

Let's look at three examples of couples making decisions about the numbers and spacing of their children. Make your decisions on these issues as if you were the couple. Then we'll think through the consequences together.

*Couple A:*

You are a thirty-year-old graduate student in clinical psychology. Your husband is thirty-four and has a solid job as an accountant in a major firm. Both of you want children, love children, but have delayed parenthood so that you could earn your doctoral degree. Two exciting things are about to happen during the coming summer. In June, you'll graduate with that degree; and in late August, you're expecting your first child. Your future career plans include a small private practice in child therapy. Your husband's job is reasonably secure. There is little chance he will be moved, but a fairly good possibility that he'll receive regular and sizable salary increases. You are torn in your thinking. You are anxious to start your counselling career, but you and your husband want at least two children. The big question: How many and how far apart?

*Couple B:*

Both you and your husband are thirty-one years old. You teach school. You have your master's degree in special education and have no desire to go back to school for a higher degree. Your husband is a sales representative for a major merchandising firm. As part of his rise up the career ladder, he is moved to a better position in a different city about every three years. He is on his third job in his third city. Both of you calculate that after two more promotions and moves, he will be at an executive level in the main branch on a permanent, stable basis. Two months after you moved to this new city, you discovered that you were pregnant. You plan to take a six-month leave from teaching after the baby is born, and are beginning to wonder if you should consider another child soon after the first and not return to work until you have as many children as you both want. Again the big question: How many and how far apart?

*Couple C:*

You and your husband live in a bustling, crowded urban area. Both of you are thirty-six-year-old professionals—you a lawyer and he a physician. Putting off parenthood has not been difficult because of your busy work schedules and many social distractions. Both careers are spiralling upward and each of you has invested your effort heavily in your career. However, you have reached the point where you both want to experience the fulfillment of parenthood as another of the important and significant phases in your lives. You have cleared your desk of potential cases for about two months after the delivery, hired an expensive but highly regarded child care person, and are sharing with your husband the exciting anticipation of the coming birth. But you keep hearing from friends and relatives about how old the two of you are, and, "If you want more children, you should have them right away." Or, "You shouldn't have just one, you know." Every time you hear these warnings, you experience a mixture of guilt and anxiety. What should the two of you do? For the third time: How many and how far apart?

Have you recognized yourself in one or more of these three situations? Are you facing the same dilemmas? What did you decide was the best reaction on the part of each of these couples?

There can be no "right" answer. Here are some potential solutions that seem both rational and healthy for the marriage and career situations described.

With couple A, there are several major considerations. First, the reason for the delay in parenthood—the doctoral degree—has been realized. The start of the private clinical practice probably can be deferred for as long as necessary to create a family of the desired size. Skills won't be lost; their use is merely put off for a time. Indeed, with these particular talents, you could offer your services, free or for salary, on a very limited part-time basis while raising a family. Your full-time child counselling practice could be started at the point where family demands are lessened or shifted to other people. Your husband's job appears stable in location and wages, so that the addition to your income immediately after graduation or after your first child won't be a serious limitation.

A possible solution for couple A: Having another child within two or three years would permit this couple to enjoy two children without hampering their career potential or progress.

Couple B is another story entirely. Again, this is a couple who desires more than one child. But the stability of the home situation is somewhat tenuous because of the moves demanded by the husband's career. However, there's a light at the end of the tunnel of packing cases and moving vans: he predicts a stable home situation several years from now. The woman has skills in the teaching field that are generally marketable wherever her husband will be moved. Both of you are only thirty-one years old. Waiting until you are settled for the second child would not make you parents of an advanced age or beyond your level of tolerance or energy.

A possible solution for couple B: These two people should have at least two children, but the second child should be carefully planned for the time when career advancements, with their unsettling moves, have come to an end. For some couples, the possibility of unexpected moves hangs heavily over the marriage. In these cases, a careful consideration whether to have more than one child is warranted. In addition, if more than one child is anticipated in mobile families, planning for pregnancy at the beginning of a new career move is most sensible, allowing a stable time for pregnancy and early infancy without the added insecurity of a different home, new job, new friends, and most importantly, new support systems of child care helpers and physicians. So our suggestion to the second couple is to wait four or five years for the next child.

What is motivating couple C to want more children: their own needs or the needs of their relatives, friends, society? For some reason, the thought that two people can rear only one child is viewed as an insufficient effort by many members of our society. It is not the responsibility of every married couple to replicate themselves in equal numbers to maintain the earth's population. There are sufficient families currently have three or more children to offer more than ample balance.

Another factor is casting a shadow over this third couple. This is the pervasive myth that only children are the "poor souls" of the world, growing up lonely, maladjusted, depressed, and defeated. That is pure hogwash. Only children can be well adjusted, productive, happy, achieving people. We will discuss this in greater detail later in the book. But cross that reason immediately off your list as a prime cause for having more than one child. If you want only one child, you don't need anyone else's permission to have one.

These two people want the experience of parenthood, but they also are deeply involved in their careers. Having one child will satisfy their desire to become parents and allow them to offer "quality time" to that single youngster. There may not be enough "quality time" in their busy lives for two children, and they should recognize this fact.

Don't forget about the cost of a three-bedroom apartment in most cities. Two children of different sexes will need separate rooms eventually. If couple C has no desire to move out of the urban area, their housing costs will rise appreciably as the family grows from one child to two, three, or four.

A possible solution for couple C: You are the ideal couple to rear one child. Having more than one child to satisfy the wishes of others or your own inner fantasies would lead to growing tensions in marriage, family, and careers. It is your decision, no one else's. You will be the ones to get up in the middle of the night, leave work when a sudden childhood illness strikes, attend the PTA meetings, etc.—no one else. If you are similar to couple C, relax. Have your only child. Become the well-adjusted parents of a well-adjusted child.

## EMOTIONAL FLEXIBILITY

As you grow older and responsibilities accumulate, you begin to find that your emotional flexibility and tolerance levels diminish with each passing year. Noisy situations that previously went unnoticed suddenly begin to annoy you. Indecision angers you. You resent having to repeat directions over again. You have become a busy, mature person whose daily career and social life have been carefully structured for a degree of consistency. You can't be as flexible or as spontaneous as you were when you were twenty. Think about those days: stop and consider the flexibility of your planning when you were twenty. Then, the future was the next minute, not the next year. And as you grow older, the elasticity of your emotional responses will lessen even more.

Now add an infant to this less flexible style. The baby will require your adaptation. You have prepared yourself to respond in as tolerant and adaptable a fashion as possible through the infancy months, the boisterous school years, the explosive adolescent period. Emotionally, you feel you can go the route one time. So you have your first child.

But can you do it twice? Three times? When will you stop being able to snap back sufficiently to have the resilience to spare for a newborn infant? These are serious questions to consider when trying to solve the problem of how many and how far apart.

You can rate yourself on your current emotional flexibility so that you can judge where you are at this moment and also where you might be in three, five, or ten years when the thought of another child comes to mind or when the idea of having three children instead of two crowds into your busy, structured day.

Select the number on the scale that best fits your current state of mind or preference:

| | | | | | | |
|---|---|---|---|---|---|---|
| NOISE | 5 | 4 | 3 | 2 | 1 | QUIET |
| SPONTANEOUS | 5 | 4 | 3 | 2 | 1 | STRUCTURED |
| ACCEPTS BEING LATE | 5 | 4 | 3 | 2 | 1 | PUNCTUAL |
| HOUSE: CASUAL | 5 | 4 | 3 | 2 | 1 | HOUSE: ORDERLY |
| LOW SENSE OF SOCIAL PRESSURE | 5 | 4 | 3 | 2 | 1 | HIGH SENSE OF SOCIAL PRESSURE |
| PATIENT | 5 | 4 | 3 | 2 | 1 | IMPATIENT |
| HIGHLY ADAPTABLE | 5 | 4 | 3 | 2 | 1 | HIGHLY ORGANIZED |
| WORKER | 5 | 4 | 3 | 2 | 1 | BOSS |
| SHARING | 5 | 4 | 3 | 2 | 1 | DELEGATING |
| MOBILE | 5 | 4 | 3 | 2 | 1 | SETTLED |

Have you been totally honest? For example, what level of noise in the hallway outside your office will you tolerate before you quiet the other people? Can you sit by and watch the clutter in your house or apartment grow before your eyes as you attend to more important matters? When three appointments are cancelled the very same day and your organized calendar goes haywire, what is your level of frustration? How many times will you return a letter or a purchase order or a work outline for corrections and revisions? These are only a sampling of the questions you should consider as you rate your level of emotional flexibility. Most people lose one point in each area every five to seven years after thirty, so that your total score will be 10 points lower in seven years time.

Now add up your score. *To become a good parent over thirty, you should have a total score of at least 25.* Certainly most of you are at that number or way over. But now subtract 10 points for where you will be seven years from now. Are you still at a score of 25? If not, think twice about having children later in life.

Each additional child also subtracts approximately 10 points from your total score. So if you scored 37 at this point and plan another child within three years, you'll probably have the emotional resilience to handle two small children into your late thirties and early forties. Why? 37 minus 10 gives you a score of 27, which is over the 25 minimum.

This scale is not a final arbiter as to whether you should or should not have more than one child or how to space your children. It's a rough guide to the types of considerations that you, as an after-thirty parent, must turn over in your mind as you debate your emotional flexibility in deciding how many and how far apart.

## SHORT- AND LONG-RANGE FINANCIAL FACTORS

What are the short-range financial factors that have to be taken into consideration when you debate the number and spacing of your children?

1. There may be a temporary or more prolonged loss of income with each pregnancy in the two-paycheck family.
2. There may be doctor and/or hospital expenses with each pregnancy if you don't have high benefit health insurance.
3. Each child needs space. This may mean moving to a bigger apartment, adding on to your house, or renovating a room currently dedicated to other activities.
4. Babies and children eat. And food costs money. As does their clothing, the furniture, strollers, diapers, etc. Not everything lasts from child to child, especially if they are close together in age and are using things simultaneously (or if clothing can't be worn by the opposite sex).
5. Pediatrician visits, shots, house calls, etc., can prove costly.
6. Last but far from least, in the two-career family, responsible child care is expensive.

With each child, the length of time you'll need someone at home to take care of the child increases by several years, escalating your expenses.

It's not true that if you have had one child already, the additional expenses of having another are halved or quartered. Expenses are reduced somewhat: one caretaker can look after two children for a slightly higher fee; clothes, some furniture, and toys can be passed on to other children, and food expenses are not raised significantly when several children are eating the same meal. Medical bills, dentistry, schooling expenses, and music lessons, however, cannot be consolidated. Each child will cost a great deal; a realistic estimate of at least 75 percent of that first child's cost should be used in planning for more than one child in your future. Can you afford these costs a second time?

Many of us who had three, four, or five children in the 1950s and 1960s had no idea what we faced in long-range financial responsibilities fifteen to twenty years later. We were not blind to the visible costs nor ignorant of the potential expenses. The cost of educating, clothing, and caring for teenage children today far exceeds that of our parents. A doctor we know had three children in college at the same time with the fourth youngster in private school. Education costs exceeded $35,000 that year. Is that figure mind-boggling? Consider the fact that every year notices arrive from colleges throughout the nation announcing that tuition has gone up again—to $4,000, $6,000, $8,000. No one can predict where the spiralling education costs will end. But for now, you must consider these future costs in making your decision on how many and how far apart. Should the children be spaced four years apart so that one will finish college after the other begins? Don't forget advanced degrees. Few college graduates will be able to attain the job they want twenty years from now if the advanced degree competition continues to intensify at the current pace. The key question is not how far apart the children should be, but how much money you think you will be able to save between now and then—and your educated guess as to what you will be earning at that time. A guess? It's a rough and imprecise estimate, but at least you're making an attempt to "crystal ball" the future in financial terms before you face a crucial decision. (Economic planning is discussed further in Chapter 10.)

## Your Age at the Crucial Times in Your Child's Development

Most of you have parents who were considerably younger at the time of your birth than you are now in relation to your own family. You're familiar with parents who were forty years old or younger during your late adolescence. Throughout your early childhood until your marriage, your own parents presented you with the role model of younger parents. You're having your first child and possibly subsequent children much later than your parents did, maybe twelve or more years later. But your more advanced age isn't important.

A thirty-two-year-old parent of a twelve-year-old Little Leaguer has no particular advantage over a forty-six-year-old parent. Possibly we're prejudiced. We're in our mid- to late forties and have boys and girls in their early and/or late teens. We feel quite as capable as the younger parents who often surround us at the ball games, school plays, and car pool lots.

Even if you have any hang-ups about being too old to do an adequate job during the growing-up years of your children, and if your negative feelings are strong enough, nurtured and strengthened by your own experiences with your younger parents (or an unsatisfactory experience with older parents), it is highly likely that you will play out your prophecy and do less than the best parenting job.

A healthy, intelligent, sensitive person in his or her thirties or early forties who makes every effort to remain in that positive condition can be a good parent all the way up through the adolescent years. Beyond the age of forty-five, parenting an infant begins to have long-range hazards of a generational gap that is insurmountable during those crucial developmental years.

Think it over carefully. If you are balking at having the second child at thirty-five because "I'll be too old when she's eighteen," you might be using the age differential as a cover-up for the real reason—you simply do not want to have another child at this point in your life. There is nothing wrong in making that decision. The most important thing is for each of you to be honest with yourself. Childrearing is not a race—it is a slow and careful walk through those important developmental years with your child or children. You are not in competition with anyone else. Only you can know with how many children you can successfully take that walk, and your age should be one of the least important considerations.

## Myths and Realities

Let's consider some of the myths and realities surrounding the number and spacing of children—issues that are of particular importance to the after-thirty parent.

*Having children close together provides them with instant friendship.*

MYTH: In most families, children born close together (two years apart or less) have the highest degree of sibling rivalry. This is a reasonably healthy competitive relationship in which there is vying for parental approval. Only later in life will these relationships mellow into close friendships.

*You should wait for the second child until the first one goes to school. Then a new baby doesn't create as much jealousy.*

MYTH: Bringing the interloper, the new baby, into the home where the firstborn has had total center stage for five or more years will often cause some jealousy and need for readjustment in the older child. Also, attending school while the new baby remains at home with you to receive attention can create school problems if not anticipated and dealt with. We are *not* against waiting this length of time. But two things must be considered: you will be that much older, possibly out of practice with babies; and secondly, the jealousy which will be felt by the first child should be recognized and dealt with beforehand and during the infancy period.

*The more children I have when I'm over thirty-five, the greater chance there is for abnormalities.*

REALITY: This is only true in the case of Down's Syndrome (Mongolism). Other genetic diseases will occur with *no* greater frequency with increasing age, but Down's Syndrome will. However, the incidence is not frequent enough for us to feel that you should give this more than a passing consideration. Check with your obstetrician for high risk fetal monitoring during the pregnancy, as discussed earlier. It will tell you what you need to know to make appropriate decisions for you and your family.

*I have to have more than one child. Only children are known to be less well adjusted.*

MYTH: As mentioned previously, only children can be extremely well adjusted, creative, achieving individuals. (We know that must be true since one of us is an only child!)

*I have a boy. We really want a girl. They tell me that your amniotic fluid cells can be tested so you will know.*

REALITY: Yes, the sex of your unborn child can be told to you months before the birth. But suppose you got pregnant a second time just to have that girl and the cells show that you're carrying your second son. What are you going to do? *Don't* have a second child to even up the sexes. If you don't get the sex you want, you can start a parent/child relationship on the wrong footing and never get back into a healthy stride. Consider adoption if your child's sex is that important.

*I should have more than one child since I'm thirty-five. It isn't fair to one child to have to care for me when I'm sixty-five and my child is just starting to live his life.*

MYTH: Who said sixty-five is infirm and dependent? Most sixty-five-year-old Americans are mobile and self-reliant. In addition, you'll have financial supports such as social security, a pension, or retirement benefits. Remember, the retirement age has often been raised to seventy; it may become obsolete. Stop planning for your vulnerable old age. You'll probably be kicking up your heels and will get insulted if your child suggests in any way that you are "old." If you want two children, have them, but not for your waning years (which may be well beyond what you predict at thirty-five). Have the second (or third) child for *now*—at this moment in your life.

*My husband and I have been thinking twice about having another child. We're both thirty-nine and have a seven-year-old. The three of us live in a two-bedroom house. I could keep the baby in our room until it was time to move it into the seven-year-old's room. But something tells me that mixing two children who are so different in age is not a good idea.*

REALITY: There is almost a semigenerational difference when seven years separate siblings. Forcing them to room together could create serious problems for the older child at first and eventually cause the younger to sense the anger and rejection within his or her own bedroom. Children need space within which to grow. If you can afford that space, you can afford a second child. But ask yourself this question honestly: at thirty-nine, which of the following is uppermost in both of your thinking, the need for a second child or the comforts that the money spent on the additional room or new home would bring to all three of you during the next five years? This question is by no means selfish introspection. It is an honest perusal of what you might be feeling five years from now. And it is essential before you make a decision at your age.

*We have thought about having a child of our own and then adopting the next child. That way my work would be interrupted only once for a pregnancy. And we could have a two-child family. But we've been warned that it is very bad to mix natural and adopted children.*

MYTH: A balanced, loving home in emotional equilibrium can adjust to the mixture of natural and adopted children. Only if the adopted child is made to feel "different" will the adaptation become difficult. However, please bear in mind that the care of the adopted child will require the same degree of attention and life adjustment as will the care of the natural child. Children need the same parental quality time and attention, whether natural or adopted.

*It really doesn't matter whether you have one, two, or seven children. You relate to the kids the same way and they adjust to each other the same way also.*

MYTH: There is a decided difference in the time, energy, focus, and communication in a home with one child, two children, or a large number of children. You, as parents, can be spread only so far. The same goes for the children. Clearly this depends to a degree on your parenting style; but in general, you will have the flexibility to experiment with time and activities more when you have only one or two children, whereas you will need much more structure, economy of motion and communication, careful organization, and time distribution as your family grows larger. Many after-thirty parents simply cannot handle a large family as well as taxing jobs and the responsibilities of community and elderly parents. But there are some over-thirty couples who are so highly organized that not only can they manage a roomful of children, they might be able to run Washington, D.C., at the same time.

Two siblings usually will be closer than four siblings. The age span and the diffusion of feelings over the larger numbers commonly cause this situation. Two, however, will be far more competitive than four (with increased need for parent refereeing in the clinches.) But we have seen families of four children who are tightly knit, caring, concerned siblings, fighting but loving to the same degree, and growing closer as the years passed. Each home is different. This is where the answer lies. The more communicative, loving, and organized the home, the easier it will be for you to have more children.

Is having only one child okay? Absolutely. See Chapter 14 and relax. But if you opt for a large family and you're after thirty, please look before you leap. There's no turning back once the children are here.

These are some of the issues and problems that must be brought into focus when the two of you sit down to decide if you are to be a one-, two-, or three-child family in your thirties and forties. The question of how close together the children should be is equally important. As we suggested previously, you are no longer wholly spontaneous people. That is one of your great strengths as an after-thirty parent, you can think carefully and maturely before reaching decisions. So you must consider what is best for each member of your potential family.

# II

*Changing
Lifestyles*

# CHAPTER SEVEN

# The Two-Career Family

Many of you have delayed parenthood because of two concurrent careers that needed attention, commitment, and time. Now you have come to the realization that the needs to nurture each of your separate careers will always continue, but time is slipping away from your potential parenting years. You would like a compromise —careers and parenthood. But you are worried: Can the two of you parent a child while maintaining the forward thrust of both of your important jobs? Most of you can. A few of you should reconsider. We can't answer your very personal and individual questions. But we can point out the problems so you can think through your own particular living/working situation.

Planning ahead is the key to negotiating the tricky balance of parenthood and careers. Often planning requires thinking of the many accommodations that have to be made to child's demands—sickness, PTA meetings, scouting, trips, etc.—and then making contracts with each other about sharing these career interruptions. Many of the child's demands are predictable. Here are some issues that you can and should discuss—and resolve—before the birth of your child.

## TIMING

When is the "right" time or the "wrong" time to consider a baby in the career patterns you have set for yourselves? Do you feel that sense of urgency, as do so many after-thirty parents, that you *have* to have children now, or parenthood will escape forever? Is the time right according to whatever future you can predict about your career? Do you have time to work out the many details of parenthood that will be thrust upon you with the new career interrupter in the home?

There are several questions you must answer for yourselves when you consider the timing of the baby in your personal and professional lives.

*First, the essential question: Is there place within that hectic, productive, energized dual-career marriage for the entry of a small child, full of his own needs, moves, demands, and crises—now?

*If there honestly is no time for that child this year, will there be time within the next five? It is not necessary to enter the parenting game when you are over thirty years old just because you feel that sand in the hourglass of time is running out—a few more grains can fall if more time will improve your comfort in parenting. If, however, you are waiting for that fabled "steady state" in job mobility and security, know that it may never come. You may have to decide to accept the difficult and disquieting sensation of balancing a struggling career in one hand and a squirming infant in the other—when your career responsibilities are a bit lighter. That could be tomorrow, or the year after next.

*Are the two of you willing to negotiate, not only with yourselves but with your bosses, the elements of time and responsibility, and to mix them with a healthy and willing seasoning of sacrifice?

You cannot graft a child onto a busy lifestyle—the child will wither and the marriage and career may perish. Time the blending of your after-thirty child systematically and intelligently into your active and exciting schedule. You will have the satisfaction of seeing not just another job well done but another essential facet of your life placed in its proper and productive order. With planning, the two careers, the two parents, and the child will grow healthy and happy together.

## THE PRE- AND POST-DELIVERY PERIOD

Several key issues will face the woman when she enters the last trimester of her pregnancy. The first: "When should I take off from work to await the arrival of the baby?" There are no pat answers to that question. A large part of the answer rests in how you are feeling and the type of job you do. Other than a sense of heaviness, swollen feet, and need for rest periods during the day, most after-thirty women are able to work up until the moment that labor begins. If you have a job that requires your presence, you can plan to be there until the time you deliver. We suspect that as a forward-moving career woman, you have not permitted yourself very much coddling along the way. You have probably been driving just a bit harder than necessary, spending long hours, worrying over issues after work, and so on. So it will probably not be difficult to tolerate some minor discomfort as you near the date of expected delivery. However, you also have to allow yourself the luxury of nurturing your body—and your unborn baby—during this period. If you work until the very last minute, slow down your overdrive, leave on time, take rest breaks during the day, and leave the office work and troubles on your desk rather than bringing them home with you. You and your husband need to engage in much planning and enjoyment of each other at this crucial time of your lives. Allow yourself the privilege of indulging your home time with yourself, your husband, your fullsome pregnancy, and your future motherhood.

Unless significant health problems intervene, it does not seem reasonable to leave work for a pre-delivery waiting period any sooner than six weeks prior to the expected birth. Some of you will want the time to prepare yourselves, your bodies, and your homes for the anticipated child. But remember, you are a mature, active career woman. Time will begin to hang heavy if you give yourself too much waiting. The days before delivery move so much more quickly if they are filled with exciting and meaningful activity.

A *big* question comes up next: "How long should I stay home with my baby after the baby is born?" There is no formula. The best solution depends entirely and completely on you—your marriage, your job, your emotional frame of mind, your financial status, and the caretaking arrangements you have been able to negotiate for the hours you are away from your child.

It is perfectly reasonable for you to return to work after six weeks of recuperation. Good caretaking, an understanding that crises will necessitate absence, and clear guidelines between husband and wife about sharing the responsibilities will make this return to work possible. If you are breast feeding, it may be difficult to continue because of the build-up of milk in your breasts during the work day. But the baby can be bottle fed in your absence. And we have known very successful career women who have solved this problem by pumping their breasts during the day at work and continuing to breast feed for six or more months while managing demanding careers. With planning, almost all aspects of parenting can be accomplished along with an active career.

Will you be harming your child by getting back to your work situation so quickly? Again this depends totally on you. If work comes home with you, absorbing your mind, taking your time, keeping you out late at night, the answer may be Yes. But if you allow yourself to spend "quality time" with your infant, and later growing child, then little will be lost for either of you. We'll talk more about quality time later in this chapter.

Some of you are thinking: I have waited so long to become a mother that I don't want to miss those exciting first months by rushing back to my job. If your career has reached the steady, safe state where a prolonged leave will be acceptable, then take your time and enjoy more hours with your baby. But recognize that most of you will very likely need to return to that career eventually. So prepare yourself emotionally to leave the baby in the hands of a competent caretaker. There can be nothing as painful as a sudden tearing apart of mother and baby by career demands without careful emotional and logistical foresight.

We caution you not to make the decision to stay home with your newborn for a prolonged period of time because of the myth that it "makes you a proper mother," or because "it is the right thing to do." You *must* want to give up your career temporarily. You should have a real desire to spend the hours away from the job at home with your child. There are no judges or juries to condemn you if you do not make this particular decision. In fact, a reluctant housebound mother is likely to give less, feel less, and want less from her infant than the one who has made the decision out of personal need rather than societal expectations. You can be a good mother either way: returning to your career within weeks or staying with your infant for a prolonged period of time. Good motherhood is not related to the amount of time you spend, but how well you use the time you have.

## QUALITY TIME

We have been using the phrase, "quality time," frequently. Quality time can't be easily defined, but we'll take a stab at it. It is time spent in the best possible manner to enrich the relationship between parent and child. It may be time spent in cuddling and rocking, or quiet listening time when a parent sits and attends to a child's thoughts and concerns, or a touch football game on the back lawn, or shopping together in the local supermarket, or a dinner where the child shares the day's events with his or her parents and listens as they do the same. Quality time is touching, holding, hearing, disciplining, sharing, visiting, or just being together without anything more meaningful happening than the quiet joy of sitting next to one another fully aware of each other's presence.

Good quality time combines many of the above. At the same time, loving and caring are consciously blended with talking and teaching. Emotions are shared. Attention is given to each other's lives. Understanding occurs. Quality time is a concept so important that we'll discuss it more later, especially in Chapter 10. It is the answer to the question: "How can I be a good parent after I'm thirty years old?"

It must be obvious that as parents, you can't offer your child quality time when you're preoccupied with other issues or activities. Being older, it is often more difficult for you to find this quality time in your busy and responsible day. But those periods of time, whether they are hours or just minutes, must be there.

Quality time can take many shapes and forms. We should like to share a story of how one older mother solved the need for quality time in her home. She was an over-forties physician. Her husband led many community organizations and frequently was out of the home at night. There were three children: five, six, and seven years old. Both parents suddenly became aware that they were losing contact with their growing children because of their extremely busy career schedules. The woman designed a plan. Every evening after homework was done, each child brought his or her shoes into the bathroom to be shined for the next day. The parents alternated evenings. Mother or father would sit on the bathroom floor with the child and together they would shine the pair of shoes, chatting the entire time. The process lasted twenty to thirty minutes depending on the things being shared. If serious problems spilled out from the particular child, the adult hands moved more slowly over the already shiny shoes. This shoe-shining ritual continued into the children's older years. Tragedy struck—the father was killed in an automobile accident. But the nightly shoe shining continued as the mother pursued her active medical career to support her children and herself. Obviously those shoes did not need to be shined every night. This woman had made time in a very busy lifestyle for sharing. These three children are now fully grown, very successful but, most important, happy and well-adjusted adults. This wise woman had discovered the true meaning of "quality time."

## HOUSEHUSBANDRY

Many of you have deferred parenting until you were over thirty years old because the wife's career was as essential and important as the husband's. This new "single standard" society has long been overdue. Now that we are watching the ascendency of the two-career marriage, in which each partner has invested heavily in his and her lifetime job, we should point out that the partnership must adapt in other ways.

The husband must be prepared to play an equal role in the housekeeping and parenting chores if both careers and marriage are to survive. You may feel that there is a great deal of mutual sharing occurring now. But with the arrival of your child, more will be needed if both careers are to be kept in high gear. Unless the husband is willing to assume a degree of househusbandry, there will be very little possibility that two growing careers can be maintained after the arrival of your child.

Another interesting phenomenon has occurred with after-thirty career parents during the last few years. Husbands have found that it was *their* specific careers that were in a relatively "steady state" and able to be deferred, while the wife's was moving forward at a fast and unbrakeable pace. Some of these men had professions such as writing, painting, composing, book reviewing, and so on, that easily permitted homebound activities. But others actually took leaves of absence or sabbaticals from careers to become the househusband and stay home with the infant child while the wife returned to work. At times this was for fiscal reasons; child care was too expensive. Others decided that one of them should nurture full time until the child reached six months or a year of age. Whatever the reasons, there has been an upsurge in husbands assuming the full-time nurturing role as househusband during the early period while the wife pursues a dynamic career.

Will this work? Of course it will work, and we approve heartily if the decision is made by *both* husband and wife with foresight and mutual agreement. "Mothering" is, of course, not confined to the female gender; males can be effective nurturers, caretakers, child rearers on a full-time basis. The stereotyped macho male with the aloof image has crippled our mental growth as a nation for far too long. It has also deprived many fathers of the joys of parenting: the holding, cuddling, nurturing, sharing. It is highly unlikely that the child during any stage of development will become confused as to "who is my mother and who is my father?" There are many well-adjusted, gender-secure young adults from families where the father has played the nurturing role, and the mother that of disciplinarian. "Role reversal" parenting does not seem to confuse children. Househusbandry and child caretaking can allow two careers to thrive.

We not only approve of the husband assuming a goodly or greater share of the child care chores, we encourage this enthusiastically. The best way to know your child is to care for your child. The same theory works for your child's ability to communicate with you. The older father may feel a sense of generational distance from that new baby; the best way to bridge that span of years is to encourage him to become a nurturer and caretaker. The years will slip away like magic as he begins to enjoy and understand his own child.

## WHO WILL GIVE UP WHAT FOR THE CHILD?

Part of the concept of shared parenting is the idea that there will be times in the two-career parenting process where one of you will have to make an adjustment, expected or sudden, for the sake of your child. Who will be the one expected to make this adaptation? If it always falls on one of the two of you, a parenting imbalance in the two-career family will occur; one career may suffer and your marriage be weakened in the process. It is difficult to plan ahead for every exigency and emergency that could arise, but some advance thought and negotiation between the two of you might prevent a confrontation between career and child at a crucial time in your lives.

We can't do this planning and contract building for you. Your marriage, your relationship, your careers are quite specifically and uniquely your own, and can't be generalized or patterned using universally acceptable solutions.

Let's share some real-life situations. Put yourselves in the roles of the couple as two-career parents—placing your specific jobs in perspective—and make decisions as to (1) how you would respond, (2) how you *should* respond, and (3) the effects of your response.

*Situation 1:*

It is 2 P.M. Wednesday afternoon. You have an important sales meeting in half an hour; your husband mentioned a lecture he was invited to give to the faculty at the university that afternoon. The phone rings. Your six-month-old has a high fever, according to your reliable child caretaker. Quickly you call your pediatrician. He asks that someone bring the baby into the office to be checked as soon as possible. What are you going to do?

### Questions to ask yourself:
**1.** Should you or your husband go? Would you feel comfortable in telling the babysitter to call a cab and take the baby to the doctor's office?
**2.** Can you wait until you get home, check the temperature again, and call the doctor a second time? Is it safe? Will you be able to function adequately at work?
**3.** Should you call your husband right before his speech to tell him about the baby's fever?
**4.** Which of you has the manageable appointment, the one that can be postponed, deferred, or missed?

### Some observations:
There may be times when you will need to depend on the babysitter to act as your substitute in crises or child-related situations. Just be certain you have selected one with good common sense. Waiting with a six-month-old with a high fever is generally not wise. It sounds like your husband is about to give an important career speech. Should he be rattled beforehand with this news? Is his situation deferrable? Not likely. Yours? No one but you can know that answer or make that decision.

*Situation 2:*
You and your wife have alternated taking your nine-month-old son to the pediatrician for all previous visits. But this time both of you are booked with important career appointments. You have called the office and the next open appointment is several weeks from now. You have tried to be punctual with the baby's immunizations. All check-ups have gone well; he seems to be healthy and happy. But you feel uneasy about asking the babysitter to take him this time. Your wife has tried to cancel her appointment, but can't. You are scheduled to be in court with an important case. Should you take the later appointment and block off your calendar since it is your turn to go with the baby?

*Questions to ask yourself:*

**1.** Are there important issues you wish to discuss personally with the doctor?

**2.** Are there any health problems faced by your youngster, or does he seem as well as ever?

**3.** What immunization is to be given and can it wait?

**4.** Do you want to begin asking the caretaker to perform duties which you feel are your responsibility?

*Some observations:*

Don't make the proverbial mountain out of a molehill. You have a healthy baby who needs a shot. If there are no other major health issues, you have two viable and rational options—either postpone the appointment until you can go, or allow the caretaker to take the baby to the doctor's office this time. Perhaps the second choice is better, for you can observe the caretaker's capacity for emergency action in a nonemergency situation. Remember, you haven't lost your turn if you don't go. Just make certain that you block your calendar for that one-year check-up. Make that appointment today. Be prepared.

*Situation 3:*

Both of you have been putting small parts of your paychecks aside in separate accounts. You want a European vacation in the future; your husband is saving for a summer home in the mountains. When your little girl is three years old, you realize that there are not enough children in your urban community with whom she can play. You investigate a reputable day care center. One of you will have to spend the money in the bank to send her to this special school. Which of you will make the sacrifice?

*Questions to ask yourself:*

**1.** What are the potentials for significant salary raises in the future?

**2.** Are there areas in your daily lives where money can be saved where it isn't being saved at present—taking lunches, smoking, car pooling, etc.?

**3.** How realistic are the two goals: the European vacation and the summer home? Which one means more to the two of you, or has the best chance of being realized?

4. Which is becoming more important: a private time away together (Europe), or a private time away from the city as a family (vacation home)?

### Some observations:

Unless you know that a raise is assured, don't plan futures on possibilities, only realities. The two of you must bear in mind that this day care center will be only the beginning of additional child expenses. Be prepared. Saving for something special in the future is part of our positive planning and dreaming. Without looking ahead, we get lost in the strivings and struggles of the present. We need those dreams; we need to plan and save for them. You may have to plan for your dreams in sequence, one before the other. Decide what is important, and save for one thing while using the rest as needed by your child.

### Situation 4:

Your five year old is in kindergarten. She has announced that parents' visiting day is next Friday. Your wife shakes her head; there is no way she can go; she has to be at a convention out of town that day. You check your appointment book; there are two sales representatives who can be rescheduled for the afternoon. But you close your eyes and see yourself sitting in that classroom, a thirty-eight-year-old man surrounded by an army of twenty-five-year-old mothers. The thought causes you a rush of sudden embarrassment. What are you going to do?

### Questions to ask yourself:

1. Is this something that you can miss? How important is it to your daughter?

2. Could you arrange to go another day?

3. Aren't there some things an older father should be spared?

4. Would it be wrong to call your mother or your wife's mother and ask either one of them to represent you?

5. Should your wife set up another day and go at that time?

*Some observations:*

Each of us after-thirty authors can remember that first visiting day when, because of our deep desire to be the ideal parent, we anxiously went to one of our children's open house days. What a pleasant shock to find about seven or eight other fathers sitting in that room self-consciously smiling back at us—a few as old as we were. What a relief! But what if we *had* been the only ones. Would our masculinity have been threatened, our role as father thrown into question? Of course not. Only three people would have cared at all that we were there: the teacher, who would have enjoyed having a father in the room; the father, who would have enjoyed watching his child; and, most important of all, the child, who would have had a parent to represent her or him that day.

*Situation 5:*

A note has come from your nine year old's teacher. Wednesday night is PTA night. She would like to see you there—Johnny is having school problems. Your husband has a community board meeting. He is vice president of an important organization and is reluctant to miss the meeting. Wednesday night is your yoga night. Somehow the relaxation you obtain then helps you get through the rigors of your job for the rest of the week; at forty-one, you feel that it is important to your work output. Neither of you wants to give up the prearranged appointment to face the music with Johnny's teacher. Who gives in?

*Questions to ask yourself:*

1. Are Johnny's school accomplishments important to you?
2. Will your husband be thrown off the community board if he misses the meeting?
3. What will create more tension in your career: losing the yoga session or discovering the extent of Johnny's problems?
4. Are you not going because you want to avoid the truth? Will what you hear mean more sacrifices in time and money? Are you fearful that you have reached the limit of both at your age?
5. Could you ignore the request and call the principal to set up a special meeting when you have the time?

*Some observations:*

There is no question that, as more mature parents, you have more structure and responsibility to your life, day and night. However, the responsibility of your child's education has few equals when it comes to your time and attention. We are quite biased on this issue. We hope you both have decided to go to the PTA meeting instead of the other appointments.

*Situation 6:*

Billy is fifteen and on the junior varsity football team. His games are every Tuesday and Friday afternoons at three thirty. Half are on the home field. He has pinned the schedule up in the kitchen and hinted that he would like you to be there. Your wife teaches school, so she can make almost every game. But your schedule at the office makes attendance at every game almost impossible. You feel guilty, but each time you don't show up, his silence worsens the situation. What can you do? You're forty-nine and people other than Billy are depending on you. You just can't drop everything—or can you?

*Questions to ask yourself:*

1. Are you resentful that your wife is the only one of the two who can cheer for your son at every game?
2. How many other times have professional duties kept you from fulfilling an obligation to Billy? Have you prepared him for those possible times?
3. Are there other ways of participating without being there?
4. Suppose you just showed up in the last quarter?
5. Is it permissible for a parent to say, "I can't be there"?

*Some observations:*

You won't miss his high school graduation. And we suspect that if he wins an award, you'll be sitting next to him at the dinner. Also if there is a special game (like a championship or playoff game), you most probably will adjust your calendar to be present, rooting him on. But reality must be part of every parent/child relationship. Billy will have to understand that your career will not allow you the freedom to attend every game. Your wife should understand this as well. However, it does seem logical that you could block off one or two afternoons to be in the stands yelling your head off. And don't forget that being interested in every play even though you couldn't be there will reassure your son how much you really do care.

These are only six potential situations that illustrate the need to think, plan, and negotiate during your child's growing years when you are part of a two-career family. If each parent works at child rearing separately rather than as a functioning team, there will be a sense of chaos. It is the mix of sharing, sacrificing, honest appraisal, giving in rather than giving up, postponing, and setting priorities that will permit the older parent to keep his or her career in motion and be a good parent at the same time.

## Hours and Minutes

Have you ever considered how you spend your time each day? Have you calculated a typical work or weekend day to get a clearer perspective on what use you make of time? Most people take time for granted. It is used to make schedules, catch planes, collect hourly wages, arrive for movies, or to make us wonder where it went and why so quickly. But few of us analyze what use we make of time. If you are an older parent, you are probably burning up time at an accelerated pace. Where are both of you busy, active, career-oriented people going to find the time that your child will need? There are only twenty-four hours in a day, and they can't be stretched or extended. Time must be found somewhere.

Why the big fuss about time? Because it is this very issue that plagues the two-career family when faced with the problems of bringing up a child or a family of children. We can only give our children quality time when there is available time to be given.

Sit down now and calculate your twenty-four-hour-day, both a typical work day and a typical weekend day. Use the following major headings, thoughtfully and honestly adding up the hours (or minutes) that you spend on each:

Sleeping
Eating
Bathing and bodily care
Work
Hobbies
Entertainment (in home)
Entertainment (out of home)
Travel (commutation, car pooling, etc.)
Visits (friends, family)
Phone
Work preparation or study
Household chores (including cooking)

Have you detailed a typical working Thursday in your life? Look at it carefully. Have you thought of all the time you spend? What does it all add up to? It may shock some of you to see that the figure exceeds the normal twenty-four-hour day!

We would like to hypothesize the time spent by a typical thirty-three-year-old career woman:

Sleeping: 8 hours
Eating: 2 hours
Body functions: ½ hour
Bathing: ¼ hour
Work: 8 hours
Entertainment (in home): 1 hour
Entertainment (out of home): 0 hours
Travel: 1¼ hours
Visits (neighbors): ¼ hour
Phone: ½ hour
Work preparation and study: ½ hour
Household chores: 1½ hours
Hours spent: 23¾ hours
Time left for child: ¼ hour

Certainly the thought of having only fifteen minutes to spend with your child seems ludicrous. However, the allotments as projected are within reason for most over-thirty career women. Outside entertainment is not even included. Where can a career woman find the time to rear a child if there are only fifteen extra minutes in her day?

We could do the same for the working day of the after-thirty father with quite similar results. Again, where is the fathering time in the busy work day?

It is there. Time is malleable; it only *seems* fixed and immobile. Where in that busy day can time for rearing a child be found? The decisions as to whether you sleep less, hobby less, cut down on time spent on household chores, spend less time on entertainment, talk less on the phone, or change other flexible parts of the work day, depend solely on you. But you must readjust and reschedule your day to find a *minimum* of one hour to devote quality time to your child during a typical working day—both of you, father as well as mother.

What are some of the concrete things that you can do to adjust your day to find more time during the work week for your child? Let's look together at that tight schedule.

**1.** That fifteen minutes you spend visiting neighbors might be postponed until the weekend. During the week we need every minute we can get when the baby is awake. A saving of fifteen minutes here.

**2.** Trying to combine evening in-home entertainment (1 hour), work preparation (½ hour), and household chores (1½ hours) within an evening when you want to spend more time with your child needs a firm reassessment. Share the household chores as a couple or be satisfied with something less than perfection during the work week, or else (if finances permit) seek domestic help at this stage of parenting. But cut down this figure to no more than forty-five minutes for each of you. It may be necessary during the work week to be more selective with your TV and reading, paring home entertainment down to an average of forty-five minutes per night. This saves fifteen valuable minutes. There is no way you should go to the office less well prepared. If you follow this regimen, you have saved one whole hour for your child.

**3.** Keep phone calls to a minimum. Share the obligatory parent calls with each other and space them every other day. Your family and friends will understand that there is a new demand, a new baby in your house. Cut the phone time to fifteen minutes. Again, a savings of fifteen minutes.

By merely programming your work nights and days in this fashion, you have found 1½ more hours to spend with and attend to your child. These are very valuable minutes. The time is there. You merely have to reprogram to find it.

The same exercise can be conducted for the weekend day. Let's take a thirty-seven-year-old career man on a typical Sunday. Does this sound like you?

> Sleeping: 8 hours
> Eating: 2½ hours
> Body functions: ½ hour
> Bathing: ¼ hour
> Work: 0 hours
> Hobbies: 1½ hours
> Entertainment (in home)
> or
> Entertainment (out of home): 2½ hours
> Travel: ½ hour
> Visits: 1 hour
> Phone: ½ hour
> Work preparation and study: 1 hour
> Household chores: 1 hour
> Reading paper: 1 hour
> Hours spent: 20¼ hours
> Time left for child: 3¾ hours
> Time left for wife: 0, if child gets all the above

It isn't too difficult to see how time can be reclaimed from this weekend to have sufficient for both child and wife.

**1.** Wife and child are also a hobby of sorts. At this stage of the game, give yourself permission for no more than one hour of private hobby time. You have saved thirty minutes.

**2.** Why not visit on one weekend day and seek entertainment on the other? You could save as much as one hour on one day and two and a half hours on the other.

**3.** The luxury of reading the Sunday paper that you enjoyed before the birth of the baby may need a slight readjustment. Your hour may have to be streamlined to a forty-five-minute deadline. Fifteen minutes saved. Insignificant? Not when the minutes begin to add up to hours of personal communication between husband and wife or parent and child.

Using this scheme, you have reclaimed from one hour and forty-five minutes to as much as three and a quarter hours on each of your weekend days. The sacrifice has been painless; the gains in family time are invaluable.

So you see, the weekend days also need careful planning if you're going to have the quality time to give not only to your child but also to each other. But this can only be accomplished if we reprogram our days carefully to allow for the entry of the other significant people: our spouse and our child(ren).

Time will not rearrange itself for you. You must be active and manipulate the minutes and the hours on your own. There is a delicate balance of time for two-career over-thirty parents. Maintaining that balance by constant realignment will keep the family comfortably on top of the tightrope of full career schedules, childhood and marital needs.

# CHAPTER EIGHT

# The Male Dilemma: What Inside Me Needs to Change?

You are thirty-three years old, still think of yourself as a young man, and you try to keep in shape by jogging or playing tennis or racquet ball. You went to college and midway through your junior year began to sense what you wanted to do with your life. After you graduated, you took a year off, worked, saved money, and finally went on to get an advanced degree. You tried a few companies until you settled on the one for whom you're now working. You've made it slowly but surely up the corporate ladder, moving from a junior executive to the lowest senior executive position very recently.

While in college, you experimented sexually with a number of women, resisting the temptation to become involved with any one particular person. While working the year before graduate school, you met someone who was also deeply involved in her career; the two of you finally moved in together during the last months of your advanced schooling and a year later you were married. You were twenty-seven when you got married; she was twenty-six. Both of you had just begun your respective careers and decided to wait for children. With each passing year, it has seemed sensible to keep putting off becoming parents. Somehow you had begun to think that the issue no longer was an important priority in your marriage.

Yesterday, over dinner, your wife announced that she felt ready to have a child. You felt shocked and unexpectedly frightened. This morning, your mind is foggy and confused. Hundreds of thoughts and images tumble about inside your head. You sense that your entire life is about to change, your responsibilities will be refocused, your freedom limited. Last night when she asked if you wanted to have a child, you answered, "Yes." But this morning you're not sure. You ask yourself: "What am I getting into at my age?"

This is the story of only one potential after-thirty father. Each of you is a distinctive, unique person, with background, career, marriage, motivations, concerns, and priorities that may differ from the individual described. But the one thing that many of you share is the final dilemma faced by this man: "What am I getting into at my age?"

What you are getting into is a new role. Gears will have to be shifted and directions changed to some degree as this new state of fatherhood is accompanied by changes in your marriage and personal life. There is *no* way that you can simply allow fatherhood to "just happen." If you do, you'll get knocked out in the process—your career, your marriage, and your role as a father may go down for the full count unless you give thoughtful preparation to the entry of a new child in your mature life.

What are you as an over-thirty man that makes you so different from your younger male friends and relatives? What characteristics do you possess that need attention before and after the birth of your child at your somewhat older age? Let's look at a successful over-thirty father.


## The Structured Professional

One major point is that the forward thrust of your career will not have to be hampered by the birth of your child. If anything, the motivation to dedicate yourself to providing for your expanding family may subconsciously raise your ambitions and achievements.

Some changes may need to be made in your previous job activities, however. For example, many career people use the after-work cocktail hours to firm up business deals, reward employees, establish important business relationships, or confer with staff members. These hours may now become crucial "quality time" hours to spend with your new child. If you are a two-career family, these after-work hours will also mean a combined effort by husband and wife to take care of the baby, prepare the evening meal, and plan the activities of the after-dinner hours. For many of you, these after-work hours that were once free and flexible will become the times of your househusbandry.

How serious is this change? Not very. Anything that can be accomplished over a drink between 5 and 7 P.M. can also be accomplished at a lunchtime meeting. Some people set up breakfast meetings, or have dinner with staff or associates on prearranged evenings. Learn to save time effectively by mixing business with pleasure.

Suppose you have to leave work on a particular day because it's your turn for the doctor's visit, your time to respond to the illness call, or your expected attendance at a teacher's conference. Are these dangers to your career? Unlikely. Most bosses are also parents. And even though they may not have had the same sharing arrangement that you and your wife have worked out, they will understand. It is highly unlikely that you'll leave the job during a crucial business conference. Other people, including your wife or other caretakers, can be mobilized at those times. Stop worrying. You have juggled so many conflicting appointments during your professional life, there is probably no better trained person to maneuver fatherhood through the hurdles of your career.

Becoming a father at your age does not mean that you have ceased being an employee. As a mature career father, you must reassess your time. Negotiate with your wife and colleagues for the essential, fixed times and assignments. Then integrate being a father into your career and marriage. Your career as a father will cause you to organize your career better as a professional.

## The Mature Spouse

You're quite different from your younger male married friends. Many of you have had much more time in your marriage to establish the role that you play successfully as husband to your wife. In each marriage, those roles are quite different. Even if your marriage is relatively new, you, as a more mature man, have been through sufficient male/female relationships and interactions to have established creative responses to your role in the husband/wife scenario.

To some degree, this comfortably structured and often flexible role within your marriage is going to change for the worse, and you must change right along with it. Your wife no longer sees you only as her husband; she is now beginning to look at you as the father of your child. There will be times when your need to tell your wife about a particularly disturbing aspect of your day as a means of releasing some inner tension may have to be postponed as you change a wet diaper. Likewise other conflicts will inevitably arise, such as when both of you are feeling particularly romantic and a three-year-old begins to cry with an earache. If your role as husband has included strength and calm during crises, you may find the roles reversed when dealing with childhood problems. If your ability to make decisions has enriched your marriage for both of you, it may change when your wife rightfully claims that ability when making decisions about the new child. If nurturing your wife has been a significant personal pleasure for you, you may find the reverse situation: your wife's nurturing of the infant may begin to spill over into a sudden additional concern about your health and welfare. Many subtle shifts will occur with the arrival of a child into a mature, structured relationship.

On occasion, the baby's arrival creates such a sense of motherhood in the wife that she begins to transcend her role; the home becomes a matriarchy to the husband. The wife assumes her role with a vengeance and tends to shut out the husband from the inner circle. This rejection causes the husband to feel unwanted. Usually, women move through this possessive period. However, if the issue can be discussed ahead of time, talked about when the first signs are appearing, and gently turned around so that the husband/father is allowed into the mother/child interaction, the matriarchal situation gradually evolves into a three-way relationship—a family. But if this turnaround is not accomplished, the father runs the risk of taking a permanent "back seat" in the family as his wife establishes a mother-dominated household. Is this common? Unfortunately, it appears to be. And the risk is much greater among after-thirty couples, where the waiting has created pent-up needs for expression of motherhood in the woman.

Try facing this particular dilemma with a two-fold approach. Allow your previously comfortable husband role to bend, mold, change, modify during the times that you and your wife care for and share the pleasure and concerns about your new child. But realize that you *cannot* give up what you were before the baby's arrival. Too many changes at a single point in a marriage can be fatal to the relationship. Maintain enough of what worked before in your role as husband to support and reassure your wife and yourself that there has not been a complete revolution in your lives. Return to these comfortable roles as husband and wife during the child-free hours. This will establish clearly that you have adapted to the arrival of the child and that you are still the same husband and lover who fathered the child months before.

## The "Only" Husband

You've heard of the only child who receives all the parents' attention and love. You are the "only" husband. For a time, you have not had to share your wife with many other people, particularly within your own home. It is true that her mother may want some of her time; she frequently owes some of herself to her own professional colleagues. As a mature woman, she probably has established several strong and meaningful female friendships. But once the front door of your own home has been closed to the outside world, you have been the center of her attention.

All that changes dramatically with the arrival of your new child. Younger couples often pass so quickly through the stages of courting, marrying, and having children that a sense of belonging to each other gets muted and diffused before it can be firmly felt by either. But the more mature couple, whether married for a long or short period of time, usually considers the belonging aspect of their relationship as primary. Belonging is not ownership, they have found. Belonging for the after-thirty couple is the realization that the other person has willingly relinquished some private time to focus on you as a partner. This makes your time together even more meaningful.

Enter the "interloper," who will be taking away some of that time. Bottles, diapers, baths, strollers, doctor's visits, illnesses, increased visits to and by relatives, will all cut into the time that once was yours. Your natural response will be one of anger and resentment.

There are two points that have to be cleared up before you can stop feeling sorry for yourself.

1. There was no way that a new baby could come into your home without your wife assuming some motherhood roles. That means giving time and attention to the baby. You knew this, even though you did not know the extent of it. You know now that you are going to have to share the time, affection, attention of your wife with your child for many years to come. But it will be a very different kind of time, affection, and attention. Parenthood takes nothing away from the feelings that one of you previously felt or demonstrated toward the other. Look for different forms of loving. Don't confuse the love between two adults with the love expressed between a parent and child.

2. The second point is equally important: What makes you think that your wife is so delighted with the shifting of *her* time and attention away from you? Remember, this is a new experience for her as well. She may be over-responding to prove that she can succeed. Waiting as long as she has to become a mother probably has created doubts within her mind about her mothering capacity. What she may need is the reassurance from you that she is doing a good job as mother and wife. She wants to relax and allow the balance in your lives to return to normal. You cannot assume for one moment that your wife has *willingly* relinquished her role as wife to take up the consuming role of mother of a new baby with-

out some deep concerns, regrets, and worries about you as her husband—and your previously comfortable marriage.

How can you get out of the dilemma of feeling rejected? How can you feel part of what is happening rather than a detached and distant bystander?

Accept the fact that the baby will be occupying much of your time. Do your share of nurturing the baby—and your wife in her mothering role. Accept her support of you as an involved father. Recognize and talk about the fact that your relationship has moved into a new dimension without discarding the important aspects of the previous one. Plan "private time" together and make as meaningful as possible the hours you and your wife spend together. Understand your wife's need to succeed as a mother. Reassure her, but also let her remain aware of *your* needs as her partner in as tactful and open a way as possible. Don't repress or hold back; keep talking to each other. This is essential if the arrival of a new responsibility within your marriage is to have a positive effect.

The key word is *share*. Share the responsibility. Share the love. Let her know how you feel; encourage her to do the same. Being a parent need not always be a relaxed, joyous experience. Letting off steam with each other along preestablished lines will bring you closer together, allow you to support each other, and solve child care problems. This can only strengthen your marriage and make having a child after thirty a challenge, not a chore.

Remember, you "only" husbands, you are *not* losing a wife, a companion, a lover, your best friend. You are entering a new phase of your relationship—one in which the element of sharing becomes the key to your happiness.

## The Private Person

You're a busy man. As an older father, you hold a responsible job. There are few quiet moments during your work day. If your wife works (and she probably does or will again in the near future), she too faces the same type of crowded career day without any time to herself. There must be some way out of this problem if you are to be an effective father. Private time allows you to rejuvenate, refresh, reassess, relax, and return with the necessary patience and judgment needed to be a good father.

So you can see that it is essential for you to make sure that you do have this private time in your life. It also becomes important that you negotiate with your wife, so that she too has sufficient time to herself during the crowded week. This private time will not pop up spontaneously; it must be carefully arranged between the two of you. Often a scheduled evening out for each of you as individuals rather than as a couple works wonders. Occasionally, taking an older youngster out to relatives, an event, or just for dinner and a drive while the other parent relaxes at home can prove equally rejuvenating.

You owe it to yourself, your wife, and your child to plan some private time in your life. You had it before the baby arrived; you need it even more afterwards. You will be a far better father and husband if you do.


## FRIENDS

Because marriage has been delayed in the case of many over-thirty fathers, it is likely that these men have developed firm and meaningful friendships with other men through the years of bachelorhood. Even men who've been married for a long time without having children will be much more prone to spend evenings out with male friends than those younger men whose children arrived in their early twenties. One of the very real dilemmas faced by the over-thirty man as he approaches fatherhood is the question: "Am I giving up my friends because we're having a child?"

Friendships are essential. Your friends help you work through problems and uncover aspects of your personality that neither wife nor child could. Without friends, both male and female, you can become a prisoner within your own nuclear family. You need the fresh perspective and insights of friends. You need their objectivity and their concern. You need the continuity that they, as well as your wife and child, bring to your life. You must allow yourself to continue your friendships even though you can't spend as much time, and you'll have to rearrange your schedule or cancel occasionally because your child needs you. Despite these changes, friendships should be worked at with vigor to keep them vital and alive.

As before, it becomes essential for you to be sensitive to the very same needs in your wife. She too has accumulated friends during her childless years. There may be no more important time in her life when she will need the support, affection, and affirmation of her friends than after the birth of a child. These friends may symbolize to her that her life has not changed dramatically; it has merely expanded to include another exciting dimension.

Work together to ensure the continuation of personal friendships after the birth of your child.

## THE SON WITH A MEMORY

It is very common for fathers to say, "You know, I'm doing the same things that my mother [or father] did. And I resented it when I was growing up. Why am I repeating their mistakes?" We repeat what our parents did because it is basically the only model of parenting we have learned. We respond instinctively with the action or word that we remember from our younger days, no matter how we felt at that time about the fairness or correctness of the reaction. We don't consider the possible options open to us as parents, which include but *expand* our own parents' methods in rearing us.

You are over thirty. Days at the office are trying. Your wife expects you to do your share of disciplining, training, counselling, advising. You arrive home tired and edgy. Your wife turns to you with a discipline problem. Your most likely response is to go back and use what you know—your own father's response. It's quick and expedient. Who has the time after a busy day at the office to sit down and consider possible options? Then you watch with dismay when your own child reacts even more negatively to you than you did years before to your father.

As mature fathers, solve this dilemma the same way you would a complex management problem at work. Use the points of strength from your past experience, avoid the known weaknesses and failures, and allow yourself the guidance of others. Listen, learn and do—in that order.

The main point here is that you shouldn't allow your memory to lock you into set patterns or conservative stands you learned a generation ago. Avoid being a boss in your home, even if you're a boss from nine to five every day in the office. Even though you may love and respect your own father very much, consider his parenting practices honestly and objectively, then build from his strengths and shift away from his weaknesses. You are your father's son, but your own man. Give your child a tradition of creative individualism by observing your actions.

## THE OLDER PERSON

One of the major dilemmas in your role as an after-thirty father is the realization that you are beginning to grow older. As your child ages, so will you. You keep wondering and worrying: Will I look older than all the other fathers in his first grade class? Will I be able to play ball with any degree of energy when my son wants to? Will I be able to keep up with his physical exuberance? What kind of role model will I be when he reaches eighteen and I'm in my mid- to late fifties?

Relax. You're underestimating your child. First of all, you *will* have the necessary energy when the youngster is small. You are not the person your child will be wanting to romp with; he wants *other children* his or her own age. You should provide your child with friends and playmates as early as possible. You can't be your child's best friend. You are his or her father, not a lifelong playmate.

Only as your child matures will he or she realize that you're somewhat older than the parents of some of the other children. But you will not be the only mature father. One out of every three fathers are older (see Introduction). And being older and more advanced in your occupation will give you the advantage of community stature and financial flexibility not possessed by some of the younger parents. In fact, the scales will be tipping in your direction as "Who's got the best Daddy?" is debated.

There is a misconception that teenagers measure us by our physical appearance. That could not be further away from reality. Young men and women measure themselves against our values, achievements, philosophies, life patterns and styles, and community acceptance, to name a few of many qualities. Our physical appearance, our age, our degree of "being with it," is not as important as what we believe in and who we are. You don't have to be a thirty-nine-year-old father to qualify as a good role model for a seventeen-year-old son. You can be fifty-three years old and be top notch as an example to him. There is a sense of style, class, achievement, and self-realization that comes with age that adds dimension to the models provided by older fathers.

If your child rejects you at any point, it will not be because you are a more mature parent, but because your fathering practices aren't working. Don't let your age offer a way out of solving any problems that exist in your home. Age is the least likely cause.

You are an after-thirty father. You are facing a number of unique dilemmas in your new role as parent. Which ones have you solved and which ones lie lurking ahead ready to ambush you as you make every effort to be the best possible father you can be for your child—and for yourself? Here are some statements which an after-thirty father who has resolved almost all of his major problems could affirm. Check off the quotes you feel that you also could affirm honestly. Then reread the ones that are not checked off and consider how you can solve each one.

* I have solved the after-thirty father problems because:

1. I realize that I want to have this child as much as my wife does.

2. I feel that this is the best time in both of our lives to become parents.

3. I realize that having a child requires work and planning before and after.

4. I have analyzed my job and have found the time I will need to be a father.

5. The role of father does not frighten me, I feel capable and prepared.

6. I know I have to adjust my role as husband without giving it up.

**7.** Sharing my wife with the baby is expected. We've talked about how we can keep in touch with each other about our own needs.

**8.** I'm ready to share responsibility for the baby's care. I can find the time, motivation, and emotional energy for it.

**9.** I know I need private time. I can manage this well and help my wife find some private time for herself.

**10.** I'm working out with my friends ways in which we can maintain our relationships despite this new responsibility in my life.

**11.** I've discussed with my wife the need for her to do the same with her friends.

**12.** I'm prepared to make a fresh start on fathering without clinging to past tradition or allowing my fixed beliefs to get in the way of flexible parenting.

**13.** I no longer worry that I'm too old to be a father. I realize that I can offer valuable, mature parenting skills. Youth isn't a prerequisite to parenting.

**14.** My ability to act as a role model has very little to do with my age.

**15.** I realize that I owe as much to myself as I do to my wife and child. My happiness will be reflected in theirs.

**16.** I know that being a parent may be one of the most difficult and demanding jobs in my life, but it can also be one of the most rewarding.

**17.** My caution and concern at this point are healthy signs of mature reasoning. I know there are hurdles ahead; I'm merely trying to get into training to clear them.

**18.** Despite the best preparation, I'll need all the help I can get. I'll get the advice of my wife, friends, and professionals without any concern that because I'm older, I should know it all.

**19.** I can plan ahead without sacrificing the need to live the essence of the moment as fully, but also as sensibly, as possible.

**20.** I have expanded my life by becoming a father, not limited my options.

These twenty statements show much of what the after-thirty father must face and resolve. Every father faces personal dilemmas on the birth of a child. When younger, these may be financial, career, or marital. The older father has different and particular age-related concerns. None of them is insurmountable. Each part of your personality will need your individual attention and readjustment. With thoughtful planning, each dilemma will find its own solution within your particular family. You'll find that despite those moments of panic before and after the baby arrives, you can do the job of fathering as well as, if not better than, your younger male friends. Being a successful father is not related to how old you are, but to whether you have a positive, receptive, willing, and sensitive attitude about fatherhood. Add planning, and you're as close to guaranteed success as is possible in any lifetime endeavor.

CHAPTER NINE

·

# Being a Woman
# and a Mother
# After Thirty

You are a unique individual. Having waited until you were over
thirty to have this child, you allowed yourself the privilege of more
education, experience, career development, community involvement, and dedication to your husband and marriage. You are about
to (or already have) add another dimension to your already full
life—motherhood. Being a mother is in no way similar to being the
wife, student, executive, community worker, world traveler, professional, or free spirit you might have been before the birth of
your baby. Being older, you are more than likely settled, mature,
sophisticated. What does it mean to suddenly change diapers, boil
bottles, and burp a crying baby? There are moments when the in-
congruity of the entire situation overwhelms you, and you begin
to wonder who you really are. A lack of definition has crept into
your ordinarily ordered and well-defined life. A major concern
deals with the worrisome question: "Can I remain an independent
woman *and* become a good mother?"

Here are some general questions that show the concerns of
the after-thirty mother.

*Question:* "If motherhood is going to be like a new career for
me, I feel uneducated. I went to school to learn what I had to
know for my occupation. But I have no degrees in the skills of

146

being a mother. What am I going to do?"

As an after-thirty mother, you most likely have spent your twenties preparing for a career, earning degrees, or broadening your experiences in many diverse ways. The one area within which you are least likely to feel formally prepared is the career of motherhood. The prospect of entering this new career without thirty credits and an internship leaves you anxious.

Relax. The first thing that you must realize is that motherhood is *not* a profession. *Motherhood is a state of being.* It is different for every woman because each woman brings her own background, personality, marriage, values, and her own unique child into the fascinating process of mothering. You can't approach the task of being a mother in the same way that you tackled learning a profession or acquiring promotions. There is no one competing with you. Your success will not be measured in promotions, salary increases, more status, titles, or your name in lights. Mothering is a very private affair.

But of course you can prepare to become an after-thirty mother. Actually, you may need the self-instruction more than your younger friends because your life has been full of *other* kinds of learning. A longer gap exists between your own childhood and your motherhood. And you have selected many friends who are childless. Thus, you *do* need to learn about the skills of mothering.

By now you are probably adept at self-instruction. Check with your obstetrician and/or pediatrician about courses in parenting. Often the American Red Cross offers such courses, as do many of the community colleges. Other resources may be available in your community and your doctors may be aware of them. Check with the nurses at the local public health department, mother and child care division; they are often the best informed about such matters. Go to the library or bookstore and select appropriate books (we mention a few outstanding ones at the end of this section). Don't hesitate to ask other women what they have done. But beware. Experience can sometimes be defined as making the same mistake over and over again. So observe their children carefully. Make certain that you want your youngster to grow up that way before you adopt the rules and methods of others.

Assimilate what you see, hear, and experience. The result will be the development of your own individual degree in mothering that best fits your own specific situation and goals. Whom do you ask? Find a pediatrician who will answer your questions. If the one you have selected is too busy for questions, seems poorly informed, says repeatedly, "Don't worry. The baby will outgrow it," or grumbles, "What are you worried about? The baby looks okay," find yourself another doctor. You've picked a pediatrician who doesn't realize the tremendous importance of educating parents and preventing future parent/child problems. Your pediatrician should help you learn as you go through each new and different "childhood developmental phase." (For more specifics on selecting a pediatrician, see page 00.)

Ask your friends, your mother, your husband's mother, other mothers who have raised kids you like. But weigh their responses carefully to determine whether any particular advice applies to you and your child.

There are excellent child-rearing books on the market. A few examples follow:

*The Parenting Advisor*, Frank Caplan, gen. ed., Princeton Center for
    Infancy. Anchor Press, Doubleday, 1978.
*Child Health Encyclopedia: The Complete Guide for Parents*. Boston
    Children's Medical Center and Richard I. Feinbloom, *et al.* Delacorte Press, 1975.
*What Every Child Would Like His Parents To Know*, Lee Salk, McKay, 1972.
And if we may add immodestly,
*Signals: What Your Child Is Really Telling You*, Paul R. Ackerman
    and Murray M. Kappelman. Dial Press/James Wade, 1978.
(A bibliography of more child care and child-rearing books appears at the end of Chapter 15.)

Read these carefully, extracting only what is pertinent and useful to your situation. Remember, for instance, that by not adjusting Dr. Benjamin Spock's sensible but very general advice to the individual child, many mothers allowed their youngsters far too much personal freedom with the resultant rebellious cry for structure, often misunderstood as anti-social behavior. But you have the maturity, experience, and self-confidence to analyze what you read and to apply the pertinent, relevant facts and advice to your own situation. Watch other mothers in action. What are their strengths and weaknesses? What will be your strengths? Never forget that your child is an individual—what looks good in another mother/child relationship may not work in yours. Be flexible enough to discard an approach that doesn't work. Join a child care group. Keep an eye out for interesting lectures or talks. Check with your local community organizations and colleges about parenting courses. You'll find out about issues you might not have been aware of and child-rearing practices that have been forgotten in the frenzy of blending career and family.

The key is: Don't approach your child as if he or she were just another difficult assignment that has to be mastered. Become a mother by being one. Discover about mothering by asking questions, observing others, attending courses, reading books, living with and learning from your own child.

*Question:* "I work hard during the day. I need time to unwind, and I know I just don't have the same level of energy I had ten years ago. What will I do with an active child?"

You don't lack the energy to be a good mother. No matter how old you are, eighteen or thirty-eight, a two-year-old on the run will tire you out. If you intend to stay at home with your growing child, you may therefore want to arrange play groups or supervised activities with other children in the area for several hours during the day. No one can keep up with your very active three-year-old better than another three-year-old. Give yourself enough time after settling down at home in the evening for some active play, but recognize that you can only take so much physical activity and plan also for quiet time, those meaningful, warm moments when your child lies curled up in your lap listening to a story or being rocked and sung to, or coloring, pasting, or playing quiet games together. These are important times in your child's life with you— as important as the buoyant physical moments. Find the balance between active and quiet times that you can manage without giving too little or too much of either to your child.

As your child grows, you will be amazed at the strength of

your maturity and your past experiences as a balance against the youthfulness and energy available to those parents much younger in age. You'll be able to romp during the first five years with sufficient verve. As your energy ebbs, so will your child's need for you to be a playtime companion. By then, your youngster will have located friends of similar age and you'll get off the hook. This is healthy and expected.

During the early years, use your energy carefully with your child. Help find friends with whom your youngster can let out some of the physical exuberance of the first five years. Share some of the physical play with your husband (and the caretaker, if you're a working mother). Don't overlook the essential quiet moments. And know that as your child grows, you will replace your lack of twenties energy with thirties and forties wisdom and maturity—which will be far more valuable to your child in the long run.

*Question:* "My mother is so much older than the younger women's mothers. I can't count on her for much help in child care, and I'm further from the time when we were mother and daughter, so I've forgotten a great deal of what went on between us. How do I manage a good relationship between my mother, myself, and my family?"

This is a crucial concern with many after-thirty mothers, a concern not often found at a conscious level. You may worry about the fact that your mother (and father) are older and therefore lack the patience for the antics of a baby or young child. This may be true if your parents are ill, but it's more often an unfounded concern. Even though your parent may be testier and more critical of you as he or she grows older, a totally new person often emerges at the sight of a grandchild. Remember, your parents can always return the child to your arms and remove themselves when the noise or problems get on their nerves. That is the beauty of being a grandparent and that is what keeps them happy.

You don't want to hurt your mother's feelings, but you feel that she is too old to be the primary caretaker of your child when you return to work. How can you tell her without wounding her?

She may be wondering how to tell you the same thing. Her feelings may not be damaged in the least; she'll probably be secretly relieved. The thought of being tied down to an infant or small child and the concept of denying the aches and pains to play substitute mother may not be quite as appealing as you imagine. If you feel that you want her to keep her role as grandmother while you hire an outside caretaker, explain this to her. She'll probably accept her freedom far better than you had imagined.

The third concern is that you may have lost much of the past mother/daughter interaction that would be a groundwork for your future mothering. Building on the positive and rejecting the negative parts of what you remember about your relationship with your mother could be the first important step in developing your mothering skills. But your relationship with your older mother has shifted throughout these last years. She has aged and grown—first more independent, but now possibly more dependent. You *will* remember much of your interaction with your own mother as each new child-rearing situation arises, and you'll be able to select those traditions from your upbringing that you feel you want to pass along to your own child.

What is important, however, is objectivity. By age thirty, most women have passed through the various stages of rebellion, anger, rejection, antipathy, or overdependence with their mother. It is at about this age that your mother begins to look like a "human being," someone with virtues as well as faults—a person to be accepted at face value. This resolution of the unsettling mother/daughter crises so often experienced by active, ambitious women in their twenties will allow a much more natural mothering process to evolve with your own child. You will not be wasting time doing things opposite to those of your childhood just to prove a point. It is essential that a woman be as relaxed as possible as a mother. Only a person who has settled her own conflicts with her mother can relax totally and be an objective and comfortable mother in her turn. As a woman over thirty, you have the best opportunity to be in that position.

A quick summary of the answers to mother/daughter concerns: Don't judge your parents' responses to your child by their reactions to you. Being a grandparent is very different from being a parent. The grandmother may be as delighted to be relieved of babysitting chores as you are concerned about offering her those chores. Not only will you remember enough of your own interactions to help you in your new role but, because of your mature age, there's a much greater likelihood of your having resolved your own conflicts and being able to enter the mothering role in a more relaxed way.

*Question:* "I've worked long and hard in my career. The best part of my job is the sense that I am a competent individual. I've fought to be valued as a woman in my job. What will becoming a mother mean to these vital issues in my life?"

For the over-thirty mother, there are several provocative problems contained in that question.

The second issue mentioned raises the question of personal identity during motherhood. Fighting to become themselves has been a major issue for so many women that a nagging fear exists that having a child will reduce them to a faceless mass of kitchen-bound clones known as "mothers." This is absolute nonsense! You are what you let yourself become. If you want to sink into anonymity carrying a baby in your arms, that's your choice. But you could have done that *without* a baby in your arms. You *can* be a mother and a very separate, distinct person at the same time. Many very famous and respected women of our time (Beverly Sills, Rosalyn Carter, Lauren Bacall, Ladybird Johnson, to name but a few) have combined motherhood and career without losing one shade of their distinctiveness.

Another dilemma deals with the issue of the feminist who becomes a mother. Is she a traitor to the movement? Has she given in to the stereotype of the childbearing image of the woman of past generations? How can she remain a feminist and rear a child at the same time? There is nothing in being a mother that means you have given in to sexism. Childbearing is not an issue of anti-feminist subjugation. Having a child when and with whom you want is the most individualistic and unique ability possessed by a woman. In this day and age, it is an action over which she has *total* control. She alone (rather than the male in the relationship) has the capacity to carry and bear the child. Becoming a mother is not the abrogation of feminism; it is the quintessential expression of feminism.

Career and motherhood can be blended successfully after planning and preparing during the months before and after your child is born. Having a baby after you have waited and developed yourself as an individual won't change your identity. You merely add the role of mother to your other images. You can remain a strong feminist while becoming a mother. These conditions are not mutually exclusive; if anything, they are mutually enriching.

*Question:* "So many of my female friends don't have children. Am I going to get submerged in a young mother society of strollers and diapers and lose all those years of investment in the older friends in my life?"

There will be a tendency for your childless female friends to drift away from your suddenly restructured life. It will be up to you to keep the relationships alive and well—if you really want to. After the first few polite questions about the baby, these friends would enjoy other topics, similar to those you shared before your pregnancy. Motherhood may be a prime topic in your life, but not in the lives of your childless friends. In fact the subject, for many, may be uncomfortable. Be sensitive and tenacious, if you want to keep those old and valued relationships.

You can't avoid the diapers, bottles, and strollers—all of the necessary parts of family life. But you can steer clear of becoming absorbed into the society of younger couples if you want to. Start planning during your pregnancy. Ask your obstetrician to mention your name to other women in his practice who are over thirty and pregnant and talk with the women you meet in his waiting room. See if appointments can be arranged on the same day. Meet in the doctor's office and test the chemistry of the potential friendship. If you click, meet for lunches or dinners. Then try introducing your husbands. Add to your list of over-thirty expectant parents and build up a new group of friends. Then, after the babies are born, there is an established link that can be strengthened over time.

You'll want to balance your social life. You'll need the continued associations of old friends, but the support and communal experiences of the new group of mature parents will become equally as vital to you and your husband. In addition, there will be professional social obligations in your careers. It will require a bit of calendar juggling to keep all these diverse elements flowing, but it can be done. And you can control your social life by being as assertive in your selection of "mother friends" as you were in your selection of past friends and professional colleagues.

*Question:* "I've been struggling to keep my figure for the last few years. It gets more difficult as I get older. I guess I might as well give up after the baby. Can I ever look the same again?"

You've been struggling to keep that youthful figure not just for vanity but because you feel that looking good is as important to your career as it is to your marriage and your own self-image. Suddenly your belly is getting larger and you are losing all semblance of your former self. The image staring back at you in the full-length mirror is not the person you ever knew (or wanted to become). But you realize that this temporary loss of body image is the price of having a child. And everyone seems to accept—even to enjoy—your changing body. But what about afterwards? Will those older cells refuse to snap back into shape? Will your more mature body settle into a matronly figure, a fullness and sagginess that you have been fighting for the past few years?

Let's face it. You are older. And you'll have to work harder to regain the body image that satisfies you. But it *is* possible to look like the same woman you were before your pregnancy. If you return to the exercises, diet, and body and face care you practiced before your pregnancy, you can return to a physical state that satisfies you and your husband. You found the time before. You can find it now—even with a new baby. Remember that taking care of yourself is as important as taking care of your new child and your husband. It enriches all three of you in the long run.

*Question:* "It has taken me several years to organize my life, my house, and my marriage. Will the baby destroy that sense of order in my life?"

It seems that the older we get, the more we need a sense of orderliness in our lives. Neatness applies not only to the appearance of the home in which we live but also to the structure of our schedules, our work pattern, and our relationships. The over-thirty mother often has established a clear and distinctive routine that works for her. What will happen with the birth of a child into this orderly existence? At first, the sense of order can be maintained. If enough time is spent during the first few months, the house will appear neat and tidy, the schedules can be carefully constructed, the sharing arrangements fairly assigned. But in time, there will have to be a degree of spontaneity allowed into this structured life.

When the child becomes ill, some schedule adjustment will have to be made. The daytime caretaker may have a personal emergency, causing a sudden shift in husband's or wife's immediate plans. A careening two-year-old crashes into the cocktail table— order is lost along with several valued china dishes. The older parent must be prepared for some unpredictability within her life with the birth and growth of a child. The younger parent usually has less difficulty accepting this because she has yet to establish her own routines by the time her first child arrives. One of the major sacrifices you must accept with the decision to become a parent is the loss of total predictability and order in your life.

You're giving up far less than you are gaining. What is wonderful about a neat room compared to the excited laughter of a young child? What is wonderful about a carefully structured appointment book compared to the trusting hand of a child in yours as you sit by the bed waiting for the doctor?

In a nutshell: Allow as much disorder into your life as you allow fresh air into your child's room. Enough, not too much, at the right time, and with consideration.

*Question:* "I have spent the last years sharing all of myself with my husband. How can I take that away from him and share it with the baby instead?"

You won't. The love and care that you have shared with your husband is a far different form of love from the love between a parent and a child. There will still be a significant part of your adult self that only your husband can share with you. You will find another part of you—a nurturing part of your personality that differs from the part of you that supports your husband. This nurturing aspect will feed your child's needs. But there will still be time in your day to share with your husband that part of you that has sustained and fed your marriage. Don't allow yourself to fall into the trap of *not* finding that important time as you attempt to balance your career and your child.

There is plenty of you to go around. As a mature woman, you have the wisdom and perceptiveness of experience. Use this maturity to foster, first, the relationships of love between your child, your mate, and you, and then the other necessary—and wanted—friendships in your life.

Cynthia Smith was thirty-one and married for eight years when she and her husband decided to become parents. She was a computer programmer; he was an associate professor of biology at a local college. Both of them went to a parenting course offered by one of the nurses in the obstetrician's office. During the course, Cynthia met several other after-thirty women and made friends with them. Gradually the women brought the husbands into the social arrangement. Cynthia and her husband had always maintained a separate evening during which each devoted himself or herself to personal friends. On this evening, Cynthia arranged time with her college friends, some married and childless, others unmarried. Both Cynthia and her husband continued this special private evening during and after the pregnancy, alternating nights for babysitting purposes.

After the baby was born, Cynthia joined a local health club and went twice weekly. After several weeks she convinced her husband to join her, and together they began swimming every Saturday morning in the health club pool while her husband's mother stayed with the baby.

Cynthia returned to work when the baby was three months old. She interviewed several applicants for the job as caretaker before selecting the person who had the best references and who she observed was best with her baby. Her husband's schedule allowed him to stay home in the morning until the caretaker arrived while Cynthia went to work early. This meant she could leave in time to come home to feed the baby at night and spend private time with it before her husband arrived home. Then he took over while Cynthia made dinner. On weekends, he became cook and housekeeper for one day while Cynthia took a day to be with friends; shopping, lunching, going to the theater, visiting a museum. On Sundays, her husband golfed or played tennis with his friends while Cynthia spent time with the baby. After the baby went to sleep at night, the couple cleaned up, finished whatever office work or classroom preparation was needed for the next day, and shared a quick cup of coffee before going to bed.

Six months after the baby was born, Cynthia had a serious marital problem. Her husband was staying away from home at nights and she had evidence that he was involved in an extra-marital affair. She had done so many things so very well. But something had gone wrong.

Where did she succeed and in what crucial area did she miss the essential issue?

### What Cynthia did right:

1. She and her husband took a parenting course together before the baby was born.
2. She found friends who were her own age with children so that she avoided a generational distance with younger mothers.
3. She maintained her friendships with past friends, keeping open lines of communication and allowing herself and her husband private evenings by themselves.
4. She kept her body in good physical health and convinced her husband to join her swimming.
5. She selected the child caretaker carefully and arranged her schedule so that she could feed her baby at night whenever possible.
6. She worked out equitable weekend arrangements with her husband so that she could get out of the house and not feel "penned in."

So much was carefully and correctly planned. What went wrong?

Nowhere in that very busy schedule did Cynthia devote time to nurturing her marriage. She and her husband took the course together, but that was child-oriented. They swam together, but that was health-related. They shared family responsibilities. But where were the special moments together, the times that every marriage needs, the sustenance of a loving relationship—the talks, the sharing, the togetherness in a relaxed, comfortable situation? Their marriage had gotten lost in the hectic mainstream of Cynthia's after-thirty motherhood. Neither she nor her husband realized what was happening until it was almost too late. He had been having trouble at the school and after repeated futile attempts to discuss the subject with a disinterested, or over-active and unreceptive wife, Cynthia's husband exploded and accused her of being insensitive to his needs. She was hurt and depressed. But she was also wise enough to reassess her priorities and find those extra minutes in the evening hours when she and her husband could communicate without the sounds of a crying child or the distractions of a health club pool, or having to whisper wearily in bed last thing at night.

It takes a very wise woman to become a mother after thirty years of age. The wisdom lies primarily in the constant careful stepping back and reassessing what you are doing, how well it works, and what you can do better to nurture you, your husband, and your child.

You have been in control of your life up until the time you decided to become a mother. There is no reason to give up that control now. Continue growing, expanding, maturing as an individual. Maintain your identity. You can be a person in addition to being a mother. Take very good care of the other relationships in your life. Keep your career or other important interests in the center of your attention whenever possible and desired. Most importantly, nurture your image of yourself as a total woman, full of the carefully established characteristics that were part of you before the pregnancy. You are still that person. The only difference is that you have added yet another dimension to your life—motherhood.

·

# CHAPTER TEN

# The Economics
# of After-Thirty
# Parenthood

*The letter lay unopened on the kitchen table when Hal arrived home that night, and his hand paused for a brief moment before he picked it up. He suspected this was the one he had been worrying about so much recently: the final tabulation of the cost of Peter's first semester in college. He turned the envelope over gingerly and opened it, hoping that he had planned correctly. He gasped when he saw the figure on the bill; it was at least $1,000 over his estimate. He stared at the numbers that spelled the difference between a first- and second-rate college education for Peter. Was it my fault, he thought bitterly, that the cost of college goes up each year so much more than I can possibly save in advance?

*Mary was worried about the financial problems of her daughter and son-in-law as they struggled to meet their debts, and, at the same time, provide for their one son. It was obvious that the couple had succumbed to living on the "American Way of Credit," and now faced the monthly agony of piles of unpaid bills. As this grandmother enumerated her children's outstanding debts, she mentioned the payment on sixteen-yead-old Tommy's car. When we gently probed the reasoning behind buying him a car at this time of financial stress, she replied apologetically: "His mother feels that he *needs* the independence of a car."

*The report card and the familiar notes from the teachers lay conspicuou ly on the kitchen table as Jonathan ran up the stairs to begin reading his new library book. His mother looked at her husband and sighed. They both knew what was in the report card and the notes. Jonathan was doing poorly in the local public school. He was bright, bored, and had a behavior problem. In a few years, the teachers predicted, he would probably become a school failure or dropout if his attitude toward school didn't change. He needed more challenge and individualized attention, with special coursework. Only a private school could offer this to Jonathan—an expensive private school. "How," they both questioned, "can we possibly afford the right private school?"

These anecdotes focus on typical dilemmas and crises in the lives of many parents. Just because they're typical doesn't make them any easier to handle. It is not possible to manufacture money to solve the immediate financial crisis. Borrowing delays the crisis. In some cases, however (like Tommy's car), borrowing may worsen the situation. These common financial crises create a lifetime of nightmares. The risk of such a future financial crisis is an underlying cause for many after-thirty people to think twice about having children. These parents anxiously try to plan to avoid these times of financial stress, knowing that unexpected expenses make crises unpredictable.

The after-thirty couple usually has a clear perspective on their vocational goals, their earning potential for the rest of their working lives, and the predictability of their income and expenditures. They can budget and plan. But how can they predict the unexpected expenses which are part of raising a child? Is it fair to the child or to the mature couple to have a child after thirty, considering the possibility that the child's financial dependence may last well beyond the parents' earning years? Will they have to work past retirement? Is it possible in today's spiralling economy to support a child until adulthood in the manner of your choice without many sacrifices? Will the child's economic liabilities offset the joys of parenthood for the mature couple? These are all questions asked by the thoughtful prospective after-thirty parent. Economic issues are often the major worries for older parents. Such parents bring to parenthood the mature sense of responsibility that has grown out

of their extended experiences at work or home or within community organizations. It is this heightened sense of responsibility that
causes the mature parent to pause and consider the potential economic factors involved; however, it is also this sense of responsibility that will act as a positive skill in planning or deciding about
a child.

The after-thirty parent can meet the economic pressures of
raising a child? The key word is *planning*. There are some facts
you should know about what your child is going to cost you. Caroline Bird, in her 1979 book *The Two-Paycheck Marriage*, compiles
some useful statistics:

*The medical birth expenses for the normal child are about
$1,500. A good medical insurance plan will probably pay about
half that amount. The total first-year cost for the baby will be
about $3,000.

*Although costs vary by geography, a conservative estimate of
the out-of-pocket costs for any child is 20 percent of the family's
total income. This figure holds with families of all incomes except,
perhaps, the very rich or poor.

*These out-of-pocket expenses add up greatly by the time a
child is eighteen. In New York City, for instance, the total cost of
raising a middle-class child born in 1979 until he or she is eighteen
is projected at $100,000.

*The College Board estimates the national average yearly cost
for a private four-year residential college in 1978–79 at $5,110. Add
a 6 percent yearly increase, and you have a total average cost of
almost $22,500 for a bachelor's degree today.

*Hiring competent, full-time child care costs $8,000 to $10,000
per year.

*The greatest expense of child raising to the after-thirty parent
is child care, whether it be paid at the rate above, or figured from
loss of income of one parent who does not work during the childhood years. The latter figure can be derived by taking the yearly
income of that parent, multiplying it by the number of years out,
and adding a 1 percent inflation/promotion factor. For a parent
who earns $10,000 a year, for example, staying out of work during
a child's preschool years (ages birth to five) would cost that family
at least $55,000.

Some families have predictable long-range expenses that increase the cost of raising children. Parents who have crooked teeth, allergies, or other predictable genetic "pass-alongs" can expect to spend thousands of additional dollars in correcting these problems in their children. Many other chronic health problems, however, will not be spotted until after birth. Thus, medical expenses for children are hardly ever entirely predictable (for budgeting purposes) until the first or second year.

These are the facts. There are some ways of budgeting for the after-thirty parent that can minimize the inevitable expenses of raising children. You can decide that the child you want is worth your loss of income or the added expenses and then proceed with both long- and short-term planning that will help you get *as ready as possible* for the support of your wanted child. These procedures can't answer all your unexpected financial needs, but they will offer you help in making wise decisions. You'll be buying more time for fun and less time for worry.

1. *Immediately place 20 percent of your gross family income in a separate bank account.* This is the account that will be used to pay for many of the out-of-pocket costs of raising your new child. The word "immediately" means that you should start this savings *before* you have your baby. Putting the money into a separate account which is not used regularly makes it less tempting for you to withdraw these savings. This process can usually be done automatically and easily, using bank procedures which regularly transfer monies from income or dividends into the same account. The idea behind the procedure is (a) to help you get ahead of the expenses of the child from the very beginning and stay ahead by a comfortable margin; and (b) by separating savings for your child from the remainder of your banking, to be able to keep a more accurate account of the money available for child raising. Budgeting will become more predictable; expenses can be monitored more closely because each payment will require a withdrawal from a separate account. This procedure will help you keep track of the child's actual expenses, and that knowledge will help you become a better financial planner.

There is another advantage. The separate account will act as a guide in adjusting your life to your new budget. After the baby is born, those child-related expenses are going to force you to re-examine your own luxuries and needs. You'll have to distinguish between luxuries and necessities. Do this before the birth of your child so that you can begin to live a little more judiciously. Adjust early to the change in lifestyle and eliminate any later resentment after the arrival of the child. Babies take time, energy, and thought, so during the adjustment period bills may be paid late and budgets kept unevenly. The sooner you put yourself on a thrifty régime, the easier it will be to give the baby the needed time and money.

2. *Immediately budget 5 percent of your gross family income into another bank account.* Should you combine this 5 percent with the above 20 percent into one account? No. This second savings account is the *college* account (or, instead of college, the business/home starter account). This is the account which needs to draw interest for eighteen years, waiting for your child's post–high school expenses. This is also the contingency account, to help you over those really tough big expenses you had not predicted but with which you want to help your child—expenses like graduate school, a wedding, a house down payment, a business failure, or grandchildren.

*Twenty-five percent?* That's right on target according to the financial experts. That is the fiscal reality of having a baby and rearing it according to your standards. The savings will become a necessity after the birth of the child, so why not start before and keep that margin of safety? If you are able to eliminate an anticipated expense (let's say your child receives a scholarship to college), you'll have no trouble budgeting the surplus money. Kids' expenses follow a universal principle: Raising a child your way will always take more money than you have.

How do you budget for more than one child? Obviously, you can't put aside 25 percent of your income for each child and still have enough money for expenses in a multiple child family. If you have time to get those savings started *before* the first child arrives, we suggest allocating an additional 10 percent per child into those "children's funds." The preliminary savings gives you a cushion. Without preliminary savings, put aside 15 percent for each child after the first. Sure, it will hurt, but you'll expect it, and that makes the sacrifice hurt much less, and financial management for your family much easier.

**3.** *Consider all the options for child care and pick the one that best fits all your needs.* If you are similar to many after-thirty couples, you already have two careers. You will also receive great pressure from family and friends to have one of you stop working and take full-time care of the child. This option, they will tell you, is the best because it is the "natural" thing to do; the traditional role of a parent, it fits the greatest needs of the baby.

The "natural" action myth is nonsense! Many children are adequately raised and loved by parents with the help of child care workers. The decision, therefore, as to the child's care must take into consideration the economic dimensions of the problem as well as the emotional factors. You should not automatically consider a wife's stopping work to take care of a baby as the best solution. It is only one option out of a number of possibilities.

These are the factors that you'll want to study in deciding the cost and kind of child care:

*How much money will child care, either full or part time, cost if you hire a competent person? What percentage is this of the family income? Can it be afforded?

*If one of the parents, particularly the mother, quits for several years to take care of the baby, will she (or he) be able to pick up a career when work resumes? This is a particular danger for the woman professional whose career is advancing in a highly competitive field. Full-time home care could end her mobility, possibly even her career. Is the potential resentment that could be directed toward the baby worth this sacrifice?

*Many women and men have waited their whole lives for the singular experience of having children. They have put off children in favor of building careers, but the careers have been dedicated to freeing them, finally, for children. If you are one of these people, then you'll probably want to remain at home and take care of your own child. Celebrate the event. Write your resignation, ready to hand in when the baby comes, and rejoice in motherhood or fatherhood. Your decision is made. Be sure it is economically as well as emotionally sound, however, before you burn your bridges behind you.

**4.** *Plan for long-term security for your child through wills,* *insurance, and investments.* Cold, hard facts force us to realize that one of the differences between the after-thirty parent and his younger counterpart is that the after-thirty parent may not live as long as the younger parent. His child may be denied an income-producing parent during some of the youngster's dependent years. Should this stop you from becoming an after-thirty parent? Not at all! It simply means you must consider long-term financial security and a definite plan for your "estate."

"Estate planning" is not only for the rich. Almost every after-thirty parent will have an estate: personal property, financial assets, and/or real estate. If you have never done so, take a pencil and jot down a quick list of the items your family would have to dispose of if you died tomorrow. You're probably worth more than you realize.

That estate, the sum total of all of the assets owned by you, will be your legacy to your child. If your child is in college when you die, he will need money, money you would want him to have. Will there be money enough in your estate to finish school? Will he be able to realize the cash as soon as it is needed? Will he have to sell your prized oil painting to meet the costs of his tuition?

These questions don't need painful answers if you consult (a) a good lawyer about your will, (b) a reputable insurance broker about estate security, and (c) a good accountant about taxes and investments.

The lawyer will help you draw up a will that will take advantage of every tax break available to your beneficiary(ies). The will should take into account the necessity for cash if you should die while your child is a teenager or young adult, and it also should provide for the event of your death when the child is past the years when there is an acute cash-flow problem. In any case, it is wise to combine insurance planning with will and estate planning.

For insurance planning, you'll be asked by your broker to estimate the cash needs of your family for the next few years, and then the broker will draw up an insurance policy that fits these needs. Check and compare carefully the different kinds of insurance policies available to you, particularly term insurance as opposed to whole life insurance. You might estimate, as we did earlier in this chapter, that you, as middle-class parents, should have insurance coverage of $125,000 to cover your child's expenses ($100,000) and education ($25,000) through age twenty-one. And you are right— *for this year.* Sign on the dotted line, if you feel you want total protection.

But can you afford the premiums for that type of insurance? There are other issues to consider as well. If you died this year, would your mate still have a career, and could he or she help to support that child? If so, you really don't need a full $125,000 worth of insurance for this year.

Consider another fact. The $125,000 was based on *this* year. Will you need the same amount in five years? Ten years? Possibly not—many of the expenses could be over if your child is older when the insurance is purchased. The wise insurance shopper, therefore, looks into a *decreasing* life insurance policy. He protects his family during their needful years and then allows himself the luxury of spending a bit more on retirement, a vacation home, travel, or other pleasures. This money can come out of lessening insurance premiums in policies of decreasing face value. You will have protected your family during the years when they need money but you don't have to make yourself "insurance poor."

Because the after-thirty parent is often more financially secure than the younger parent, he can invest more capital, plan more benefits, consider earlier retirement, or design long-term financial plans for himself and his family. You'll need help in making these decisions because of today's complex tax laws, investment schemes, and financial regulations. A well-versed accountant is a great help to the after-thirty parent. You can discover more possibilities for investment, optional retirement, additional sources of income, and child planning than you may realize are possible. A professional can assist you in almost all of your major financial decisions.

How do you find this well-versed accountant, the understanding, capable lawyer, or the insurance broker with your best financial interests at heart? We asked several of these professionals how they picked their own support people in these fields; and each told us of the long and difficult problems they had encountered in finding the trusted, knowledgeable professionals who were just right for them. But a few general principles emerged from our discussions with them:

\*   \*   \*

\*Conduct an intensive word-of-mouth search. Ask many people who use these professionals extensively. Look for recurring names.

\*Interview *more than one* professional whom you might consider. Enter this interview armed with questions and ask that professional for his or her candid appraisal of how your particular concerns might be attacked. For example, ask an accountant how he or she feels about deductions in the "gray" areas of the IRS regulations and question him or her about the accountant's role in a tax audit. You should hear the answers that are appropriate for you. Ask an insurance salesman about the less expensive options to estate management for the next few years versus long-term plans. Note how well versed an attorney is in long-term legal management of money, estates, trusts, and wills.

\*Check the educational backgrounds of the professional to see if he or she graduated from a notable school. This criterion should not be definitive, of course; but it may add a measure of confidence if you recognize the school as one that produces outstanding graduates.

\*If a professional is recommended by a school or university, make certain that the person suggested also practices extensively. You need experience as much as you need theory.

\*Finally, if you have several choices, consider the efforts of the various professionals to update themselves. Accountants should attend IRS briefings regularly; lawyers and insurance brokers would do well to take classes that update their knowledge. If this information is unavailable, pick the younger or newer of the professionals. Why? Chances are good that he or she will have the most current information because of recent education.

The cost of raising a child seems huge at first, but the long-range picture is optimistic. The cost is indeed high initially, but diminishes steadily until just after high school, when expenses again become quite heavy. Most of the costs occur during the period of your greatest productivity financially. You may have to change your lifestyle today, but eventually you will be able to readjust to your present luxuries—and more! And you will have the joy of knowing that you have raised, in the meantime, a wonderful child.

There are ways to cut down on daily expenses in child raising. Long-range planning works well; but wouldn't it be great to be overplanned and overbudgeted—to be able to be ahead of that projected sum at the end of the year? It can be done, if you begin thinking about the usual childhood expenses and when they should occur.

Or *if* they should occur. One of the problems in modern child raising is the constant seduction of parents and children by advertisers to buy everything on the market—each product advertised as more educative, more stimulating, more necessary than the one you already have. Children leave the television set and immediately begin to make out their Christmas and birthday lists. The issue is not whether a child wants these advertised items, but whether the child *needs* them. Many busy parents practically break their bank accounts every Christmas or Chanukah trying to provide the child with what he wants, only to note in January that half the toys, games, and other gifts are broken, untouched, and cluttering up the house.

Buying clothes for children also presents the *needs versus wants* quandary. Knowing that some children can have cheap clothes at some times in their lives, cheap toys at other times, and that there are periods for expensive items, allows a parent to plan better. It has to be the *parent*, not the child, who determines what is wanted and what is needed.

Here's a chance to predict some of these wants now, and to project your child's needs. You'll be able to know when you'll need to spend more money than usual. You'll learn something about your philosophy of child rearing, too.

This list contains many items that will be presented to you as "wants" by your child; for example, a bicycle. First, estimate the age at which this item might be needed. Then decide whether the item, the bicycle, is a want or a need. If you live far enough from a school and bicycling is a must, then a bike at age six is a need. If you live near an overcrowded highway, then a bike is unnecessary at least until the child is old enough to handle it wisely. Then, estimate the costs. Many children own up to three bicycles but *they don't always have to be new*. Like clothes, they can be purchased second-hand, repaired and touched up, and loved as well as a new bike; so estimate your costs based on that assumption. Then you'll know at what age you'll have to start thinking about bicycles for your child. Try it with some of the other significant childhood items (crossing off those you never expect to purchase). Here is a partial list that you can use as an example of the way you need to plan your future child-raising expenses.

Having pinpointed future major expenses, you'll know when to expect them. But look at the list again and see what you have crossed off, what you will delay buying, what items you will buy cheaply, and what items deserve a larger investment.

Economics for the parent after thirty is a vital matter for discussion and decision. Because older parents usually have had experience in the business world, and because they have needed to budget and plan, they can approach the challenges of economic planning with greater insight and skills than their younger counterparts. The children of parents after thirty are fortunate. They'll feel secure in the stable economic base of their future. Money problems won't be a constant burden. They'll be free to pursue their full potential. And parents who plan for the economic security of their child will know the unbounded freedom of enjoying the child totally *as a child*, not an economic liability.

| Items | Age | Want or Need | Cost | How Often? | Yearly Total Cost |
|---|---|---|---|---|---|
| playpen | | | | | |
| baby carriage | | | | | |
| stroller | | | | | |
| dolls | | | | | |
| train sets | | | | | |
| bicycles | | | | | |
| musical instru- ments | | | | | |
| pets | | | | | |
| educational games | | | | | |
| music classes | | | | | |
| dancing classes | | | | | |
| drama classes | | | | | |
| books | | | | | |
| records | | | | | |
| theater tickets | | | | | |
| sports tickets | | | | | |
| concerts | | | | | |
| radio and stereo sets | | | | | |
| personal TV set | | | | | |
| formal party clothes | | | | | |
| private tele- phone | | | | | |
| motorcycle | | | | | |
| automobile | | | | | |
| foreign trip(s) | | | | | |
| summer camp(s) | | | | | |
| luggage | | | | | |

# III

---

*Parenting
from Birth
Through
Adolescence*

.

# CHAPTER ELEVEN

# Preventive
# Parenting

The common fantasy of the after-thirty parent is to be the "best mother or father on the block."

Most after-thirty parents are counting on their maturity and experience to help them be objective about their child and wise about their responses to the usual childhood needs. The joy of after-thirty parenting stems from the fact that this objectivity and this wisdom truly *can* work to help you be a better parent than your younger counterpart. But it is up to you to channel that objectivity and that maturity into your family life. This is the challenge of the after-thirty parent, a challenge not easily met because of the other demands in your lives: your career, your social obligations, your outside interests, and your need for adult relaxation. This challenge, to become an effective parent amid the requirements of a very busy life, requires thorough and careful planning. "Preventive Parenting" will help you meet the challenge successfully.

In order to practice effective preventive parenting, you should decide which important values and human qualities you'd like your child to possess as an adult. Then design a style of parenting that will achieve your goals. This practical philosophy of parenting will be distinctively your own. It must include ways to prevent the many obstacles and detours that will occur along your child's path in early life. Every after-thirty parent wants to be able to help his child prevent or solve a myriad of inevitable problems. Preventive parenting is an individual concept that helps you think through your own actions, ask yourself the reason for your responses to your child's needs, and modify your lifestyle so that you become an effective and, more important, an *efficient* parent. With your busy life, you will have to make every moment of your day count in realizing your parenting goals.

Most children need open communication with their parents. They need to know the limits of right and wrong, what is permissible and what is forbidden, and why. They need to know their parents as role models for adult men and women. They need to know that they are loved. They need to see themselves as unique individuals, with the strength to make decisions about some problems, seek advice about other problems, and eventually act in their own behalf. They need to be able to give and receive love. Your parenting, then, has to make effective use of your available time to fill your child's needs.

Several basic principles have worked for us. They could provide a beginning in your determination of your own preventive parenting style. Write down your principles, your own unique Preventive Parenting Plan. Refer to it often. Check yourself on your consistency. Try to look for milestones in your objectives (e.g., when your child tells you he feels loved). Criticize yourself for not following your own plan. Above all, don't become so caught up in the process of parenting that you forget the most essential part—sharing fun together with your child.

Here are some of our personal preventive parenting principles. You may want to live the same way with your children:

1. *Establish a daily time for contact with your child and the child's caretaker*

You have a busy schedule, and if you aren't careful, you're going to begin to feel guilty for not spending more time with your child.

Time is an essential framework within which you must learn as much as you can about your child and be available so he or she can do the same with you. It will be important for both you and the child to be able to talk, touch, romp, or just listen, but with your schedule this too may almost have to be pencilled into your appointment book.

If so, "pencilled in" it should be, for you both need that time. It will be easier, however, if you can select a regular time for the contact, possibly after work, after dinner, or just before the child's bedtime. But allow yourself one proviso: Schedule that time when *you feel best*. Don't plan the child's time for immediately after you come home from work if this is the time you feel like winding down. Save the contact time until you're more relaxed, more communicative, and less preoccupied with other issues. Schedule it for when you will be able to concentrate on the child, to listen aggressively, to hear feelings and "between the lines" concerns, to give the child counsel, and just talk—sometimes for extended periods—or play with your child.

Give yourself a parenting treat—daily contacts with your child's world.

**2.** *Get to know your child's external world*

Often your schedule won't permit you as much exploration of your child, through his or her eyes, as you want. Your picture of your child and his progress is incomplete without knowing his environment and its effect on him. But you can discover his world by meeting the people who have important contacts with him. These meetings can be scheduled to conform to your schedule.

Is your child being taken care of by a caretaker? Stay home a few hours for several days to observe the interaction between child and caretaker. Reassure yourself that the person you hired is the person you want to help you raise your child. You could discover that you want someone else to do this vital task. Work together with your child's care provider so that you share a common and consistent set of guidelines in dealing with your child. This is essential for reinforcement of your Preventive Parenting Plan. Then you can be more relaxed at work, more assured of a solid home front consistent with your parenting philosophy.

If your child is in school, get to know his or her teachers. Undoubtedly the school will have a parents' visiting night, but this isn't necessarily the best way to get to know your child's school environment. The whole atmosphere on parents' nights is parent- rather than child-oriented. The only way to see your child in action in an environment is to see this for yourself.

We usually requested permission (sometimes grudgingly given) to visit the classroom. This is a prerogative guaranteed by the public schools to all parents, but known to few. When we visited for a morning and sat in the back of a class, we learned a great deal about this aspect of our child's environment. You can see how your child responds to the authority of the teacher, the stimulation of other classmates, and the situation of having a parent present in his "other world." You can see how articulate your child is in explaining concepts, and you can compare him to his peers. By seeing the environment that fosters the growth of your child when he isn't with you, you can decide how to supplement that environment at home with other activities of importance to your child. If you enter the class with a desire to cooperate with the school in the learning needs of your child, and if you relate this to the teachers, you'll rarely find difficulty in communicating—and in learning important facts about your child.

A final source of information about your child will be found in observing a child's friends and peers. When your young child is playing in a group, pay an unexpected visit. If your child is over five, invite the friends in for milk and cookies after school. En- courage your teenager to invite friends to dinner or "overnights," and offer the family room for occasional parties. If you don't know your child's friends, you're ignorant about the most signifi- cant influences in his or her life. And if you don't cultivate trust and respect with your child's friends, you are missing a vital source of information you might need someday. To modify an old but true saying, "A child is known by the company he keeps."

3. *Establish a system of punishments and rewards*

Every child needs discipline. Growth consists of learning what one can and cannot do—and why. Children first test the limits tolerated by their family, and then what is tolerated by the outside world. Thus a child, to find out where he fits into society, must have some rewards and punishments along the way—rewards for being unique, creative, and self-fulfilling, and punishments for breaking rules, harming self or others, or demonstrating lack of respect or responsibility.

Most parents impose discipline as the situation arises, at times punishing either too harshly or too gently, or not rewarding the child's good behavior sufficiently. The busy after-thirty parent runs the risk of reacting expediently due to the pressure of time, so increasing the danger of inappropriate rewards and punishments.

Sit down with your child (or the caretaker of your young child) and together design a system of rewards and punishments. It's much more meaningful to a child to be disciplined when he expects it and to be punished with an anticipated action, rather than having to face an unexpected, inconsistent, spontaneous, and angry reaction every time. You have established a contract of behavior and consequences with your child. You both now know the rules of the game.

The same is true for rewards. Too many children are "bought off" by material things when they accomplish something positive, rather than being given the reward of sharing quality time with their parents. Planning rewards ahead allows the child to participate in selecting the types of sharing time most valuable to him or her.

Your child's participation in considerations of reward and punishment is necessary. This is the key action that tells the child the seriousness and importance of the consequences of his actions.

So, write down what you and the child consider fair and equitable punishments and rewards. This "contract building" very likely will teach you a great deal about your child's preferences and fears. You are liable to discover that the punishments and rewards (as viewed by your child) are related to *you*. Punishments, for example, could well consist of deprivation of a promised ritual (having to eat dinner alone instead of with the family), rather than the expected loss of an entertainment (watching TV or a weekly movie). This would clearly indicate that the child feels that not having that special dinner with you is a far greater punishment. Conversely, you may find that the reward system also revolves around you. Undivided time for an outing with your child may have greater reward value than money for good grades. A weekend at the beach may provide more motivation to stay on the honor role than the gift of a new bicycle. One of us discovered that attending a lacrosse game changed a father/daughter relationship far more than a special afternoon at the theater. This is very individual and depends entirely on you and your child.

The next step in writing your list is to divide the punishments and rewards into those that are major and minor. Perhaps, if your child has reached the age of being articulate, you can talk at that time about the types of behavior that would necessitate punishment or earn rewards, major or minor. In doing this, you may uncover philosophical differences between yourself and your spouse that will need thorough discussion. Perhaps also you will learn more about yourself during the process. In any event, you will be a step closer to eliminating the most negative quality in preventive parenting—inconsistency.

The design of such a reward and punishment system—which of course can never satisfy all situations—will offer as much consistency as possible between parents themselves, parents and caretaker, and parents and others (grandparents, teachers) in the child's life.

4. *Find out what your child is learning*

Contact with the child's teachers, friends, and caretakers will give you a superficial idea of what your child is learning in many fields; but you as a parent must continually try to find what the child is learning in two extremely important areas: values and independence. You are responsible for your child's learning values and independence.

How do you find out how the child is progressing in these areas? By his or her actions. You must observe a child playing to find out how much he actually demonstrates the values of caring, sharing, honesty, helping others, and so on. You must also observe a child in the community to find out how he is progressing in his independence, adjustment to society, comfort in new and strange situations, willingness to accept new responsibilities, and so on. Often these values are tested in situations over which you have no control, for example, your child's playmate tries to talk your child into stealing a comic book at the local drugstore. You can capitalize on the event when it comes to your attention. Talk about it with your child. Articulate clearly and at the age-related level of your child your point of view. Extrapolate the value system being analyzed to other situations.

The exploration of values with your child doesn't have to be confined to an accidentally discovered situation. Many TV programs and movies are based on themes in which there is a clear conflict of values. The early Walt Disney movies are rich in moralistic themes—lying in *Pinocchio,* friendship in *Dumbo,* importance of family and loss in *Bambi,* etc. Seeing these and their modern counterparts will provide you with a background for rich and thorough discussions in values. Quality time spent with your child attending these entertainments will enrich his or her repertoire of principles and values.

Likewise, how much do you know about what your child will do in situations involving the skills of independence? When you are walking with her, do you ever ask her to decide when the two of you should cross the street? Does your child pay the bill at the hamburger franchise? Do you ever ask your son to prepare his own lunch, and yours as well? It is easy to help your child become more independent by setting up specific situations in which independence is needed and can be taught with gentle supervision. Most often you will be teaching by remaining quiet, by letting your child experiment and learn from each experience. He or she will learn in an atmosphere of reassurance. Your child will have you nearby if he needs you; that is the best learning experience possible.

5. *Encourage love and affection in your home*

Many after-thirty parents are so concerned about being the correct disciplinarian, the proper example, and a role model in their child's life, that they find little time to enjoy the child fully. In a hectic schedule, it often seems out of place to relax and just experience the exquisite pleasure of holding and caressing a child.

This experience of sharing love with your child might seem foreign. Possibly it wasn't part of your own childhood, but it is part of the pure fun of having a child. It's okay and emotionally quite healthy. Today's child psychologists encourage it. If it doesn't fit into your schedule, schedule it.

A child also has to know how to love. He needs the experience of being loved before a sense of self can be formed. The child who has never experienced the sense of being loved will have great difficulty giving the same feeling to another person when he becomes an adult. The child who knows he is deeply loved will become the adult who has a clear sense of his true worth. As a result, he will be better adjusted. These truths are often forgotten by parents who are either too busy, or too modest, or too inhibited to take the time to demonstrate emotion and physical love to their child.

If this is your case, build a love philosophy into your style of preventive parenting. Create situations for you and your child that will be fun for both of you, like a movie outing, or reading, or a visit to the local ice cream parlor. Come home with unexpected gifts once in a while. Do "special" things together. Touch. Speak gently sometimes. Kiss. Talk about future enjoyments. Hold each other close. Talk about past pleasures. Never turn off the physical or emotional part of your love for each other—even when your child has become an adult.

Allow yourself the infinite pleasure of loving your child and being loved in return.

6. *Look at situations positively as well as negatively*

When you get reports on your child, you'll often hear the negative aspects. And why not? You probably appear too busy to hear everything about a situation. You will only be given the facts that require decisions because you have limited time. These facts sometimes can paint a somewhat negative picture of your child. You'll worry; you might, in fact, overreact.

But remember that there are both positive and negative sides to any human situation. Your child is no exception. You do your child an injustice if you take all reports about him or her, even the most positive ones, at face value. Try to accustom yourself to weighing both sides of any issue concerning your child. Ask your child for positives as well as negatives or, conversely, negatives as well as all positives. What is your child's viewpoint? You are striving for objectivity in learning about your child. You are weighing consequences and determining motivations. Both are complicated processes. You'll need all of the information (especially your child's perspective) to be fair, objective, and accurate. Look at your child's behavior from all sides.

7. *Establish the concept of quality time*

Most successful after-thirty parents find that improving the quality of their time with their child is the most valuable parenting practice.

How does quality time work? Take an average situation faced by an after-thirty parent. Both parent and child find themselves alone for a few hours one afternoon while the spouse is out Christmas shopping. Some parents might use the afternoon to take a nap, call a friend, or take care of business. The parent concerned with improving the quality of time with the child, however, will see this as an opportunity to be with the child both physically and emotionally. Probably, that parent will suggest an activity. How about a walk to the drugstore for Christmas wrapping paper? On the way, the two can talk about Christmas and gifts and giving as well as receiving. And in the drugstore, the father may urge the child to select the paper, pay the cashier, and check the change. On the way home, the father shares with the child the secret of the gifts he has bought for her mother.

You can see how this parent has worked the values of sharing and loving into the walk to the drugstore and how the transaction in the store will become a learning experience for the child. This is a parent who has improved the quality of a brief period of time spent with his child. The parent was not manipulative, merely efficient. Time and situation were tailored to meet parenting goals. In addition, it was a period of fun and caring between parent and child.

One of the most important actions you can *ever* take in parenting your child effectively is to decide to improve the quality of time you spend with your child.

Improving the quality of your time, however, isn't easy. You have to decide what you want to accomplish during your time with your child: lessons to be learned, information to be shared, questions to be asked and answered, caring to be offered and accepted, and that vital listening to your child and *hearing* what he or she is really telling you.

Here are a few suggestions for quality time issues that have proven to be valuable starting points for parents and children:

*Get to know the child's internal world*

This difficult but worthy goal is one of exploration with your child of how he or she perceives the world, and you. Such insight is not easily obtainable, because the youngster may not be sufficiently verbal to tell you and the older child may be too guarded to expose his inner feelings with ease. You must, therefore, watch your child and attempt to put yourself in his place. "Why did he do that?" is a question you should be continually asking yourself. Often when you can't understand your child's actions, the best policy is to ask him directly what it means and he may tell you just as directly. At other times, he will let you know that he simply doesn't know why he did what he did or how he feels inside, that he may be dealing with habit or impulse. You must look for patterns, for repetitions that indicate clearly that the child has evolved a consistency —perhaps a principle—which governs his actions. You play with your son and set up situations which tell you what you might have suspected or considered about his behavior. You watch your daughter in new situations and observe how she puts her world into perspective, how she brings things together. Yo do *not* have to be a child psychologist to know your child's inner workings; just a patient, interested, caring, and perceptive adult.

*Offer anticipatory guidance*

A child needs a parent's counsel. Sometimes the child can express this need, sometimes not, in which case the parent has to be sensitive to the unspoken need. Whenever the parent knows that the need exists, or perceives the need, he offers help in the form of anticipatory guidance. Often a parent can discuss a potential sequence of events using the first-person-singular approach. "I know what it's like the first day of school, Jimmy. I remember when I went that first day. I cried hard because I didn't want to leave my Mommy, and the school was a strange building to me, but I found out I had to go anyway. So I just put on my coat and walked to school, and when I got there . . ." This gives Jimmy a framework from which to ask questions comfortably. It gives him a chance to see his role model in a similar vulnerable situation. The conversation establishes a rapport that allows the child to talk about his own feelings. This father opened up the road to anticipatory guidance.

*Show the child that she is loved*

How easy, yet sometimes how hard. How soon after punishment? How frequently? How much of it physically? How much only verbally? How openly? These are not questions answered easily because they must be specifically addressed by each parent for each child. But if you work on these issues during your quality time, they will eventually be resolved to the emotional satisfaction of you and your child.

*Display your values*

Does your child really know how you feel about sharing, lying, violence, religion, politics, etc.? How often do you display or explain your values to your child? How can you work values into his or her life? When and how can he or she differ, dispute, and argue with you about values? How can you make them meaningful to a young child, and when do you give the responsibility of a value system to a young adult? Make these issues a quality time item with your child.

*Reveal yourself as a role model*

Does your child know the real you, or does he know the idealized you? Or the grumpy you? Or the permissive you? Your child needs to know the total you, including faults, in order to have a model against whom to compare himself and other people. The slow revelation of the total you to your child needs careful preparation and work. Be sure you know who "you" really are, and be sure you can share yourself. It's not an easy process, especially with your child. Can you take that exposure? Consider it a quality time subject.

*Explain rules and compare them with other options*

Young children are simplistic and concrete in determining the rules under which they live. Something is right or wrong, good or bad. But right and wrong are often situational and/or relative. A parent must talk about rules, abstract them, compare them, intellectualize them, and conceptualize them. A child has to learn about their complexity and their abstractness. As his parent, help him or her through this maze during quality time.

*Finish all interactions with your child*

Often interactions with a child, like interactions with a spouse, end up unresolved and can create a very real and debilitating anxiety. Always try to conclude interactions with your child. Or, be sensitive enough to end an interaction with a *promise* of resolution or a statement that a certain problem has no resolution. Avoid creating anxiety in your child. Let him know that not everything can be resolved; but don't allow indecision and unresolved feelings to become the trademark of your relationship with him.

There will be times when your own ingenuity fails you and you search for ways of enriching those times you and your child have together. Let us refer you to a very worthwhile book on that subject. It is entitled *What To Do When There's Nothing To Do*. It was written by the members of the staff of the Boston Children's Medical Center and Elizabeth M. Gregg. The book is now available in Dell paperback.

Preventive parenting requires you to have a clearly stated philosophy of parenthood. You know what you want your child to become and you are ready to act on that belief. As an after-thirty parent, your wisdom, maturity, and experience will balance the paucity of your time and the greater span of years between you and your child. To be successful at preventive parenting, you must "practice what you preach," and assess and improve your "quality of time" with your child. In doing this, you will become a more efficient and effective parent.

·

# CHAPTER TWELVE

# Maintaining Healthy Children

Are you very different from your twenty-year-old parental counterparts in your desire or ability to maintain and rear healthy children? Absolutely not. So why is this special chapter dedicated to the topic when there are numerous child care books available on the shelves of your local bookstore? There are several unique situations in child health that might apply to an over-thirty parent more than to a younger parent.

## How To Handle an Emergency

First, it is not unlikely that both of you are working parents and rely on the daily services of a child caretaker. This places a great deal of the responsibility for the child's health care in someone else's hands when you are out of the house. Dilemmas often occur: when should one of you leave work to be with your sick child? How serious does the problem have to be to require your presence? How long will you have to stay away from your job to care for your youngster? Who should call the doctor?

Let us look at the last question first because it is one of the most important: Who should call the doctor? This decision must be based on several important variables:

1. Are either of the two parents accessible to a return phone call from the physician? You must remember that pediatricians often don't answer calls until office hours are over; or you may call while they are out making hospital, teaching, or home rounds. If your jobs keep both of you away from a central telephone for long periods during the day, the best decision is that the caretaker should communicate with your child's physician. You can check with the doctor after work, but *do not wait* until then to make the first call. You may not be able to see the doctor later at night if the situation is not an emergency, and you are penalizing your sick child by holding your conception of a "parenting role" ahead of your child's welfare. If either of you can be reached easily by the physician, it is preferable, of course, for the parent to call the doctor in a non-emergency situation.
2. How sudden is the illness? Be flexible enough so that if your youngster develops a high fever, a sudden pain, or otherwise seems quite ill in a short time, and you can't be reached on the first try, the caretaker should have the authority to call the doctor and not wait until you come back from lunch or a meeting.
3. Is there an emergency? Children fall and injure themselves. There will be infrequent times when an injury or illness—possibly a potential poisoning—occurs. An immediate call, or taking the child to the nearest health facility, would be the most sensible response. In these instances, the daily careaker must have the green light to use discretion and judgment, acting not out of concern for your feelings but for your youngster's health.

Because there will be times when the caretaker must move quickly in getting your child to the doctor or the hospital, be prepared so that these occasions will be handled efficiently. Post the phone numbers of your offices, your parents or close friends (should both of you be unavailable), your pediatrician, the local hospital, and the ambulance crew. Make certain that there is contingency money in the house in case your caretaker must take a taxi or buy medicine before you can get home. Always be sure that your Blue Cross and Blue Shield (or other third-party health insurance coverage) policy number is posted so that care can be expedited in the doctor's office or the hospital.

Be sure to have the phone number of the local Poison Control Center in clear view. Give the caretaker a note of any allergies to drugs or other medical or emotional history of your child. If you know your child's blood type, include that in the background information. Be as thorough as possible in anticipating a sudden event in your child's life when you are not available. Then both you and your caretaker can rest easier. And your child will be protected from the delays and errors of poorly informed medical staff in an emergency.

The issue of when you should leave work to respond to your child's illness is a difficult one. Some of you will want to be with an ill or hurt youngster immediately; often both parents feel the personal need to respond. Others will wait until the severity of the illness suggests that the presence of a parent is indicated. A few of you may have sufficient intrinsic faith in the caretaker that you respond only in severe emergency situations.

However, there are several issues that should be considered when you are making these decisions: (a) When do I leave work? (b) When do I stay home? (c) Should both of us be there? and (d) How long do I stay away from the job?

1. *What is best for the mental security of your child?*—This issue is of great importance. There are specific instances when there is very little question but that you *should* be with your child. What are they?

*During a short hospitalization.

*On those occasions when frightening procedures such as suturing a wound are necessary.

*When pain of a significant degree accompanies the problem.

*When there is an honest fear on the child's part caused by certain aspects of an illness. (For example, the first attacks of asthma, when the child becomes worried about his ability to breathe.)

*Obviously when the illness is serious, life-threatening, and may require hospitalization.

Use your mature judgment and not your emotions to make these decisions. Why? Children with working parents sometimes come to enjoy the chance of unusual intimacy with their parents during a time of illness. This extra attention may motivate the child to overemphasize his or her illness, become accident prone, or use ill health as a tool to bring the working parents close. Running home every time that Johnny sneezes, runs a low-grade fever, or skins his knee will create an abnormal emphasis on health as a manipulating factor in love. Come home when he *really* needs you, and stay at work when the problem can be solved quite easily by a competent caretaker.

2. *When you have a new caretaker*—This also has significance for both the mental and physical health of your child. You should test the judgment and common sense of the new caretaker in other, less important areas before you experiment with the response to your child's illness. Be certain that you are dealing with a thoughtful and appropriately reactive individual before you turn your youngster's state of health over to this stranger. Also bear in mind that it takes a good deal of time before your child can develop the same sense of trust in this new caretaker that he has in his parents. Having a stranger guide a child through even the most minor illness or injury can be both a frightening experience and a moment when the youngster truly feels a sense of abandonment.

3. *Office visits to the doctor*—These visits are not merely to reaffirm that your youngster is healthy and to give immunizations or change formulas and diets. They also provide an environment for you as parents to ask and answer questions with your child's doctor. It is essential that one or both of you be available to go with the youngster to the doctor's office for these regular checkups. If you wish the daily caretaker to accompany you, this is quite acceptable. But the caretaker should *not* routinely be sent to the pediatrician's office without you. On occasion, when the child is unexpectedly ill, the caretaker may need to go to the office alone for minor problems. But regular visits are *your* responsibility.

4. *The nature of the illness*—This should be self-evident. The more severe or chronic the illness, the more likely you both will be home, sharing nursing chores. You don't have to stay away from work until your child has *fully* recovered, however. Knowing that

the remainder of the recovery is mere convalescence should be sufficient to allow you to return to your other important job.

## SHARING AND REHEARSING

Dividing responsibility for a child's health with a caretaker requires two major interactions between parents and caretaker: we call them sharing and rehearsing.

Sharing the responsibility means that *all* parties must feel the same degree of responsibility for the child's welfare. If for one moment you *doubt* that the person you have selected for your child feels a great deal of personal responsibility for that child, then you have made a very unwise choice and should look for someone else as soon as possible.

What do we mean by rehearsing? It becomes very important for the parents and the caretaker to know what important information will be needed by the doctor to make an intelligent assessment before treating a child's illness or injury. Therefore, a standard set of observations and actions should be outlined to ensure an accurate description of the problem both to the parents and to the doctor. Here are some crucial observations that will serve as examples of the "rehearsing" concept of shared caretaking:

*What is the child's temperature? Has it changed over the past few hours?

*How active is the child? Is he/she restless, listless, unresponsive, or twitchy?

*Are there digestive tract problems? Has the child vomited? How often? Diarrhea? How many bowel movements? Describe color and consistency. Is the youngster becoming dehydrated? Is the mouth dry? Has urination slowed down? Are there tears?

*Does the child appear to have a cold? Is the nose stuffy? Any pulling of the ears? Any breathing problems like noisy breathing on inhaling or wheezing on exhaling? Is there a cough? What does it sound like? Using the second hand of a watch, count the number of breaths per minute.

*Are there rashes on the skin? Bruises, pinpoint bleeding,

blisters, or other skin eruptions not seen before?

*If the child is under eighteen months old, is the "soft spot" depressed or bulging? (Depression could mean dehydration, while bulging might herald meningitis.)

*How sick does the baby seem to you?

These are simple but tremendously important observations of a child who appears to be ill. Injuries also have a similar list of basic questions that can be pinned up on the wall for easy reference for all those responsible for the child's care:

*What was hurt? How was it injured?

*Is there any bleeding? How profuse? Can the bleeding be stopped?

*Was the head involved? Is the child conscious? As alert as usual? Complaining of pain? Vomiting? Are either of the pupils dilated (enlarged)?

*If a limb was hurt, can it be moved, touched, turned? Will the foot bear weight? Is there a limp?

*How deep is the wound? Are the edges separated and requiring suturing?

*Could there be internal injuries? Does the child have pain, vomiting, look pale and sweaty, or is he passing blood through nostril, mouth, ear, or rectum?

Again, these key questions will give very important clues about the severity of the injury. If all of the answers are No, then it is very probable that caretaker and parent can relax. But if there is a Yes on more than one observation, call the doctor or take the child to the nearest health facility. But you can't get to that decision point without quick and accurate assessment. It's much easier for the caretaker to have these observations listed clearly and concisely in a convenient place. It's reassuring to the working parent to know that if such an illness or injury occurs, there will be instant communication on exactly what is happening with the child, not only between the caretaker and the parent, but between the caretaker and the doctor as well. And it's much safer for your child.

One further vital issue is the concern harbored by more mature parents about asking the pediatrician "silly" questions. Because of the maturity of the parents and their position in the decision-making community, they feel foolish coming into the doctor's office with a list of what they might consider insignificant questions, questions that they are embarrassed to ask because they believe they should know the answers themselves.

Why? Because they are thirty-two, or thirty-five, or forty? What makes older parents think that their MBA or Ph.D. degree or even a nursing or medical degree provides them with all the information necessary to become a totally knowledgeable parent? Be prepared *not to know* a helluva lot. Work from that basis and don't be afraid to ask all the questions you wish to pose to your child's doctor. Some of the most distressing parent/child problems in physical and mental health result from mature parents' unwillingness and inability to admit their need for help, information, and advice. *Don't* fall into the trap. Leave your professional career image outside the door when you walk into the pediatrician's office. Forget the "responsibility" of being older and wiser. Allow yourselves to be exactly what you are—parents of a young child who have a great deal to learn about this totally new adventure in their lives. Ask those "silly" questions without one moment of concern.

## The Importance of Consistency

Consistency is the key word to the successful rearing of children. And the area where consistency plays the most essential part is that of discipline. As mature parents, several factors may mitigate *against* consistency in your child-rearing practices. As we list these danger spots, assess your own situation so you can avoid each of these pitfalls:

*Significant differences in disciplinary actions between the mother and father. Each of you may be an excellent manager in your own line of work, but use extremely different methods of maintaining discipline on this job. Bringing this difference home to your child will only confuse and confound the youngster. *From the beginning,* you must be together on the rules and limits in your home.

*Differences between the discipline of parents and caretaker. This can create a serious problem for the young child who may not understand that what was acceptable at three o'clock in the afternoon is no longer okay at 6 P.M. when Mommy and Daddy come home. You should select a caretaker who is willing to help rear your child using *your* set of disciplinary goals and values. If a rift occurs in this area, it may be necessary to seek another caretaker. Consistency is *that* important to the mental health of your child.

*Differences in the day-to-day way you manage your own child which reflect the fallout from the stresses of your work day. Despite your fatigue, business worries, or rushed social/business schedule, you can't change the rules to fit your moods. When your child reacts by demonstrating severe swings in moods that are very unpredictable, your own inconsistency may be his model.

*Differences in your expectations regarding your child's behavior in the presence of others versus your home/neighborhood environment. If you are a consistently relaxed and mature parent but you worry about taking your child to a colleague's more structured home, you have only two options: Leave the child home, or allow the child the same freedom you permit him or her at home (warning your colleague in advance). If these different expectations are a problem for you, then you must stop and assess your own child-rearing patterns. Should you still wish to adhere to them, you'll continue to face a problem in the homes of others. Incidentally, the same problem applies to your child's behavior in the grandparents' homes. Your parents are older and the noise, chaos, and permissiveness that you accept may not be tolerable for them. Don't punish the child by expecting different behavior in the grandparents' homes. Don't punish the grandparents by keeping the child in their home for an extended period of time. Leave while you are still ahead of the game, before you get caught between the two widely separated generations.

## GROUP ILLNESSES

As after-thirty parents who are probably both working, you're faced with an irony in child health care. You feel, correctly, that your young child should have excellent day care and begin to share and learn from other children his own age. So you enter him into a day care center at three years of age. Soon he is ill every few days with a never-ending march of bacterial and viral infections that force one or both of you to stay away from work or call in the previous caretaker and pay double for child care. Worry and lack of sleep, which go hand in hand with your child's ill health, can also affect your job performance. Did you make the wrong decision in sending your youngster to day care? Was he better off with his in-house nursemaid?

You are not caught in a Catch-22 situation. What is happening to your child happens to most first or only children when they initially go to a school or play group. In the past, the number of external contacts who could have spread infection to the child were minimal. Suddenly the entrance into the group situation has multiplied that exposure many times. But whether it was at three years old in nursery school, or five in kindergarten, your youngster would have had to face this "group entry" health problem. Be prepared to spend the first six months to a year after your youngster goes to day care, nursery school, or kindergarten taking care of minor colds, fevers, and childhood illnesses. In time, your youngster will have built up enough defenses against the common health hazards to be at no greater risk than other children.

The advantage of entering your child in a relaxed but well-supervised group process as early as possible cannot be overstressed. As mature parents, you move in a sophisticated adult world. Your reactions with your child tend to be less spontaneous and more measured. Your child needs the company and the world of other children his own age. It is by being with them, learning to relate and communicate with them, testing his individuality on them, and using them to release his childhood exuberance, that he will learn to discriminate sensibly and sensitively between their child's world and your adult world.

The advantages of letting your child play in a group fully compensate for the inconvenience and worry of the sudden emergence of minor but incapacitating temporary illnesses. It is going to happen eventually. Just be prepared to be both parent and nurse (male or female) for a time. Being forewarned is being fore-armed.

## Speech Is Vital

No matter how tired you are when you come from work, talk to your child. Start immediately after you bring the baby home from the hospital. Do *not* talk baby talk. Speak gently, clearly, lovingly. Convince any caretaker that talking to your child frequently throughout the day is an absolute prerequisite for looking after your child. Encourage the flow of conversation from your child. Save your private, silent moments for the hours after your child has gone to bed. Share with each other when the youngster is not center stage.

Speech is the bridge over which we meet each other, first family and then others. It is also the basis of intelligence. You must, therefore, talk to your child—and your caretaker must also do so—when the infant is being fed, diapered, washed, held close, or rocked to sleep. Speech must be an integral part of the very youngest life. The understanding of speech can only follow listening to speech. You and the others who care for your child must imprint on your child early the sounds of your voices, the sounds of words, the sounds of communication freely offered with love. It seems so natural, so much part of what parents should do. But it does *not* happen often enough. To deprive a child of the sound of your voice is a major deprivation.

Make much of the quality time that you spend with your child verbal time. Even though you speak all day long, and silence seems relaxing to you, it is withering to your child's development. You can never be too old to speak to a child. If you wonder about that, watch your parents as they manage to cross a much wider generational gap, laughing and cooing with your youngster.

Speak to your child every chance you get and your child will find his own voice, will discover the words early that he needs to express himself. You are investing in his future—a future of articulate and comfortable self-expression.

Last but far from least, don't expect your later-in-life child to conform to your preconceived fantasies of who or what he is or will be. Your successes are yours. His will be his. Your beauty is distinctively yours, not his.

You have waited somewhat longer to have this first child, and, therefore, have greater expectations. He is very "special." But he is special because he is himself. The sooner you, as a parent, recognize and accept the individuality of your child, the fewer problems in communication and interpretation you will have in the future. Begin to respect and observe your child as his own person from the very beginning. Don't compare him to yourselves at any age. Don't compare him to friends' children. Compare him only to himself.

Allow your child the same freedom you have been fighting more than thirty years to attain—give him permission to be himself.

.

# CHAPTER THIRTEEN

# What Your Child
# Is Really Telling You

Jimmy's dinnertime behavior was particularly annoying to the Greens.

Both parents worked in difficult and stressful jobs; each was in their mid-forties and at the peak of demanding careers. They could barely tolerate the forty-five-minute ride home, usually spent swaying from an overhead strap. Once inside their home, together they prepared dinner, often not pausing for an "unwinding time" because of Jimmy's need to start his homework after the meal. Finally when the meal was ready, Jimmy was called. And called. Then called once again. He was reading. Or riding his bike. Or out romping with the dog. When he at last showed up, the meal was overcooked and his parents impatient and edgy. But the two adults forced themselves to attempt conversation so that dinnertime could have the "feel of a family." But Jimmy repeatedly ruined the meal for the Greens. Although twelve years old, he played with his food, holding it in his mouth for long periods, then swallowing quickly and belching. As soon as this occurred, he would erupt with raucous laughter, spraying the table with food and shattering the attempts at gentle conversation. Despite warnings, threats, and occasional swats, Jimmy would often interrupt his parents' conversation with loud comments of his own, usually completely irrelevant to their topic. He appeared to demand the center of his parents' focus, but used all of the wrong methods to gain their attention. The Greens tried to ignore his behavior, trying not to reinforce it, but even that didn't help. The adults would finish dinner in absolute frustration and exhaustion, unable to be civil to Jimmy or each other the rest of the evening. A family was coming apart at the seams. They needed and sought help.

"Is this characteristic of twelve year olds?" they asked.

Such behavior is *not* characteristic of twelve year olds—unless they are signalling.

Jimmy was sending a signal to his parents. He was trying to tell them something that he could not say directly to them. He wasn't saying, "I'm a slob," or, "I'm immature." We found out, through long conversations with Jimmy and his parents, separately and together, that Jimmy was signalling something more profound. He was really indicating to his parents: "Hey, Mom and Dad, I need your undivided attention for a few minutes. I need to have you recognize that I belong to your life, that I am as important as your jobs, that I need to be included in your interests, your worries, and your world." And at a different level he was saying, "I got more attention when I was younger. If I act as if I were younger, maybe I'll recapture that attention once more."

Jimmy's signal—immature behavior—contained a number of messages to his mature parents, either messages too painful or difficult to tell them directly, or messages that he knew they would have great difficulty in receiving or understanding during this time of great work stress in their lives.

But, through help, Mr. and Mrs. Green came to understand the messages and correct the situation. They could not, of course, condone Jimmy's immature behavior. They were able to recognize, however, the message of Jimmy's continual need for their attention. The Greens planned activities that all three of them would enjoy together. After a thoughtful investigation, they discovered mutual interests in arts and crafts and began planning joint projects. The parents reinstituted their private relaxation time after work and requested that Jimmy, at first, eat by himself. This clearly indicated to Jimmy that they had no intention of accepting his usual dinner behavior. In addition, they could unwind, and afterwards give more and a better quality of time to Jimmy. Jimmy, on the other hand, discovering that his parents finally understood the need for spending more quality time with him, and also finding the isolation of eating by himself unrewarding, asked to be allowed to rejoin the family at dinner. His behavior was more mature, his conversation relevant, his belonging understood. The signal was given, the message understood, and the situation remedied.

Unusual? Not with after-thirty parents. Ofen you have high-powered jobs, external obligations, frequent commitments, and find yourselves with less time for your child. Because of the increased age difference between you and your child, there may be a wide gap in common vocabulary. This communication problem often will cause a child to act out his or her problems symbolically, thereby giving you a message using a different communication style —a signal.

Because the after-thirty parent is more prone—and more vulnerable—to receiving signals from his or her child, discussing signals, learning how to interpret their messages, and discovering how to answer those messages in a healthy and productive way will be valuable for you. Analyzing signals helps parents to learn what their child is really telling them. This will not only be useful for the minor signals (e.g., first attempts at lying and stealing, fantasy friends, temper tantrums, etc.) but also for the later and more dramatic signals (e.g., running away from home, school phobia, excessive attachments to others, and anti-social behavior). (More detailed explanations of these and other signals can be found in *Signals: What Your Child Is Really Telling You*, by the authors, Dial Press/James Wade, New York, 1978.) As you are challenged by your child with dramatic, unexpected, and annoying behaviors that you don't understand, recognize your child's actions as a signal to you, and together try to analyze the meanings. When you find what your child is really telling you, you can respond in the best way possible.

There are five characteristics of signals that may help you in discovering and then analyzing them:

1. Signals almost always make you, as a parent, uneasy, anxious, or angry. The jarring behaviors are, in reality, confrontations, but

they are one-sided because you don't fully understand them. Your child has acted or reacted in an unexpected manner. His behavior does not "fit" with what you know, or expect, from him. You feel that the actions are personally directed at you, and you are naturally upset and annoyed.

2. Signals often challenge well-established family rules or parental values, hitting your "soft spots," the exact points where you are most vulnerable. If you are compulsively neat, for example, a usual signal will be untidiness. If you are a religious churchgoer, expect a rebellion on Sunday morning. When you label signals by their overt behaviors—e.g., "lying," "stealing," "promiscuity," "male effeminate behavior," or "failing in school"—you will have negative feelings about these words. You'll have to look beneath the labels to the real message and recognize that the shock value of the signal is *to get your attention.* The degree of parental reaction is significant. The more uptight the behavior makes you, the more important it is to the child that you receive his or her message.

3. *Any* behavior can be a signal. There is no limit to the creative ways children can convey hidden messages to you. Signals can be physical or mental, short-term or long-term, anti-social or gregarious, simple or complicated, behavior committed or action omitted—the possibilities are endless. But they have one common element—your negative reaction. You can't predict the type your child may choose, except to be certain that the signalling behavior will find your most vulnerable spots.

4. Various kinds of signals are more significant at one age than another. Every young child lies at least once in early childhood to test the limits of the family rules, but a teenager who lies constantly is sending you a dramatic signal for help. Bedwetting is not a cause for alarm in a healthy four-year-old, but needs attention at age twelve. Fantasy friends are cute at three years old and potentially dangerous when the same child is nine years old. A signal cannot be generalized; it must be interpreted within age and maturity limits as well as the context in which it is sent (and received).

5. Signals often aren't easy to perceive. In Jimmy Green's case, he used the dinner table as his showcase, hoping to focus attention on his needs when his busy family was together. Many signals evolve

in such a way. And because the behavior provokes such reactions as guilt, embarrassment, and anger, you may be struggling so hard with your own feelings that you fail to recognize your child's actions as containing a hidden message. Another reason for blinders in this area could be that you're busy trying to deny the importance of the signal, as did the Greens. That is natural, but it makes analysis more difficult, the signal more insidious.

What do you do when you think you are encountering a signal? You become a detective. You must analyze the signal, but not by the intellectual process you use with other adults. You must try to get inside the mind and feelings of your signalling child. Try to place yourself in his position, to feel what he is feeling, to sense what is happening or not happening in his life. Begin to think like your child by stepping back from your role as parent and becoming young and inarticulate once again. Become Jimmy Green. Then you must try to ask yourself, "What would I be trying to say if I were Jimmy?"

Obviously you can't ask Jimmy for a direct answer. If he could tell you, he wouldn't have to signal you. So you must look for the signal and observe its characteristics. Here are some clues that might help you in your role as the parent detective trying to find the "motive" for the signal:

*When does the signal occur? Does it happen at a certain time each day? Many children signal at one of the mealtimes or just before bed, for these are times when the whole family is present. One of the major observations you can make is whether the signal occurs *in the sequence* of some other event or entrance of a person. Does some act, or some person, trigger the signal? Do *you* trigger the signal?

Billy, aged four, complained of stomach aches every night about midway through dinner. He would cry loudly and disrupt the family meal, causing his work-weary parents to gulp down their food and turn away from the six-year-old brother to focus on Billy. About an hour after dinner, the pain seemed to subside miraculously, and Billy always felt well enough to watch his favorite TV programs before bedtime. What was the abdominal pain at the dinner table signalling? Both a time and a person.

Billy's older brother had entered the first grade. The dinner conversation for several weeks before the stomach aches began had centered on the older boy's school day, his excitements and accomplishments. No one noticed that Billy was fading further and further into the background of the dinnertime family conversation. Billy took care of this issue very dramatically; he signalled his abandonment by focusing attention onto himself through the signal of his mid-meal abdominal pain. Realizing the *why* of the physical symptom and adjusting the dinnertime conversation so that both boys could become involved removed the need for the signal.

*In what setting does the signal occur? Is it inside or outside your home, with you or with neighbors, with adults or with peers, with people or alone? What is the stage on which the drama of the signal is played? Once you have identified the stage, then look for the scenery, for that may be the clue. A signal usually occurs to force the other "actors" into dialogue. Identify the stage, and very likely you will have identified the supporting cast.

Marianne was a bright, charming, verbal youngster of seven who bubbled her enthusiastic chatter throughout the home and the neighborhood. Therefore, it came as quite a shock to her parents to receive a note from her teacher relating that Marianne was virtually mute during the entire school day. Marianne had just entered the second grade. The previous school years had not been troubled by any lack of communication in the child. Her mother asked if she could visit the classroom after Marianne tearfully refused to discuss the situation with her parents. Sitting in the second grade room, it soon became obvious to Marianne's mother what Marianne's verbal withdrawal in school signified.

The teacher demanded strict discipline. This was something that the irrepressible little girl had never before experienced in home or in school. Her mother watched as the teacher reprimanded the other children sharply for talking out of turn, whispering to each other, showing excitement when they knew the answer, even when they made a mistake in answering a question. Marianne had closed her mouth permanently out of self-defense. She knew herself. She understood that she would draw the teacher's anger if she spoke out in her usual effervescent manner. The little girl had protected herself by becoming mute. She was signalling distress by her silence.

Marianne had no reason to change. In fact, her mother was delighted with the life within her daughter. It was obvious the teacher wouldn't change her rules, so Marianne's mother negotiated a change in class with a very quick return of Marianne's voice in school. The silent signal was received and the message understood by a perceptive parent.

*Who is most generally affected by the signal? That person is the receiver of the message. The signal may not be meant for you as the child's parent. The child may be signalling others in his life: relatives, siblings, or peers. Whoever is moved by the signal is the person about whom you must ask, "What message would my child want to send to this person?"

Monica's mother couldn't understand what was happening in her home. Her only child was literally harassing her, being provocative until there were loud and tearful confrontations between the two of them, doors slamming, angry looks, verbal accusations. However, Monica's father seemed to have no difficulty in maintaining a very clear and comfortable balance of discipline and affection. Monica's mother checked at the school. Her daughter was described as a "perfectly behaved young lady."

Finally, the woman sought the advice of her own mother. "What am I doing wrong?" she pleaded. The grandmother asked quietly, "What are you doing now to keep her in line?" Monica's mother sighed. "That's what I don't understand. I don't do very much to stand in her way. I let her do what she wants most of the time. I'm the easy one. Her father is the tough disciplinarian. And yet she doesn't give him any trouble at all." The grandmother nodded slowly. "What do you think she might want from you?" Monica's mother threw up her hands in despair. "I don't know." The grandmother frowned. "I do," she said quickly. "She's trying to force you to become her mother and stop trying to be her girlfriend."

Sage advice, indeed. The signal of disruptive, angry behavior was Monica's way of trying to force her mother to play that very necessary role. For the mother, looking into herself and realizing that she was the only one who was getting the brunt of Monica's behavior was the first step in interpreting this complex but important signal between mother and daughter.

*Why can't your child send a direct message rather than a signal? If the child is beyond the very early years, has a good vocabulary, and has become accustomed to talking directly to his or her parents, then the fact that he feels the need to signal has serious connotations. A signal in adolescence often is more serious than one from a six-year-old first-grader. Teenage signals have to be approached as more complex in nature and more complicated in the underlying message. One fact should be quite clear about signals: they almost always involve feelings, for feelings are the hardest concepts to convey in words—at any age. Look for a feeling tone to the signal; that will represent the origin of the message.

Randy was the fifteen-year-old son of two fifty-year-old teachers. His father was a full professor at an Ivy League college. Randy's mother taught tenth grade English in the local high school. Randy was the older of two boys. His younger brother, aged fourteen, did adequately in school but excelled on the athletic field. Randy was the scholar and not the athlete. Suddenly, he brought home a warning slip that his grades were falling. His parents punished him; yet within weeks, his report card reflected several failing grades. His parents were stunned. Randy showed no remorse. He seemed to be challenging them by his school failure. In addition, communication seemed to have dried up to a trickle between parents and son. They couldn't get to the bottom of his problem.

One day, Randy's father was called by the librarian at Randy's school. The woman asked if she could stop by the university to chat with him about his son. When she appeared in his office, Randy's father was shocked to discover that she was very young and attractive. "Randy is one of my favorite people," she began, "but he's very troubled lately. I think his grades are only the result and not the cause." The professor begged the young woman to tell him anything that might help him understand what was going on inside the boy. "He told me something strange the other day," the librarian said quietly. "He told me that failing at something was so much easier than succeeding. Especially when succeeding was impossible. He said that he felt more like a failure before his grades fell than now, because then he was really trying."

The feeling described by the librarian struck deep into Randy's father, and he suddenly understood the essence of his son's failing signal. The message was in the excessively high standards his son perceived that he and his wife expected. There was truth in what Randy felt, and only with a compromise in the level of expectations could the signal of Randy's failing in school be turned around toward success. Who had cut off the flow of communication? Attitudes, past history, and current role models had led to assumptions which were half-truths but still strong enough to frustrate, thwart, and paralyze the feelings of this teenage boy.

*How do you respond to the signal? Whatever way you habitually respond to a particular signal or behavior is the way the child unconsciously expects you to respond. Your analysis of your response to the signal will give you a clue as to the motivation for it. Because of your child's behavior, are you forced to pay more attention to the child? Does the signal make you anxious? Who is punished by the effects of the signal? Does the signal postpone a dreaded event, bring sympathy to the signaller, give the child an excuse for undesirable behavior? These messages can sometimes be discerned by analyzing who receives the signal and the expected response.

Beth's mother returned to work when Beth was six years old. Suddenly Beth began having severe headaches during the day in school. At first the school nurse told her to lie down in the office. But when Beth's mother heard about the headaches, she became distraught and took the youngster to her pediatrician. He checked the young girl, found nothing, and suggested that the family merely observe her for a time after checking out her vision as a possible cause. The eye exam was totally normal. But Beth's mother insisted that the school call her every time one of the headaches occurred, and she then left work and took Beth home. Within weeks, Beth was missing three and four days of school each week and her mother was about to lose her new job.

The next time Beth's mother came to pick up the girl from the school nurse's office, the nurse asked if she could chat with the older woman. "Why are you so obviously upset by these headaches?" the nurse asked.

"They could be serious." Beth's mother replied defensively.

"But the doctors found nothing. Beth is well in a matter of hours. And the headaches never come on the weekends." The nurse watched as the mother's face reddened. Finally she touched Beth's mother gently on the arm. "I wonder if Beth would continue to have quite as many headaches if you didn't reward her so predictably by rushing over here from work and taking her home. Let's try three weeks without sending her home." Beth's mother reluctantly agreed.

Beth didn't give up her headaches readily. But the school nurse placed her in the bed and went about her business ignoring the girl. By the third week, the headaches were less frequent. The nurse pleaded with the mother to continue the treatment of minimal attention. As Beth lay in bed hearing the excited voices on the playground, her headaches slowly disappeared. The predictable reward response to her signal for more maternal attention and fear of mother being away from home at a new job slipped into the background. A wise nurse and a willing mother had intercepted this signal.

*How uncomfortable does the signal make you feel? This information, although subjective, will give you a clue as to the importance of the signal to your child. The more anxious you feel about the signal, the more important it is to your child. If it's meant to attract your attention, it will do so dramatically. If the behavior is truly a cry for help, you will likely experience a dramatic reaction to what your child has done. Judge the seriousness of the underlying message by the quality of your reaction.

Colin's father was a former professional football star. He had married late, and now that Colin was sixteen, his father was reaching fifty. But the older man still exercised regularly, refereed college games, and was a constant sidelines observer at all the local athletic events. He had tried from the time that Colin was a small boy to interest his only son in one sport or another. But Colin was not as well coordinated as his father. He grudgingly kept up his swimming lessons and ran track at high school so that his father would be pleased. But it didn't seem to be enough.

Right before Colin's seventeenth birthday, while he was a senior in high school, his behavior began to change dramatically.

His overall demeanor took on a decidedly effeminate air. His voice rose, his hips swayed, his wrist was more limp than before. His father was almost psychotic. He railed, screamed, pleaded, retreated, did everything to try to reverse this unacceptable behavior. There was nothing that could have upset him more. Obviously Colin knew this. One day, Colin's father asked him outright, "Are you a fag?" Colin smiled sweetly and answered, "Maybe." The older man became apopletic. "Just stay out of my sight!" was his reply. "Gladly," Colin replied. "Now I can do what I want with my life."

The father and son didn't see each other very much. But Colin's mother noted that the effeminate behavior subsided quickly and returned only when the two men were together. Finally she confronted her son. "Why are you tormenting your father? That's not how you act at school. I checked. And you don't act that way around me, only around your father. Why?" Colin sighed. "It's the only way he'll get off my back about being another superstar like him. I just couldn't take it any more. I'm not his clone."

Colin had picked on the thing that would make his father most uncomfortable to try to signal the fact that he was his own person, with needs, preferences, and lifestyle very much his own. It took his mother several weeks to convince her husband that the play acting was merely that. Sadly, the message was never understood by the father. Colin was not the son he had wanted. But he left the boy alone, and Colin stopped the performance. College separated the two men, forever. The tragedy lies in the fact that even after the signal was interpreted, this message could not be understood and accepted.

A subject as complex as signalling can be covered only superficially in one chapter, but let this chapter be sufficient to alert you to the fact that you, as an after-thirty parent, will be especially vulnerable to signalling by your child. In order to raise your child so that he or she possesses valuable, open, honest communication skills, you must interpret and act on such signals during his or her growing-up years. Take comfort in the fact that all parents receive signals from their children. It's the after-thirty parent who usually has the wisdom and experience to interpret and act on these signals with dispatch.

·

# CHAPTER FOURTEEN

# The After-Thirty Parent
# and the Only Child

It seems logical that many of you will want to have the experience of being a parent once during your busy and productive lives—but only once. This decision may not be easy or comfortable. You are plagued by endless stories about the horrors of an only child. Do only children suffer from more emotional and social problems than children in bigger families? What can you do to guarantee the healthiest possible emotional environment for your only child?

The fear for the emotional health of the only child had some basis in earlier scientific reporting. After the turn of the century, most psychiatrists regarded the state of being an only child as a decided disadvantage. But in the 1950s a large-scale review of writings and research about only children was done by R. A. Clark and H. V. Capparell, who found an almost total inconsistency about the characteristics ascribed to the only child. The most important factor in your child's life will be your individual parenting skills.

Only children can be high achievers. The *Basic Handbook of Child Psychiatry* notes the high intelligence and strong verbal abilities of only children, along with their generally higher motivation to achieve. This textbook specifically calls attention to their eminence in fields requiring scholarly and creative effort. Why?

Because only children have greater material and financial resources (in addition to more parental attention) to help them reach the top of the class. This analysis of the only child's potential for becoming a high achiever states *two* conditions—the child's ability and the child's resources. You are his or her resources. Are you ready for that challenge?

You're special. You're over thirty years of age, vitally active in career, social life, and community. Into this world of maturity arrives the only child. You have significant chances to help the emotional growth and development of your child, and much of what happens will be strongly influenced by your age.

Let's look at some of the areas of concern and work out ways you can avoid mistakes that might cause future problems.

*Situation 1:*

Johnny was seven, the only son of a two-career couple (both aged thirty-nine) living in a city. Johnny went to a progressive private school, but spent most of his evenings and weekends with his parents and their friends. He accompanied his parents to parties, theater, opera, and vacations. He had few close friends of his own. One day, Johnny's mother was called at work by Johnny's teacher, who requested an appointment. The teacher was concerned that Johnny was a "loner." She also said that he was becoming difficult to teach because he was beginning to deny the teacher's classroom authority. He often criticized other children. As a result, he was being bullied at recess time. Johnny's mother was shocked. She knew none of this. She was terribly confused as to how this situation had occurred and what she and her husband could do to correct the problem.

Johnny was feeling the effects of *forced maturity*.

Because he was their only child, Johnny had been included from his early years within his parents' daily social life. Not only was this plan more expedient and easier, but Johnny's parents also felt that the stimulation and education passed on to their son from their own friends and cultural activities would enrich and enhance his young life. But his parents forgot something: they forgot that Johnny was still a child. He needed to behave, think, react, and live as a child. He had to be surrounded by people his own age,

learn *their* language, experience *their* competition, discover how to
cope and react and rebound within a child's world. Instead, he was
being prematurely thrust into a very mature, sophisticated world,
where he unsuccessfully mimicked the posture and attitudes of
maturity. He had missed those wonderfully spontaneous years of
childhood and, as a result, he was very different from the other
children in his neighborhood and school. This early maturity—
frequently a problem with the only child of after-thirty parents—
created insurmountable social barriers between Johnny and the
important world around him, the world of his own peers.

What are some of the prevention points that you can in-
corporate into your child-rearing practices to avoid this potential
only child problem?

**1.** Encourage your youngster to have friendships with children
his own age.
**2.** Express pleased acceptance of your child's young friends and
games and demonstrate interest by discussing what your youngster
is doing with his friends. Encourage the inclusion of your child
into adult gatherings when other children can be present. Carefully
select the times when your child joins your own friends, such as
holidays, birthdays, etc.
**3.** Select the activities that you share with your child so that the
higher percentage of these outings are right for your child's age.
**4.** Acknowledge and accept the "best friend" relationship so frequently seen in only children.
**5.** Look at your only child not as an extension of yourselves but
as a growing individual who is still in the formative period of his
life. Remember your "Johnny" was not born fifteen years old, he's
the same age as the infant of a teenage mother. You're the one
who was older and must wait more patiently for your only child
to "catch up" in the style of life, education, and social/cultural
activities enjoyed by you as mature adults.

*Situation 2:*

Melissa was lying on the floor of her mother's friend's living
room, arms flailing, feet kicking, screaming—having an old-fash-
ioned "temper tantrum." Should her mother be concerned? Many

very young kids try this ploy to attract attention. But Melissa was five years old, too old for such actions. Why did this happen? Her father was forty and her mother thirty-eight years old. They had waited impatiently for Melissa and were thrilled at her birth. During her early years, they invested a great deal of themselves in the growing child. But unconsciously they worried as she grew older. Slowly she was drawing away from them; she was becoming more independent and didn't seem to need them as much any more. Since they had resolved to have only one child, they began to fight this loss by drawing her closer, making most of her decisions, devoting more and more free time to her, and allowing her more freedom than most parents. Now they were embarrassed and perplexed by her failure to appreciate the extent of their love. She bit, kicked, tantrumed, and reacted more like a two-year-old than a child her own age.

The basis for Melissa's problem was *prolonged immaturity.*

Your after-thirty only child is the only one on whom you are going to be able to focus all of your parenting love. As she grows older, she will assert her need to be independent just at the time in your life when you had planned (often subconsciously) to enjoy fully her dependence and nurturing. Some parents may tend to infantilize the child, stop the emotional growth process by babying, giving in, and denying the first feeble attempts at childhood independence. Then they are faced with regressive behavior and more serious social adaptation problems with other people.

There are prevention points to help the only or first child to grow at a normal emotional pace:

1. Allow your child to experiment with his surrounding world. Supervise him, but don't warn your child constantly about every potential danger. You'll frighten him into paralysis.
2. Let your youngster begin to make the simplest decisions within her life, such as which skirt to wear, or how much to eat, or which friends to invite to a birthday party. Then extend this as your child grows so that she can make her own decisions on such things as who her friends will be, how she will spend her allowance, when she will go to bed, and how she will spend her weekends. Each of these decisions come with advancing age, but it is essential that you

sense the right moment to "let go" and give your only child some decision-making independence. You'll know the correct time by the sense that your child is ready to try the new experiment.

**3.** Accept the fact that your youngster has to make his or her own mistakes. We can't protect our children from the pain of failure. We only delay the process and prevent the adaptation until it is much too late in their lives, and their maladjustment to a lack of continual success becomes crippling.

**4.** In both overt and subtle ways, express to your youngster your honest faith and trust that your child has the ability to take control of his or her own life gradually.

**5.** Encourage peer relationships as early as possible and don't interfere during times of conflict or crisis among children. Allow the youngster to fight his or her own battles. Be available for advice, but take off *your* boxing gloves.

**6.** Your child is not always right. Be aware of this when a youngster returns to you from the outside world full of complaints. Listen impartially. If your child needs to adjust, suggest this in a tactful but clear manner. Kids don't need constant supporters; they need advisers.

**7.** Growing up does *not* mean growing away. As your child grows older, he or she will be redefining your role within a changing life continually. It's only when that role *never* changes that you have failed as the parent of your only or firstborn child.

*Situation 3:*

Billy was the nine-year-old child of two highly skilled parents. His mother at forty-one was a senior executive in a major firm; his dad was the head of the department of physiology at the state medical school. Billy cut school three days in a row. When confronted by his distressed parents, Billy shrugged and said sadly, "What's the difference? I'm so dumb. It doesn't matter if I'm there or not." Billy had been getting B's and C's, but there had been a gradual yet noticeable decline in his work recently, so his grades had fallen. After much questioning, Billy finally admitted to the school guidance counsellor that the year before, when he had gotten one A and four B's on his report card, his father had asked him why he had not done better, while his mother had reminded him how difficult it was going to be for him to get into a good college if he didn't work harder. Billy became so distressed at this response that he simply stopped trying.

Billy's parents had *too high educational expectations*.

Many after-thirty parents deferred parenthood to attain educational degrees—some advanced—in order to compete successfully in the job market. Education has become an integral part of your lives. You have one child. You want him or her to get the very best education possible. It's likely that your spoken or silent dream is that this single human investment will pay you the dividend of becoming a professional. As older parents, the cost of this education doesn't frighten you as much as it might younger parents. You're earning more and savings can be focused on only one child. But so can the stress, the strain, the constant surveillance, the over-expectation, and the criticism. These, too, are focused singularly on one small head. If you place the educational hurdle so high that your youngster feels there is no chance to top it, he'll stop trying to reach that level. He'll simply quit the contest.

For ambitious parents, these prevention points may seem simplistic, but may also be difficult to realize without a great deal of effort on both parents' parts:

1. Adult approval is extraordinarily important to your only child. Place your educational approval level easily within his or her reach.
2. The only child fears failure, and especially facing you with failure. He must be reassured that his occasional inability to perform a task is not a disaster, but acceptable. Help him to understand it by viewing it in the context of his successes.
3. Appraise your only child's abilities realistically. Allow your youngster to proceed and to achieve at the rate that is *best for him*.
4. Help your child to understand that he is achieving to satisfy *himself* and not you as his parents.
5. Permit your youngster freedom from a preordained career or even college. Allow these decisions to percolate up through the only child's thinking as he works his way from one educational level toward the next. When you project too far ahead with very high achievement goals, you can frighten and confuse the only

child into educational immobility or retreat.

6. The essence of the advice for the mature parent of the only or firstborn child is that you have not cloned an individual to live out all your educational goals or career fantasies. You have created a person, who should be allowed to find his or her own educational level without predetermined parental expectations. In other words, leave the kid alone so he can become who and what he wants to be. He knows what you want from him, even if you don't say so. Your silence gives him the freedom to please and surprise you. It's a positive reward.

*Situation 4:*

Ellen was the nine-year-old only child of career parents in their early forties. They lived in a midwestern city; there were few children Ellen's age in her neighborhood. Her local school drew youngsters from a wide area, so that although she had some girl friends in her class, she needed transportation to go to their homes after school or on weekends. Ellen's parents came home around seven in the evening. Dinner was later. By the time dessert was finished, it was often too late to visit a friend. On weekends, Ellen's parents traveled with her to spend quiet days at a mountain retreat several hours out of the city. Ellen didn't invite any of her school friends on these weekends because she sensed that her parents wanted peace and quiet and wouldn't tolerate much spontaneous behavior from her during that time. Gradually Ellen began to retreat into her own bedroom, often refusing to come out for meals. Finally Ellen's mother took her to their pediatrician, who scheduled a special half-hour appointment to discuss the problem. After talking to the girl, he called her mother into his office and confronted her with the problem.

Ellen was suffering from *the loneliness of the only child.*

Loneliness can be a natural spinoff of being an only child. No matter how full of friends the child's school day may be, there comes a time when the only child must return home to a world of adults—in this case a world of tired, older parents. School is the breeding ground of peer friendships. There must be a nurturing outside the school environment for friendships to flower beyond the acquaintance phase. Only children desperately need friends of their own age. They need release from the adult world they live in.

This loneliness of the only child of older parents should be anticipated. There are a number of prevention points that should be begun very early and that will go a long way toward minimizing the pain of loneliness:

1. Plan as early as possible to involve your only child in some type of peer group activity, whether it is a play group for two year olds, nursery school, or weekend outings with friends. By arranging these sessions, you can teach your only child the skills of being part of a group during the early years, so that by school age your only child will be able to adjust to the new school group.
2. If you include your child in your own adult-oriented visits or functions, try to select those times when a child of similar age can be present. Cousins, nephews, and the children of friends come in very handy.
3. Realize that your only child will likely develop a very close friendship often quite early in life. These very close friendships occur commonly among only children. They are very important; don't minimize their significance. Encourage a close friendship and nurture the relationship by having the other child to your home for dinner and weekends. Allow your child the freedom to visit the friend.
4. Ellen's parents should have encouraged their daughter to bring friends with her on the weekend trips. If they did not want the responsibility or the noise or the extra concern, they could have considered leaving their youngster at home to stay with one of her own friends. There are times, which increase as the child grows older, when your company is far less important to the healthy emotional growth of the only child than the presence of her own friends.
5. Summers and holidays can be hell for only children. When you are older and more settled, summer vacations tend to be less dynamic and more geared toward rejuvenation and relaxation. Your only child has no need for this type of vacation. She needs life, excitement, activity, and lots of children her own age. Either take along a friend or select a location where you are certain there will be a number of other people the same age as your child. During the holidays, consider having special days for parties for your child's

friends. Many holidays should be spent with the intimate, nuclear family. If there are relatives with children of a similar age, share part of the day with them. If not, allow your child to plan part of the holiday time to fit her childhood needs, rather than following the traditional adult celebration. Create a childhood summer that includes friends, camp, and special opportunities to meet other children.

6. The two of you, as after-thirty parents, have more responsibilities. You have become preoccupied with business and marital problems. Finances take some of your evening time. Grandparents are aging and needing more support. Suddenly you realize that within this maelstrom of worry and preoccupation, someone has gotten lost—your only child. Your preoccupation robs the child of that "quality time" with the parent that helps to fill the friendless hours. Try to remember always that your child needs your presence and attention for some part of the day.

A quick synopsis: Don't try to be too much of a friend to your child. She needs young friends early and frequently. But also try not to forget that she will always need some of you despite the other pressures in your life. Remember you're likely to be over forty when she is almost ten years old. It's rather difficult for you to be ten again and impossible for her to be forty. In three quick words: she needs friends.

*Situation 5:*

Bobby was three years old and kept misbehaving in public, causing intense embarrassment to his over-thirty parents. They sat down with him after each episode and explained why his behavior was not what they wanted from him. Often the young boy would run away in the middle of their talks, yell at them, or strike them. Tom and Janet, his parents, were concerned. Somehow they weren't getting through to their son. They talked to his caretaker, who informed them that she had no such problems with the boy. She punished him for each of his misdeeds. Both parents were troubled. He was to be their only child and they did not in any way want to harm the relationship by using physical punishment. They hoped to reason with him. Finally Janet asked her mother what she thought might be the answer to the problem. The older woman smiled and answered, "It's about time you asked somebody. The solution is obvious to anybody who's been watching the two of you bring up that little boy."

Then she used two crucial words: *inconsistent discipline*.

This is another only child problem found more frequently among mature parents. We've discussed it before in Chapter 12, but we'll reiterate briefly because it is such a major problem for the only child. You have always attempted to talk, explain, reason, elaborate verbally without punishing or disciplining. But it hasn't worked. Why?

Because the most insecure child is the child who can't count on the consistent monitoring force of his parents, the child who has no guidelines as to what is right and wrong and also as to what will happen if he crosses the line separating the two. Verbal explanations to a young child are about as effective as whistling in the wind. The child needs consistent firm discipline, not adult discussion. He learns nothing from the words; it is the consistent application of discipline, both verbal and physical, that is the best teacher.

What about that worrisome issue of his "love"? The relationship between parents and child can be seen as a three-tiered pyramid, each level building on the one below:

LOVE

RESPECT

CONSISTENT DISCIPLINE (FEAR)

First comes the sense of fear. This is the same fear that prevents a child from running in the street because of the harsh sound of the parent's voice. The knowledge that these rules and the consequences of breaking these rules are consistent from day to day creates, in time, a growing respect for the parent. Emerging from this sense of respect are the tendrils of continuing love. It's very difficult to love another human being fully over a period of time

whom you do not respect. This extends to parent/child relationships as well. It is essential to be a consistent and fair rulemaker if
your only child is to appreciate you fully, both as a parent and as a
person.

The caretaker summed it up best. "When he's bad, he gets
punished. He knows that. So he's a pretty good boy. We get along
just fine."

*Situation 6:*

Every night before six-year-old Mandy went to sleep, there
would be a discussion about which parent would put her to bed
and read her a story. The discussion often became heated, and
finally Mandy would cry and run into her bedroom and close the
door. The same thing happened when her thirty-nine-year-old parents vied for her time on Saturdays. She would be asked whether
she wanted to go with Daddy to the Zoo, or with Mommy shopping or to the movies. Again the child would run out of the house
in tears. At her school check-up, Mandy told the doctor that her
parents were making her cry. He sat her down in the chair next to
his desk, and while they were alone together in his office, she
blurted out her pain at being placed in the middle of her parent's
competition over her. Despite the obvious nature of the problem,
it took several visits to the pediatrician before Mandy's parents
could resolve to work together at bringing her up rather than fighting to get into the driver's seat.

Their problem was *competing instead of co-parenting.*

When you're over thirty and out in the world of business or
the professions, you are attuned to the daily competition. Many
of you are accustomed to supervising younger people. There is a
natural spirit of "oneupsmanship" that you integrate into your
daily working world. You learned to leave it at the office during
your childless days. But now with that child waiting for both of
you at home at the end of the busy day and over the weekend, the
competitive spirit returns, and the two of you begin vying for your
child's time and affection. No one wins in this game—the biggest
loser is your child.

There is plenty of love in that single child for the *two* of you.
Your only child can love each of you equally and intensely. It is

most important to spare the child competitive conflict. What are the sensible prevention points that each of you should apply to your parenting so that you can avoid or overcome your naturally competitive nature in rearing the child?

1. There are no stereotyped roles of mother and father, particularly in the two-career family. Mother may do office work while father cooks. In the same regard, attempt to adjust your child to the many nurturing skills each of you possesses. The competition will diminish since your youngster will see both of you in the same light.
2. Decide what each of you does best and focus on those positive areas. This applies to every other area in your marriage, as well.
3. Arrange for each of you to have an adequate amount of your child's time and attention. Don't forget to leave sufficient time for your child's friends as well as private time for the child. Don't consume your child's time in the frantic effort to be equal co-parents.
4. Try not to argue about child rearing in the presence of the child. Never take the child's "side" in an argument involving your spouse in front of the child. This begins the insidious and dangerous practice of manipulating one parent against the other, a game played by some only children which can have serious consequences for a child—and a marriage.
5. Don't buy your child's love. Don't reward your child with material things. Together, as a couple, love your child. Reward with praise, affection, and ways to enjoy things together as a family. At times, special favors done for one parent deserve special acknowledgment. But in general, reward time is family time.

Your motto in this case: "We are individuals acting together for our child."

*Situation 7:*

Karen couldn't sleep at night. Her forty-year-old mother took the nine-year-old to the pediatrician.

"Why can't you sleep?" he asked Karen directly.

She smiled softly and sighed. "My head is so full, I can't fall asleep."

The doctor raised his eyebrows, "Full of what?"

The little girl leaned forward and said excitedly, "All of the things I have to do the next day."

The doctor asked her to elaborate on what she was thinking. She told him about her dancing class, her piano lessons, her ice skating, her extra school projects, her religious instruction—the list seemed never-ending.

Karen's problem was *overstimulation*.

You may both be over-achievers. You have waited to have this child because you wanted to experience as much of life as possible. You had goals to reach, achievements to be realized, projects or degrees to be completed. For the most part, you did a great deal of this before your only child came into the world. But then you obviously didn't just stop achieving; you continued working, experiencing, living life to the fullest with the role of parenting as an added dimension. Two important questions must be asked at this point. First, when are *you* going to slow down and enjoy who you are at this juncture of your life? Secondly, and equally important, why does your only child have to accomplish within her childhood everything it took you forty years to do?

It is very common for the affluent after-thirty parent to want his or her only child to have the maximum of life's experiences. She is the only child on whom the two parents can lavish this training. She is the only dividend from whom they can reap the rewards of their efforts. But how about the poor kid? She's exhausted and overwhelmed, and she is being set up to fail. It is impossible to be the "best" in so many activities, difficult even to succeed in that many ventures. Stretched so thin, she won't be able to reach her highest potential, or get a full sense of accomplishment, or learn how to make the personal decisions of self-containment that are so important to an active, productive life.

How can you prevent this overstimulation?

1. Find out what your child really enjoys doing.
2. Be sure that she has the talent or motivation to succeed before thrusting her fully into the venture.
3. Limit the extracurricular activities to those that consume *no more than* 25 percent of her free time. More than that can be exhausting as well as destructive to her essential friendships.

**4.** At no time indicate to her that you expect her to be the "best."
**5.** Allow her the flexibility to drop one activity and start another without a valid reason. Part of growing up is experimenting with your own skills at making decisions.
**6.** Expect your child to perform any task at a level of someone her own age. Too many older parents of only children go to the class play expecting their daughter to be the next generation's Julie Harris.
**7.** Accept the fact that your only child is going to grow up to be an individual quite different from you (and probably quite different from your fantasies of his or her future). Your child is not your clone.

Your only child is just one single person who can live through only twenty-four hours a day. Those twenty-four hours are *her* hours, *her* day. Allow her the privilege of having a significant voice in the quality and quantity of the activities assigned to her valuable time.

There are many myths and fallacies about the dangers of having or being an only child. But research has shown minimal, if any, differences in adult mental health that could be clearly connected with birth order. That there are special problems and concerns with only children is acknowledged by everyone, including the parents of only children. But being an only child doesn't condemn anyone to a greater likelihood of maladjustment. The key to adult success is the nature of the parenting received by the child. The informed and sensitive parent can rear a perfectly well-adjusted only child. Many important people in our society were only children.

You have the maturity to do the job. Be continually alert to the potential problems of the only child—particularly the only child from somewhat older parents. By mastering the seven key issues highlighted in this chapter, you'll be well on your way to being the satisfied older parent of a well-adjusted only child.

BIBLIOGRAPHY AND SUGGESTED READING

Arlow, J. A. "The Only Child," *Psychoanal. Quarterly*, 41:4, 507–536.
Clark, R. A. and Capparell, H. V. "The Psychiatry of the Adult Only Child," *Am. J. Psychother.*, 8, 487–499, 1954.
Hagenauer, F. and Tucker, H. "The Only Child," in *Basic Handbook of Child Psychiatry*, Nophitz, J. P. ed., Basic Books, 1979, pp. 388–393.
Hall, G. S., *et al.* "Aspects of Child Life and Education," in Smith, T. L. ed., Ginn, 1907.
Kappelman, M. M. *Raising the Only Child*. Dutton, 1975; Signet Books, 1977.

·

# CHAPTER FIFTEEN

# How Do I Parent
# Infants and
# Preschoolers?

Parents over thirty who raise children are no different from pre-thirty parents in their need for knowledge about children. And that knowledge is similar for both pre- and post-thirty parents; after all, children are universal in their growth patterns, needs, and problems.

The after-thirty parent does need more information. He usually reads the same child care books as the pre-thirty parent, seeks out advice from experienced child caretakers like grandparents, other parents, and lecturers, and then assimilates all of this knowledge into a useful and consistent set of actions for child rearing. But books, other parents, and lecturers often leave certain gaps unfilled, personal questions unanswered, and anxieties unresolved. After-thirty parents want to know the impact of their specific situations on their child's development. What are their specific and unique situations? They have busy schedules, established career patterns, and lowered energy levels.

The following two chapters raise the questions asked most often by after-thirty parents. This chapter covers questions about infants and children through preschool age. The next chapter covers questions asked by parents of school-aged children. They are important questions, often elicited slowly from mature parents who are embarrassed to have to ask them, for they feel they should know the answers. Such parents do *not* have to be ashamed; there are too few books dealing with their particular questions.

## FEELINGS OF THE AFTER-THIRTY PARENT

*Q*: I have a beautiful week-old baby and I should be the happiest woman in the world. Why do I feel so depressed, so dependent on my husband?

A: These are the famous "postpartum blues." Many physicians feel that some of the causes are physiological, the body's readjustment after pregnancy. Others feel that since a baby represents a major change in a family's life, the mind is getting used to this change through a type of withdrawal, a mild depression. A third possibility is the temporary "letdown" after nine months of expectation—finding the joys mixed with sudden responsibility. These "baby blues" will usually be only temporary. You can quicken the return of your normal emotional state by forcing yourself to get out, visit a friend, begin some constructive task or activity and, perhaps, permit yourself some self-indulgence. Ask your husband for a little more reassurance. Be dependent. Let him baby *you* a little. You both deserve it after all those waiting months.

*Q*: I usually feel guilty because I'm too tired to romp with my child after work. Is there any way to get more energy?

A: More energy is not the answer, nor is romping always necessary for a happy family. If you feel that romping is pleasurable and necessary for you and your child, do it when you feel you can. It's okay to tell your child that you are too tired to play at a certain time and postpone the games until later. The child knows that he is not being raised by Superman or Wonder Woman. Romp after dinner, when you feel more rested, or wait until weekends. Or hold the child on your lap for more sedentary activities like reading, playing board games, or the like. The value of romping is the contact, the loving touches, the sharing of those joyful moments. This can be done in many ways—even without physical exertion. Conserve and allot your energy. And don't feel guilty about a lost frolic. You will be remembered for your love, not your skill at hide-

and-seek. Your child can find friends for the games. He has only two parents from whom to receive that special love and affection.

Q: I'm always saying No to my child. Am I too harsh a disciplinarian?

A: How old is the child? And to what are you saying No? There are times in every baby's life that demand a fairly constant No. When a child begins testing the limits of the household rules, when the child begins to take all sorts of objects into his mouth, or does other damaging acts to himself or others, or when the child begins to dominate the attention and conversations of other children or adults, No is a must. Your child may be in one of these periods of exploration that frequently demand that No be used liberally. But carefully observe what you are "No-ing." Are you bothered by playful behavior that stretches your nerves because of the noise? Are you saying No to infant curiosity? Are you saying No to touching? If so, perhaps the answer is to raise your own tolerance. Take a relaxation break before you play with your child. Practice tolerance for a higher noise level. Consider the rapid passage of the childhood years. Baby-proof your house so that it's safer and less tempting. Postpone adult interactions until after your baby's bedtime. Plan your life to permit your child the privilege of curiosity. Docility is not a virtue for an active, inquisitive, creative child's mind.

Q: My two-year-old says No to every question and every direction. It's driving me crazy. Where have I gone wrong?

A: These are the fabled "terrible two's" and you are experiencing what every child goes through in passing from babyhood into childhood—testing every limit, rule, and command. The child wants to see just how independent he or she can be. Kids at this age must find out what it feels like to be in control, not only of you but of themselves. The best way to discover how to control your environment is to say No to everything. This, too, will pass, generally in about six months.

## PARENTAL BABY CARE

*Q*: I'm not going to breast feed my baby. Will I be depriving her of being held or fondled as babies are supposed to be?

A: No. You can hold and fondle your baby many times during the day. Nursing a baby is not the only reason to have contact with it. Children are much happier when held lovingly and frequently. You, your spouse, and your child caretaker can hold and fondle the baby. Most parents do this naturally. The desire to touch and hold their infant as a loving gesture should be encouraged. Holding the baby with its head on your left shoulder may give it more security because the infant can hear your heartbeat much as it sounded in the womb. Swaddling (wrapping a blanket tightly about the baby) in the early weeks may heighten the infant's feeling of security. Whatever your preference, be natural and spontaneous in your physical communication with your baby. Love will be communicated.

*Q*: Should I feed my baby on a regular schedule or on demand?

A: Most of the recent baby care books suggest a "flexible demand" feeding philosophy as the best for a young infant. This method recommends offering the breast or bottle to the infant whenever the baby makes the request by crying—but with reasonable modifications. Parents who adopt this feeding routine learn to recognize the infant's requests for food and to honor these specific food cries. These parents also stop feeding the baby when the infant pushes away from the source of milk. They determine the baby's feeding schedule using this method, and from the schedule they are able to estimate the amount of time between feeding usually requested by their infant. Once this schedule is determined (and it changes rapidly in the first two weeks), the baby's routine can be adjusted in a flexible manner to adapt to the parent's own personal needs for such basics as sleep and meals. If the baby is on an approximate every-four-hour schedule, it will be fed six times per day—but not always on a strict schedule and not always at the exact time requested. A telephone call, an outside visitor, a trip to the store, or mealtime need not be interrupted by feeding. Allowing the baby to cry for a while until feeding becomes convenient is permissible. It is good exercise for the baby's lungs and frees the parents from infant domination. In addition, the baby can't sleep through one feeding period and demand twice as much attention and milk the next feeding. Parents and child create a dialogue, an initial contract for feeding based on need. This unspoken contract allows both the parent and the child to obtain a bit more freedom and self-determination. As a result, despite some increased crying, the climate in the home remain basically more relaxed. Flexible demand scheduling appears to be the most relaxed and most adaptable method for all concerned.

Q: My baby cries a lot. Is that because he misses me while I'm away?

A: It depends on the age of the baby, when you separated from him, and how long you are away. If you started (or continued) working before the baby was three months old, chances are the baby is crying because of colic, gas, or some other distress. But after three months, the baby does sense separation. He may miss you. That does not mean, however, that you have to drop everything to stay home again. The baby will get over the separation fears if you have a warm, loving caretaker in the home. Babies have the capacity to attach to more than one warm, loving person. So you relinquish little of your baby's love—merely provide an adequate substitute when you are gone. It's okay to be away from home for work or other commitments. It is not okay to "lay a guilt trip" on yourself every time you must be away from your child. You, your spouse, and your child will be healthier if you realize the rights—and needs—of both parents and children.

Q: When should my child be toilet trained?

A: Only when the child's sphincter muscles around the anal opening are under the child's control. When this occurs, the child can postpone a bowel movement for a short while by holding the sphincter closed. The child must also be able to tell you his need for a bowel movement. These two conditions generally don't occur until well after the first year, usually weeks after unsupported walking begins. Sometimes it may not be practical to toilet train until the youngster is a year and a half to two years old. Often, when training occurs earlier, the person trained is not the baby but the

parent, who reacts to the slightest indication that a bowel movement is imminent.

Toilet training is complete when the child spontaneously goes
to the toilet by himself and manages on his own.

Q: How should I toilet train my child?

A: Experienced parents find that the following rules work
best:

*Do not begin toilet training until several months after your
child has begun to walk. Then the muscles that enable the child
to control his bowel and bladder should be fully functional or at
least working well enough for control.

*Then introduce the concept of individual responsibility to
your child.

*Teach in a positive, helpful, rewarding way so that the
youngster will understand and accept his role.

*Be patient but consistent. Remind, do not command. Stimu-
late, do not bribe. Reward with a show of joyful pleasure when the
child succeeds. Never punish toilet-training failure.

*Allow your youngster to observe you performing the same
function. Explain as the curious child watches.

*Bear in mind that no child can be rushed, forced, coerced,
bribed, or convinced to be toilet trained until he is ready.

*Use the potty chair if it works. Use the toilet seat if it works.
Fit the method to the child. But again, be consistent, vigilant, and
relaxed. Remember very few five-year-old children are not toilet
trained.

Q: Will my child be harmed if I toilet train him too soon?

A: Most authorities discourage toilet training at too early an
age. You should wait until your child is ready. This is often incon-
venient to a working parent or caretaker. As a result, children of
working parents may be coerced into early toilet training. This
forced training could have negative effects in the child's later bowel
and bladder control and may have subtle psychological effects that
won't show up until later life. So why risk it? Besides, the disad-
vantages of too early bowel control training may be offset by the
pure pleasure and satisfaction that you and the child get when he

first announces triumphantly: "Look, Mommy, I went in my own potty!"

Q: Can toilet training really be accomplished in twenty-four hours?

A: Some experts, using reinforcement (both negative and positive), advocate this technique. We don't. We prefer to see it as a natural developmental milestone of childhood, arrived at when the child is physically and emotionally ready, and shared by child and parent in a relaxed manner. Reducing it to a mechanical act, to be accomplished without appropriate love and praise, robs this training of the importance of being one of the first shared tasks of successful childhood learning. Brainwashing and toilet training should not be synonymous.

Q: My child won't eat. Am I being punished for not being around?

A: It is important to remember that when children reach the age of one to one and a half, they tend to eat less. They aren't growing as fast as they did during the first few months and don't need as many calories. Decreased appetite during this second year is quite common. But you should be aware that there could be other reasons for your child's diminishing appetite. There could be physical problems. Many childhood illnesses involve digestive disturbances and poor appetite. If your child's eating problem lasts longer than two weeks, it would be wise to consult your pediatrician. Be sure that your walking youngster isn't raiding the icebox or sneaking food before you ring the distress signal. Perhaps he has a different idea of what tastes good. Children's aversions to foods such as spinach, broccoli, and other green vegetables are legendary. However, individual children have individual dislikes, and these should be honored as long as they are not too inclusive —i.e., all meats. Try to encourage your youngster to experiment with new tastes. This may take time, but be patient.

Finally, you will have to examine the atmosphere at your table at mealtime. Also look at your relationship with your child as a potential problem. Is mealtime at your home a pleasant time or are chaos, anger, and stress served up as an appetizer? Do you worry excessively about the eating habits of your child to the degree that you "hover" over the plate, counting bites and worrying over every morsel of leftover food? If this is true, then you could be the prime target for the child's eating idiosyncrasies. Children find parents' soft spots quickly and learn to exploit these vulnerabilities when they want to punish, control, or manipulate their parents. If your child's failure to eat creates problems *for you*, your youngster will quickly begin to use mealtime to gain your attention, manipulate you, or signal you (see Chapter 13 on signals). If you don't perpetuate these problems, if you just relax with a healthy, finicky eater, you will find that the eating problem ceases after a time. The more you worry and fret visibly, the longer the non-eating will continue.

## BABY CARE BY A CHILD CARETAKER

*Q*: What kind of a person should I look for as a caretaker for my baby?

A: Someone mature enough to share your values as a parent and experienced enough to know the basics of child care. Start with your spouse. Consider the current flexible working hours in many jobs. Can you stagger your hours so that maximum parent time is spent with the child? Would the father consider being a househusband? Or what about your parents, in-laws, or other relatives as caretakers? If none of these is possible, check with local mothers who might not mind caretaking another child. Finally, check the agencies for a competent babysitter or nursemaid. Check each reference. Telephone, explain your situation, and ask for their appraisal of the candidate's ability. It will be necessary then to have talks with the potential caretaker about what should be done in both a daily normal routine and an emergency. Look for a warm and loving person, one who will touch, talk, and hold the baby. The caretaker should be a person who can be counted on to call you at the first sign of anything abnormal in the child. You need someone who will report to you on the child's activities, his progress as well as his problems. Picking an adequate caretaker will be one of your most important decisions, both for you and your child. It may take time and patience to find the right one, but perseverance is in order—for your child's sake.

Once you think you have found the right person, stay home with that caretaker for a few days. See how she takes routine care of the baby; assure yourself that she will take good care of the baby before you return to work. Establish a daily time of contact with the person. Supervise your parenting surrogate; don't abdicate your role as parent.

Q: Will my child assume the personality of the caretaker?

A: Your child will have his or her own personality. The youngster may mimic some of the characteristics of the caretaker, as he will do with you and your spouse. During adolescence he will seem like every other teenager. These are normal phases. Don't worry. Neither you nor the caretaker has claim to the child's personality. Ultimately, he will be absolutely himself.

## PLAY GROUPS AND PRESCHOOL

Q: What are the values of play groups?

A: In these groups, which are usually formed with the parents of children of your child's age, parents take turns supervising the group for a day each week. Thus a play group of five children only needs supervision by a particular parent one day out of a work week. In addition to the convenience for a working parent, the play group gives your child exposure to other children, allows you to observe your child with other children, and permits you to exchange child-rearing tips with other parents. Unfortunately, the close contact also exposes your child to the many minor childhood illnesses. But that disadvantage is far outweighed by the advantages. A good reference on starting play groups is Harriet Watts's *How to Start Your Own Preschool Playgroup* (Universe Books, New York, 1973). You should also consider babysitting pools, where you as parents agree to babysit for other children in exchange for having your child taken care of by another participating parent. Each parent works for "points," so there is little expense. One parent must be the bookkeeper, and receives points for that; each point is worth time when others will babysit your child. This is a good way to have an evening alone with your spouse and at the same time assure your child an experienced caretaker/parent. This shared babysitting can also be used during the day if caretakers don't show up, or if you go out of town. This is a safe and expedient child care method. The cost is minimal; the exchange is time, not money.

Q: How do I select a good preschool for my child?

A: By visiting. There are few defined standards for either staff or physical facilities of preschools, so the only way to get to know a good preschool is to pay a visit, talk to the head teacher, and observe the school in action.

What should you look for? First, take the time to meet the person who will be working with your child. Is he or she the type of person with whom you will feel comfortable leaving your child? How does she relate to the other children? Does the school employ men as well as women so that your youngster can observe role models of both sexes? Do the children have varied backgrounds, or are you going to be duplicating the population of the neighborhood from which you brought your child? Does the school offer planned educational experiences that will teach your child something about the world in which he or she is growing up? Does the school stress morals and values? If so, are they in line with your philosophies? Will the school use you as part of their educational program and report to you frequently on your child's progress? Will the school call you with any problem, and can you trust them to act swiftly and sensibly with any medical emergency? These are all questions that you will want to ask the potential teacher of your child. Only you know the answers that you want to hear; every parent has different educational goals for his child. Talk and listen, then decide.

Consider, also, that you may not want an educational program for your preschool child. You may be content with day care, with its more limited educational goals. What do you want for your child? What fits that child best? Stop and consider. Then after you have placed your child, assist the school or day care center to help him grow and flourish. Become their partner in rearing your child.

## LEAVING THE CHILD LATER

*Q:* Is it bad to leave an older child with a babysitter too often?

*A:* Not if you know the babysitter personally or by reputation. And not if you use forethought in your preparations for leaving the child. Tell your child in advance in a positive way. Try as often as possible to employ the sitter the child likes best. Leave detailed instructions for the sitter about your child's routine, places you can be reached, and any special considerations. As after-thirty parents, you'll need some time to yourselves. Don't feel selfish if you take it. It is as important to your child as it is to you that you be individuals with lives of your own.

## SEX ROLES AND STEREOTYPES

*Q:* In the modern family, what role is the father expected to play? And the mother?

*A:* Today, the typical roles of father and mother seem to be blending. Economics, increased technology, changing work patterns, and women's liberation are challenging the old sex-related stereotypes. Mothers can now make more money than their husbands. Fathers can be sensitive and artistic rather than always macho and rugged. Children are offered unisex dolls and television programs exploring various roles. Sex roles are learned: the classroom is the family. After-thirty parents in the 1980s are more likely to retain the expectations of sex roles they were taught by their parents. This may not be true among the younger generation of parents.

What roles should the mother and father play in the modern family? Whatever roles fit best with their concepts of themselves. The child whose parents offer him a variety of successful roles will be better prepared to establish his own image as he approaches adulthood.

*Q:* I found my preschooler and another child playing "Doctor and Nurse." What should I do about it?

*A:* Nothing, if this is the first time. If you interrupted them, try to talk about it with them, answering any questions they might have about the other person. If you did not interrupt them, don't talk to them about it and don't worry. It is only natural, a common exploratory phase. Only if it is continued should you seek advice from your pediatrician. Don't you remember when you played the same game?

Q: How can I keep my child from having racial prejudices?

A: By not having them yourselves, and then demonstrating your acceptance to your child. You should socialize with persons of other races and religions. Invite them (and their children) into your home. Attend theaters and sports events where races freely mix. Select social institutions (churches, schools, etc.) where there is racial and religious heterogeneity. A child has to meet, and like, persons of other races in order to combat the insidious and subtle prejudices of adults. Provide your child with every opportunity to meet and like others of different races, and you will be offering him a chance for a fuller, more exciting life.


## Resources

Q: Are parenting classes really helpful?

A: The answer to this depends on the class, the teacher, and your needs. Almost everyone finds parenting classes helpful before the baby arrives. Basic knowledge about how to feed, bathe, and nurture the baby is taught. How about during the infancy period? Are you concerned about understanding your child's behavior? Parent Effectiveness Training might be the answer. Are you interested in observing the "ages and stages" of your child's growth? Try a child development course at the local community college or university. Do you have a special interest in children's reading? Try a children's literature course at your local public library or college. Shop and choose; you don't have a lot of time for courses of marginal interest. Some, in fact, are quite biased toward nonworking mothers and offer obsolete stereotyping. So check what you're buying and get your money's worth.

Q: How do I select a good pediatrician who will understand my situation?

A: The selection of a pediatrician is almost as important as the selection of a good child caretaker. The pediatrician can be located through several sources (other than your satisfied friends): through (a) the local medical society, (b) a medical school's department of pediatrics, (c) city or county health departments, (d) another family physician, or (e) the *Directory of Medical Specialists*, which may be found in the medical or science sections of public libraries. Look for a child specialist who also teaches, for these physicians *have* to keep up with the latest developments in the field. Then, when you have narrowed the field to the two you think you want, make appointments and go for "prenatal," or childless visits. You'll be free from struggling with a baby and can talk to the physicians about your family's health patterns, your needs as after-thirty parents, your concerns about the baby, appointments (usually monthly for six months), immunizations, feeding, and similar concerns. Be candid. You are interviewing a sympathetic, understanding person who should be able to respond to most of your questions. Select on this basis. You must be satisfied with nothing less than what is best for your child. You have the maturity and experience to be talked to as an adult by another adult, and you should use that as the basis for your rapport with the pediatrician.

## Toys

Q: What kinds of toys should I buy for my child?

A: There are several toy guides on the market, but one of the best appears to be Chapter 10, "Plays and Playthings," by Frank and Theresa Caplan (founders of Creative Playthings) in *The Parenting Advisor* (Frank Caplan, gen. ed., Anchor Books, New York, 1978). Books and articles often list the educational needs of children at different ages and suggest the best toys. In addition, however, you will need to examine toys for their safety, durability, and usefulness. Almost all experts agree that toys of violence (guns, monsters, etc.) foster such values and should *not* be purchased for children. And don't forget that often the best toys are those that stimulate the unbridled creativity and imagination of the child.

Thus homemade blocks, leftover boxes of all sorts, colored wrapping paper and string make excellent and stimulating playthings for children. Don't miss the obvious in your search for the exotic.

## Child Growth and Development

*Q:* I'm embarrassed by baby talk, but should I try to use it to communicate with my infant?

*A:* Absolutely not. The child patterns his speech after yours, so make it the best (and most comfortable) you can. The only modification you need to make at first is to use simpler words than you would with adults.

*Q:* When will my child be less dependent on me or the caretaker?

*A:* Physically, the child is less dependent at about three, when he can dress, toilet, and feed himself. Psychologically, less dependency is seen at about seven or eight years of age, when the child goes into a "latency" period (which will be talked about in the next chapter).

*Q:* Is there something wrong with my child if he doesn't play with others?

*A:* Not if your child is under two. Usually, up until about that time a child prefers playing by himself. After this, a stage of "parallel play" emerges, where a child won't really interact with another child but will share the same space, playing his own games with his own toys. At about three years, the child begins to play with other children. If your three year old persists in being solitary, or actively withdraws from playing with others, you should get advice from professionals about his social development.

*Q:* What are some tips for decorating a nursery?

*A:* When you bring an infant home, it's fun to put it into a beautifully decorated room, one which will eventually show the baby that you loved him enough to go to that effort. But remember that your baby will be curious and very active, so pick furniture that will be durable. Use temporary furniture like cribs and playpens that can be disposed of as the baby grows. Make the room as open and as uncluttered as possible, using bright colors to give it interest. Use only simple mobiles over the crib, install unbreakable mirrors, have a play corner with blocks and boxes that are nontoxic, and purchase a few extra chests with drawers in which the child can store favorite toys, clothes, mementos, stuffed animals, and so on. Put in a rocking chair—for you and the baby. Make certain that the paint you use in the baby's room is lead-free. When the baby is young, you may want a ticking clock or a music box near the crib to lull it into sleep. Change the room as the baby grows into a child. As the baby develops more of a concept of self, the room should be decorated to match the emerging personality.

*Q*: How long should thumb-sucking be allowed to go on? Isn't it bad for the placement of the teeth?

*A*: Thumb-sucking appears to be a normal reflex in most babies, a precursor of putting other, often more dangerous objects into the mouth. It usually starts before three months, peaks about six months, and is gone by about twelve months. If thumb-sucking is prolonged beyond that period, it may do some damage to the teeth, but many dentists feel that damage done to baby teeth is not permanent. Therefore, don't be concerned if your child sucks his thumb in the first year. If it continues after fifteen months, consult your pediatrician.

*Q*: I have a skinny baby. Aren't fat babies healthier?

*A*: Babies are healthy unless proven otherwise. Actually, the latest research shows that fat babies who are fat because they are overfed are often in serious trouble as adults. They can't stop gaining weight and remain obese and unhappy adults. Thin babies may come from thin parents. Skinny babies, however, could be suffering from hidden chronic health problems so that they cannot gain weight even though they are good eaters. Only your pediatrician can tell you if your fat or skinny baby is healthy.

*Q*: How important is it to keep records of a child's physical and mental milestones?

*A*: In addition to the joy you will have in sharing this information with your child in later years, your pediatrician will find it very useful for you to keep such records. If something in your child causes a developmental lag, or if your child seems highly intelligent or creative, the records will show it. What are some of the items to keep in the baby log? Family tree information, birth certificate, immunization data, medical illnesses, allergies, height and weight (at least on birthdays), and dates of crawling, walking, first words, first sentence, first tooth, etc. Put in photos and you'll have a book that you and your older child will enjoy looking at time after time.

Q: My four year old stutters. What can I do?

A: You should do nothing right away. Many four year olds go through a period of nonfluency, a development in their speech patterns where they can think faster than they can talk. It is best to wait patiently until the child is finished with his thought, without correcting him, and answer in a relaxed way. If the stuttering keeps up for more than six months, check with a speech clinician about your child.

Q: How can I help my child become more intelligent?

A: If you follow an exact definition of intelligence, you will know that you can't help a child have more potential than that with which he was born. But almost no one uses that exact definition because modern behavioral science does not seem to know how to measure a person's *potential* for wisdom accurately. Therefore, books that are written about how to raise intelligence in young children really deal with raising their intelligence scores, or increasing their vocabulary, or elevating their math skills, and so on.

Only one action appears to help the child with developing skills for later life—reading to the child. Start very early, long before the child knows all the words. Read to him or her before bedtime. Read regularly. Read during relaxation periods. Build the child a library; you can purchase inexpensive books through the school. Help him obtain his own public library card. Encourage reading when the child is older. Discuss what you are reading with him: words, thoughts, ideas, concepts. These are the gifts of greatest value from the parent to the child.

Q: If I want to know something about my child's measured intelligence, how do I find out?

A: Don't. Intelligence scores have been treated as a game for too long, and the results have been the basis for some disastrous conclusions which have harmed children. Talk over your reasons for wanting this information with your pediatrician, and then accept his recommendations. Only if you both are worried about your child's developmental progress will he be likely to suggest testing your child.

Q: My child is wonderful! Can a child be "too good"?

A: There are periods in a child's life when that child is, and should be, very difficult. The aforementioned "terrible two's" is one of those times, and the four's are another. If your child demonstrates no negative behavior at these times, he may be unusually placid and even-tempered, or he may be delayed in some natural transitions. You should talk this over with your pediatrician. Sometimes children can be forced to be good by overly rigid caretakers or parents, and they repress their independence with great fear of rejection or punishment. This can only result in a damaged psyche. When your child is being difficult to handle, wait patiently for the in-between years. Enjoy them fully. Another trying time is surely on the horizon.

Q: How can I help my child appreciate the arts?

A: Many parents who feel the arts are a vital part of their lives expose their children to them too early. Young children who have to sit through incomprehensible operas or frightening movies will not feel rewarded by them, no matter how enthusiastic Daddy or Mommy is, or how good the ice cream at intermission.

But early exposure to the arts is fine—indeed, preferable—if the arts are good children's theater, puppets, local school productions, etc. Pick plays, music, and other performances that you know are appropriate for your child's age. Invite other children to go with your youngster the first time, so that your child can see the value of the experience to others. Explain the presentation to the child before it is seen and talk about it afterwards. Build up anticipation for the next performance. The arts are more enjoyable when we know something about them. Help your child learn about them and you will have opened up new worlds to him.

Q: When is the best time to get a pet for a child?

A: Probably not before the child is three years of age. At that time the child is emotionally ready; but remember that a three-year-old isn't old enough to assume full responsibility for the pet. That probably won't come until the child is about nine years old. If *you* can care for a pet when your child reaches three years, it is a good idea to get one, especially for the only child. Help the child adjust to the new pet and watch for the love that will soon develop. Your child will have a true friend.

## Bibliography and Suggested Reading

Ackerman, Paul R. and Kappelman, Murray M. *Signals: What Your Child Is Really Telling You.* Dial/James Wade, 1978.

Akmakjian, Hiag. *The Natural Way to Raise a Healthy Child.* Praeger, 1975.

Apgar, Virginia. *Is My Baby All Right?* Pocket Books, 1974.

Arnold, Arnold. *Teaching Your Child to Learn from Birth to School Age.* Prentice-Hall, 1971.

Boston Children's Medical Center and Feinbloom, Richard I., *et al. Child Health Encyclopedia: The Complete Guide for Parents.* Delacorte Press, 1975.

Brazelton, T. Berry. *Infants and Mothers.* Delacorte Press, 1972.

Brazelton, T. Berry. *Toddlers and Parents.* Delacorte Press, 1974.

Child Health Centers of America. *Your Child: Keeping Him Healthy.* Jackson, Tenn., 1971.

Gilbert, Sara D. *Three Years to Grow.* Parents' Magazine Press, 1972.

Gordon, Thomas. *P.E.T., Parent Effectiveness Training.* New American Library, 1975.

Hymes, James L. *Teaching the Child Under Six.* Bobbs-Merrill, 1974.

Kappelman, Murray M. and Ackerman, Paul R. *Between Parent and School.* Dial Press/James Wade, 1977.

Kappelman, Murray. *What Your Child Is All About.* Reader's Digest Press, 1974.

Kaye, Evelyn. *The Family Guide to Children's Television.* Pantheon Books, 1974.

Neisser, Edith. *Primer for Parents of Preschoolers.* Parents' Magazine Press, 1972.

Princeton Center for Infancy. *The First Twelve Months of Life.* Grosset, 1973.

Princeton Center for Infancy. *The Parenting Advisor.* Frank Caplan, gen. ed. Anchor Press, Doubleday, 1978.

Shiller, Jack. *Childhood Illness.* Stein and Day, 1973.

Watts, Harriet M. *How to Start Your Own Preschool Playgroup.* Universe Books, 1973.

·

# CHAPTER SIXTEEN

# How Do I Raise
# My School-Age Child?

Just when you think you have childhood under control, along comes the school-age period, four through twelve years, and you find yourself faced by a whole new set of surprises, challenges, and frustrations. This is a time when after-thirty parents often resume two careers, undisputably turn middle-aged, and begin to look forward to more occupational and personal stability. There is a tendency, during this period, to think about turning over the raising of your child to the school. But it doesn't work that way. The child still depends on you for guidance, values, and wisdom. The school's primary function is to educate your child and, therefore, it will be a "babysitter" of variable and questionable effectiveness. You will still be the most important person in your child's life.

It will often be hard to recognize this importance, however. During this period, usually at about seven years of age, the child reaches one of those stages in his life that psychologists call "latency." This is the period where the child "lays back" from parents, establishes his identity with peers, teachers, other adults, and starts to take some control of his life in general. During the latency period, which usually lasts until about twelve, the child seems to place more emphasis on social contacts with peers than with parents. His world seems to center on school, church, hobbies, sports, pets, pranks, and television. *Seems* to center on these things. Actually you, the child's parents, are very much in the forefront of his or her world. He is judging life's experiences against your rules. You are being compared to others. Friends are being tried, accepted, or discarded; your judgments on friends, movies, values, school are being carefully listened to, but translated into the language of the child's everyday life. Don't be deceived by this "latency" period. As a parent, you often may be out of sight but you are rarely out of mind.

By the time a child reaches this age, many parents are feeling rather knowledgeable about childhood. Yet there are still persistent questions that arise out of being an after-thirty parent with a school-aged child. Here are some of those most frequently asked us by mature parents who have school-aged children.

## FEELINGS OF THE AFTER-THIRTY PARENT

*Q*: Most of my child's friends' parents appear to be younger than me. What problems will I have in relating to these younger adults?

*A:* Depending on how social you are, you should have no trouble relating to these other parents *about raising children.* This is the one problem you share, the one area in which you both want and need to talk. You will enjoy sharing stories about the milestones in the growth of your children, how you solved certain universal childhood problems, and how you're going to solve expected new ones.

But unless you are exceedingly gregarious, your conversations will usually stop at that point; you will very likely have little else in common. If you are a single after-thirty parent, you may not even make it to the "let's discuss the children" phase of conversation because of the difficulty some couples have in relating to a single parent. So why fight it? Your child is not counting on you to be socially involved with all of his friends' parents. You need to have a social life that is rewarding to you and fits your schedule and your age. Accept this. You only need to concern yourself with balancing *your* social obligations. Enter into conversations with other parents, sharing anecdotes and concerns about children—theirs and yours. But save your friendships for those people with whom you wish to share much more.

Q: How do I explain to my child the difference in ages between us and his friends' parents?

A: "You were born when we were older." A simple fact, and usually all he wants to know. Don't apologize. Often our after-thirty parent friends have told us that they have heard their child comparing them with his friends' parents somewhat like this: "My dad really feels and looks like a dad, but Joey's father seems like his big brother." It can be both a positive and negative comparison—depending on the day, the mood, and the company.

Q: How "responsible" can I expect my child to be?

A: Assign a child a task that he can understand, explain to him all the options that he has, and then trust him to carry it out. If responsibility is treated as a progressively more complex series of tasks that can be learned with increasing maturity, then a school-aged child can be responsible for a great number of tasks at an early age. Notice the several variables provided by this answer. If you want a responsible child, your child must understand clearly what you expect of him. He should be physically and mentally capable of assuming this particular responsibility. The mental capability for responsibility in a child generally comes before parents expect it. Offer the child experiences in responsibility of increasing complexity, and then follow through to see that the task was done, outlining the consequences if it was not done properly, and praising the child if he showed genuine responsibility. Both praise and punishment are necessary. Be sensitive, however, to the "overly responsible" child, who is forced into mature responsibility patterns before he has a chance to be a child. But a child with a mature sense of responsibility to add to his childhood achievements is well prepared for the tasks of later adolescence and adult life.

Q: What do I do if I don't have enough energy to cope with my school child's high activity level?

A: Conserve your energy to do the things you can. A generation ago, when parents grew up feeling that they had to be "pals" and "girlfriends" to their children, they spent a lot of time worrying whether they could play ball every night with their boys, or shop for clothes with their girls. Many of those parents who succeeded in being great pals produced a generation of flower children—young people without strong adult models, striving rather aimlessly for revolution against amorphous authority figures.

Children need to know parents as adults—as persons who are unique, mature, responsible, and at times authoritarian. Children need role models for later life. They need to know our strengths and weaknesses, not so they can judge us, but to help them select those guidelines for themselves which fulfill their self-image. We can be ourselves—and being ourselves includes being exhausted and distant, being irritable and edgy after a harassed day at work. You are a human being. Your child knows this; it's no secret. Simply learn to say, "I'm sorry," or, "I was wrong," and he'll learn that as well. Today's parents are models for tomorrow's adults, and the best way to help is to communicate with children what being adult is all about. Don't be afraid to be busy or tired or preoccupied occasionally. When you have it, use that energy. When you don't have it, explain—without guilt. You will then be offering them a realistic model of an honest adult.

## SCHOOL PROGRESS

Q: How much should I bother the school about the progress of my child?

A: It is your responsibility always to be fully aware of your child's school progress and how that progress compares with the child's ability. Public schools are financed by taxpayers, but traditionally teachers have been somewhat adversarial in their relations to parents, treating them as people to be tolerated and patronized. Now public schools, faced with federal legislation that mandates freedom for parents seeking information about their child, are beginning to realize that parents can be a valuable ally. If becoming a partner in your child's education is your reason for asking for information from a school, and you share this reason with them, they will probably share facts and valuable insights about your child with you. If you are adversarial, however, you may back them into a corner so that they give you only the most basic facts, which will not be significant in helping you to help your child. Maintain a good relationship with your child's school. Monitor your child's progress frequently, but appear as an *educational team member* to the school personnel. You and your child will both benefit from your attitude.

Q: Shall I send my child to public or private school?

A: The first question you have to ask yourself is an economic one: Can I afford a private school? If the answer is Yes, or, "Yes, if I have to," then you should move on to the next questions: "Does my child need a better school than the local public school?"; "Is there some final goal for my child that would be accomplished better by a private school?"; and finally, "What about the schooling process needs to be modified to suit my child?"

To make a decision on which school to choose, you have to know a certain amount about your child and your local public school. What do you know of your child's abilities? What have his preschool or kindergarten teachers told you? What have you observed from watching him at play with other children? What have professionals such as your pediatrician told you about your child that might make you want to put him into a private school? If you have this information, then talk to the principal of the local public school. Give the school a chance to explain its position. If it still appears that the public school can't meet your child's needs, you have two options: either transport your child to a public school that can meet his needs, or consider a private school.

Many parents, knowing that suburban schools are generally better than urban or rural schools at this time, move their families into good school districts. Others simply transport children to these schools, which is costly, but less expensive than private schools. Some parents stay where they are and assert their rights, fighting for better education until the public schools improve.

What are some of the reasons for choosing private school? Some private schools have a better record of college entrance, gearing their studies to meet entrance requirements. Some private schools have a more heterogeneous population than the local school, and you might want your child to have this broad exposure. And some private schools have better teachers, lower class sizes, more diverse curricular offerings, or more individualized guidance than the public schools. If your child needs any or all of these things, you must consider a private school that meets these needs.

Start with word of mouth; then go to various listings. Write to all the private schools you are considering and study their brochures. Ask about class size, college preparation, teachers' credentials, special programs, and so on. Most private schools will be glad to answer these questions. If not, cross them off your list.

After you have narrowed your list, visit the selected private schools *with your child*. Again, those private schools don't allow you to visit and talk should be eliminated. Talk to teachers; observe a class in action. Do you feel good about it? Look at the older children; do they represent a satisfactory future image for your own child? Notice how your child reacts to the school and to the other children. Get his/her opinions. How does he/she feel about the school? That is essential.

Whatever you decide, whether it is public or private, stay involved. Protect your investment in your child's education.

Q: How important is it to become involved in school/parent organizations?

A: If you are the usual busy after-thirty parent, you will find organizations like the PTA, Fifth Grade Mother's Club, and the Jr. High Boosters difficult to manage within your schedule. If you have to pick and choose, we recommend the PTA, because local, as well as state and federal issues, are discussed at most PTA meetings. If the meetings at your child's school are not issue-oriented, question the usefulness of your attendance.

Most organizations are geared for the parents who are home with the children, mothers who can drive, fathers who have weekends free for camping trips, and so on. That more than likely is *not* you. You'll have to say No when asked to join these organizations, and you'll have to accustom yourself to refusing graciously. Don't worry; you aren't damaging your child, particularly if you allot that time to spend with him. You owe it to your child—and to yourself—to budget your time so you can be together as much as possible, even if that means excluding traditional forms of communicating with the school and other parents.

Q: What should I do about school if my child is handicapped?

A: This may sound strange, but if your child is handicapped, he or she is one of the few children in this country who is guaranteed an appropriate education by federal law, at *no extra cost* to you. You should immediately contact the principal of the local school and he or she will advise you. If he can't, then contact Closer Look (Box 1492, Washington, D.C., 20036), which is a national parents advocacy organization. They will give you full particulars about your rights, the child's rights, the individual educational program that the school must provide for your child, and the names of other parents and organizations that work with children like yours.

## PARENTING A SCHOOL-AGED CHILD

*Q*: How much guidance will I really be able to give my child once he/she enters school?

*A*: Much more than you think. School still deals, primarily, in academic subjects, not life. Most schools, for example, don't offer good sex education courses. So you must teach intimate human behavior on a daily basis to your child. You have values: honesty, responsibility, courage, candor. Discuss your value system with your child. You might be able to help your child with some of the school subjects, but wait until he/she asks for your assistance. Many parents have hurt rather than helped their child with conflicting methods of doing math; take your child's cue on these subjects. Most schools don't have adequate fine arts programs, so include your child whenever possible in visits to the theater, dance, art exhibits, and the like. Many schools can't, or won't, advise children on extra-school learning like dance, drama, or music courses, or activities connected with scouting, hobbies, or religion. You can give assistance in all these areas. Your child will need increasing guidance from this point forward into adolescence. He will have to make many more choices each year, and you will be needed to help with these personal decisions. Don't abdicate guidance to the school. The school can only go so far; you can go all the way.

*Q*: How much time will be expected of me during the school-aged years for jobs like chauffeuring, camp-outs, etc.?

*A*: More than you can give—even if you were a full-time

houseparent with unlimited energy. Practice now: "I'm sorry, I'd
like to if I could, but I'm busy that night with work. Can I offer
some Saturday when I'm home?" Offering to reimburse for the
gasoline used by those parents who drive most often may help in
offsetting your lack of chauffeuring availability. Early use of bus
and bicycle by your youngster should be encouraged to help the
child transport himself to an event or to the house of a "chauffeur."
It's important to share these logistics with your child and gradually
ask him to assume more responsibility in planning. Whatever compromises must be made, let your child know of your efforts first to
do the task and, if that's not possible, to help him solve the problem. Let him know that you care, even though sometimes you can't
help.

## Child Growth and Development

Q: When and how do I start sex education with my child?

A: Sex education begins at infancy. Babies explore every part
of their bodies. Soon they discover their genitalia and the pleasurable sensations when they touch themselves. The parent who slaps
the infant's hand then is starting the youngster on a negative sexual
journey in which one's own body is off limits. As the child grows,
there will be things in the environment that will raise sexual questions. "Where are babies carried?" "How do they get there?"
"Why do you have something there and Mommy doesn't?" All
questions should and must be answered. There are no subjects that
are taboo at any age once they are raised by the child. However,
you must be careful to frame your responses in both the language
and the context that will be understood by your child. You don't
give a six-year-old child the same response that you would give
to a twelve year old asking a similar question. Too much in too
sophisticated terms will only confuse and frighten the child; but a
"birds and bees" answer will only result in turning the child away
from the parent as a reliable sex educator.

Don't be afraid to allow conversations about sexuality and intimate human behavior to surface at any time within your home.
Handle them with ease. Sex is a natural, normal biologic part of

our existence. It is vitally important that the child sees sex in that perspective. Delaying the conversation, taking the child into another room to whisper your response, or demonstrating by your face or the contortions of your body the state of your discomfort only gives the subject of sexuality a sense of discomfort. It may take your child years to overcome the fear that such an orientation toward sexual issues instills within him. He may never succeed fully in releasing himself from the sexual inhibitions that you unwittingly (because of your own upbringing) placed within him.

So relax, and try to be an informed and comfortable sexual informant for your child. Allow others who are qualified within the schools or church or medical profession help you. There are very good books that can help you in this task; a list is provided at the end of this chapter.

When your youngster approaches adolescence, prepare him or her for the dramatic changes within his/her own body. Talk straight. Try not to instill fear. Don't pass on myths, only solid information. Share experiences. Listen and answer questions honestly. Discuss not only anatomy, but function and sexual techniques as well. If you feel shy and uncomfortable, use the resources of your physician, your clergyman, your school, and your library or bookstore. Always remember that the better informed you are, the less chance there is for a mistake, and the less chance there is that your child will rely on someone else to tell or show him or her the meaning of being sexually mature.

*Q*: Is physical punishment needed for the school-aged child?

*A*: Occasionally a loud but gentle swat to the posterior is indicated as a punctuation to discipline. It should be quick, soft, harmless, and to the point, used only for very special and serious transgressions. But physical punishment is *not* recommended. Sit down with your child and decide which punishments would be meaningful, and when and for what they should be administered. The child, thus, has a role in his own discipline. He also knows what to expect from his behavior well in advance. The agreed punishment probably won't be physical. Almost every child needs punishment at some time or another during the school year. He *must* test the limits and will exceed them occasionally. When he does, make the punishment meaningful and civilized—rarely physical.

*Q:* What are the most important things I can do at home to help educate my child beyond what the school is doing?

*A:* Talk. Communicate. Listen and respond. Share experiences with your child; use words to paint pictures, create images, travel distances. Allow your maturity to open new vistas for your child through the use of language. And keep those channels open.

Books will add to your child's education far more than you could ever dream. Books should have top priority for special purchases for everyone in the house. It's not costly, for children can borrow books from friends, school, and libraries. Children read—a great deal. They read because reading, books, and the written word are valued in their family. These words add immeasurably to their education.

## RESOURCES

*Q:* How do I know when and where to seek help for problems with my school-aged child?

*A:* The pediatrician may not be the best person to start with when your child is of preschool age and the problems for which you seek help transcend the purely physical. If your pediatrician has been trained as a behaviorist, you are lucky. Few have until recently. Therefore, your pediatrician may be unfamiliar with and inexperienced in such issues as a child's adjustment to school, educational resources, psychological needs, and developmental problems.

If your pediatrician can't help you, don't stop looking for help. Where would you turn for assistance if you suspected that your child was mildly mentally retarded, might have a learning disability, appeared emotionally disturbed, or had a chronic visual or hearing problem (to name but a few of the serious developmental-behavioral issues)?

Diagnosis is the first important step. You'll need to find a diagnostician who has experience with schools, since any chronic problem in this area will have educational ramifications. If your child's school is working with you, ask the school principal to refer your child for testing at the school's expense or to recommend a private psychologist. Local mental health clinics often have professionals with the proper credentials, as do private schools for special children. Another resource is university departments, which specialize in training professionals in psychology, child psychiatry, special education, or speech and hearing pathology. Often these centers have clinics in which excellent attention is given to diagnosis and treatment as a means of teaching tomorrow's professionals. Your child could benefit from this environment of combined service and education.

Once you have located the diagnostician for your child, be prepared to discuss your child's problem openly and candidly. After the testing reveals the type and locus of the problem, ask the professional to explain how the specific defect manifests itself in your child. Discuss the relationship of the problem to behavior. And don't forget to ask exactly how the problem relates to future expectations in school, in the home, and in society. Additional help can come from books specifically written to help parents understand the specific developmental and emotional problems of children. The authors' book *Between Parent and School* (Dial Press/ James Wade, New York, 1977) has a chapter dedicated to each of the problems mentioned above, as well as many others, and relates these to what might be expected from the child in school and from the school for the child. This gives parents guidance in what they can do and expect for their special child. But you might want to go further for information about the specific problems diagnosed in your child. In that case, we suggest that you write the following agency—a parent's agency funded federally—to get their suggestions on appropriate readings and articles:

Closer Look
1201 16th Street, N.W.
Washington, D.C., 20036

Closer Look will send you an annotated bibliography of many of the newest and most helpful books that deal with your child's problem. You'll save time and money plus the heartaches that can be caused by misinformation.

If your child has an educational problem serious enough to warrant a specialized learning program, then your primary resource throughout his or her schooling years is going to be the school system (federal, state, and local), in particular, the Division of Special

Education. Get to know who runs this division and where it is located, and be prepared to advocate for your own child at that level if you must. Federal law now mandates that every child who requires special education be given a "free and appropriate" education through the public school system. Because of the new law, there are many more professionals available to serve you and your child today than there were several years ago. Don't be shy about your child's right to services. Both you and your child will benefit by your attention and persistence. If you have a special child, make certain he or she is getting very special and appropriate educational care.

The school-aged years are exciting ones for a parent. The child expands his world; his mind is turned on by language; and he begins to grow intellectually and socially. You can share this dynamic experience with your child. It is a thrilling time for both of you. Enjoy this golden age from seven to twelve.

## BIBLIOGRAPHY

Ackerman, Paul R. and Kappelman, Murray M. *Signals: What Your Child Is Really Telling You.* Dial Press/James Wade, 1978.

Block, William A. *Dr. Block's Do-It Yourself Illustrated Human Sexuality Book for Kids,* Prep Publication, 1979.

Boston Women's Health Book Collective. *Our Bodies, Ourselves.* Simon and Schuster, 1973.

Child Study Association of America. *What To Tell Your Child About Sex.* Pocket Books, 1974.

Gordon, Sol. *Facts About Sex for Today's Youth.* John Day, 1973.

Hettlinger, Richard F. *Growing Up with Sex.* Seabury Press, 1971.

Kappelman, Murray M. *Sex and the American Teenager.* Reader's Digest Press, 1977.

Kelly, Gary. *Learning About Sex: The Contemporary Guide for Young Adults.* Barron, 1977.

McCary, James L. *Human Sexuality.* Van Nostrand and Reinhold, 1973.

Pomeroy, Wardell. *Your Child and Sex.* Delacorte Press, 1974.

Sorenson, Robert C. *Adolescent Sexuality in Contemporary America.* World, 1973.

·

# CHAPTER SEVENTEEN

# Adolescence—
# Realistic Roles
# for the Mature Parent

Adolescence is that rocky, transitional phase between childhood and adulthood through which we all must make our way. Adolescence may begin before the teenage years in a few youngsters and extend well beyond the twenties in others. But in the vast majority of young people, adolescence is the process that takes place between the ages of twelve and twenty.

These are not easy years. More change, more disruption of body and mind, more self-doubt and self-discovery will be compressed into this period than at any other time of life. These teenage years are much like a rickety wooden bridge across which a child must make his way to reach his adulthood on the other side. The bridge is shaky; the supports present, but not always connected; the length of time taken by each individual to cross that bridge and exit as a fully realized adult varies from one person to another. Some will sway precariously on the bridge of adolescence for the rest of their lives.

Often we do not remember our own adolescence very clearly. Many of us have blocked out its painful, self-deprecating, hostile, selfish, embarrassing, and seemingly endless moments; we prefer to recall the foolish and the whimsical times. These happy times were fewer and less frequent than the moments of anguish. But we successfully block the hurtful times of growing up because the memory brings back all too clearly the uncertainty and the pain.

Two very important points must be made to after-thirty parents about adolescence:

**1.** You will be farther away in years from the time of your own adolescence. So much has cluttered your life since then. Your memory fails more frequently than a younger parent's to give you the necessary insights, understanding, and compassion about those years.
**2.** It is very possible that you will be in your fifties or close to them when your youngster reaches adolescence. There is the real likelihood that your patience, tolerance, and flexibility may have diminished considerably as you've grown older. Yet these are the three qualities that are essential to the rearing of a normally complex and mercurial adolescent.

Here are some examples of the phases of adolescence your teenager will be passing through, and how you can best adapt and relate to these periods of change in your youngster's life, beginning with very early adolescence and progressing to the phases of late adolescence.

## The Diminishing Parent Image

Early in adolescence, the "perfect" parent suddenly becomes a human being. In other words, our children discover our many faults —failings that are intrinsically normal for any balanced person. But to the thirteen-year-old child, these faults reach monumental proportions. Where the younger child believed in what we said, copied what we did, cherished our approval, and retreated from our criticism, the adolescent cynically questions us. Blind allegiance has been compromised by the realization that parents are fallible beings. Because of the youngster's increasingly acute observation, keen sense of becoming an individual person, and need to draw away from us in order to find himself, a bright spotlight is suddenly turned onto our every fault.

The young adolescent becomes angry at what he or she perceives as treachery, adult "cover-up," intentional illusion. The resultant anger causes the youngster to withdraw from the parent and seek counsel and help elsewhere. Anyone over thirty becomes suspect at this point.

Because you are older and possibly more accustomed to running the show, you might fall just a bit harder from that pedestal during this period in your child's life. It could hurt a shade more because you have outgrown the self-doubt phase in your own life and have entered the middle years of self-realization. Suddenly your teenager is telling you about every minor flaw in your personality and behavior. And he is rejecting you at the same time. It may sting more than it would if you were younger.

What can you do? First and most important, do *not* try to change. You are who and what you are. Actually, you probably would not succeed in making yourself over. You're too firmly established as a specific human being, and tomorrow your adolescent will want you to become someone totally different from the day before. You must remain as the stable center around which the indecisive dance of adolescence is being performed. It is the teenager who doesn't know his own mind—not you.

You can acknowledge the youngster's right to disagree with you, not like what you do or say, have a different opinion. This recognition of the teenager's right to think and act differently *does not* mean the total relaxation of discipline or supervision. The most dangerous action the older parent can take in response to the sudden loss of their child's respect and affection during early adolescence is to pull away the structure and security of consistent rules and regulations. Every teenager needs a "catcher in the rye" and you, as the parent, *must* fill that role.

## FRIENDSHIPS

The need to "belong" is strongest in the teenage years. Your adolescent will begin to regard friends as far more important in every regard than parents. The advice, the company, the affection of other teenagers becomes essential to the adolescent.

As a more mature parent, you're accustomed to being asked for advice. Often this is an extension of the role you play in your professional life. You pride yourself on your objectivity. Giving your own child the advantage of your experienced counselling skills compensates in your own mind for your lack of younger-parent attributes, and now that rug of security has been pulled out from under your feet. Your teenager is going to his friends for advice.

You have the money, experience, and inclination to expose your youngster to cultural and sports events which younger parents may be discovering for themselves for the first time. You wisely spent your quality time in sharing some of the excitement in your world with your youngster. Now your teenager is no longer interested in doing these things with you. He would rather be with his friends, hanging around.

Some of the friends selected by your youngster at this early stage may not meet the critical standards that you have consciously (or otherwise) developed for him or her. And yet the slightest criticism causes your teenager to explode with anger. His friends can do no wrong, but you, despite your age and experience, "don't know what it's all about any more."

What is your course of action?

The first thing you must do is realize that this is a natural and expected phase. Grit your teeth, and determine to remain rational through these years. Your bright and talented daughter will lose herself inside a band of anonymous, indistinguishable teenagers. Accept this behavior as the younster's need to be accepted by others in that group and find her individuality over time before she can emerge as a distinct and realized young adult.

Be available. There will be times when your advice will be sought. Offer it only when asked. And listen more during this period than you ever have in the past. Listen without offering advice in return. Adolescents often need a human wall off which to bounce their thoughts and ideas. It could be the beginning of a strong future relationship if you allow yourself to be that wall of *silent* acceptance. It will be difficult. As an after-thirty person, it's not your style to stand by and do and say nothing when a professional colleague, client, employee, or friend comes to you with a problem. Relax with your teenager and accept the fact that in your home you are a parent—not a boss, healer, manager, counsellor, or any of the other professional roles that occupy your working days.

Accept the fact that your teenager will not want to go with you as much as before. Develop "contracts" about essential times when the youngster *must* be with you. These will differ with each family. Some insist on church every Sunday morning; others mandate Friday night dinner together. Families may choose holidays, birthdays, or other significant times when the teenager knows that parent/child togetherness is the *rule*. On other occasions, be flexible and accept a No when you invite your teenager to go with you on an outing that you always shared in the past.

The best way to handle unacceptable friends is to bring them into your home as often as possible, to dinner, over weekends, etc. Treat them respectfully and allow your youngster to evaluate them within the family setting. If the friendship is less than you feel your child warrants, this continuing comparison between the friend's values and the long-standing, ingrained family standards will help your teenager decide by herself to get rid of the friend.

## RESPONSIBILITY FOR SELF

It is a strange and frightening feeling when the teenager suddenly realizes that he is responsible for what happens to him in this complex world. No longer can he expect his parents to bail him out when he makes a mistake. He faces the realization that if he fails in school, the Fail grade is on *his* report card and there's nothing his parents can do to erase the stain. If he drops out of school, *he* will be the one without the education. If he steals, *he* will go to jail. If he has sex, *he* may make his partner pregnant or *he* may contract venereal disease. His parents can no longer carry the load for him. Often there is an unexpected retreat, a regression into more immature behavior as this mammoth personal responsibility becomes a fearful reality.

It's easy for many of you as older, respected members of the community to hold onto the teenager's world just a bit longer: step in when he smashes the car; intercede when she is caught smoking pot in school; call a physician friend and get the drugs to treat the "obvious" case of gonorrhea. We could go on and on. *Do not do any of these things.* Allow your teenager to grow up at the same rate of responsibility as every other youngster his age. It is never easy to watch your child pay the consequences of actions, but if he doesn't learn during these years that he is personally responsible, you could be paying for his behavior for the rest of your life. And who will take the responsibility for your child when you are no longer able to do so? If you start early and allow your child to assume his own responsibility for himself, you'll be doing your child and yourself a big favor.

## Decision Making

During the teenage years, the burden of decision making is subtly shifted off the shoulders of the parents and onto the adolescent. Even though the older parent may be reluctant, there will come a time toward the end of adolescence when the teenager *must* take over this chore. As parents, you can't be in the classroom when your teenager makes crucial decisions: Am I going to work hard enough to get into a good college? Am I going to college at all? You can't be in the back of the car or in the vacant apartment when your adolescent faces the decision: Will I have sex with this person? Nor can you be inside your youngster's head when such crucial questions arise as: Am I going to go along with the crowd and smoke pot? Should I leave the party to meet my parents' curfew when everybody else is staying? Am I straight or gay?

These *are* mind-boggling decisions, and your teenager must cope with such problems from about age fifteen onward. Much as you would like to help your teenager make these decisions, you will have to wait until the youngster comes to you for advice. Even then, if you are lucky enough to be asked, your advice may not be heeded. Learn to accept this role of counsellor-in-waiting, for it is a role you'll be playing for the rest of your lives together as parent and grown child.

## NEED FOR PRIVACY

There comes a time when you'll unexpectedly face locked bedroom doors, whispered telephone conversations, and long retreats into the bathroom. Why the sudden retreat from the family? The teenager has a tremendous need for private space and time. As an older parent who has similar needs both personally and professionally, you should be able to understand this need fully. Your youngster is retreating to a place where he can think, discover, and thrash out in his mind the many complex dichotomies and contradictions of adult living. This is not a retreat from you; it is a retreat into himself. Don't intrude into that special space or that quiet time. Understand that a tentative adult will emerge from the contemplation and confusion into a world where he expects you to be waiting to receive him.

## MOOD SWINGS

You lead an ordered life. As you have grown older, you've needed predictability so that you can organize your time and your emotions. Suddenly your teenager is beginning to behave in a totally unpredictable fashion, disrupting the tranquility and orderliness of your life. You are probably becoming increasingly angry.

Teenagers veer wildly from one mood to the other. A girl may be laughing and start crying suddenly the following moment. A father may hug his son, only to have him refuse to speak to him the following hour. Defiance follows compliance as readily as night follows day. There are few moments when the parent of a teenager can be assured of a predictable response. This can create havoc in the older parent's life.

*It will happen.* Accept the need of the adolescent to experience rapidly changing moods. But set a few rules, and make them stick:

1. Stable behavior is essential in the company of the parents' professional and personal friends.

**2.** Grandparents are not to be subject to the shockwave of these unpredictable moods.

**3.** No matter what the mood swing, respect between parent and child *must* be maintained.

**4.** Extremes of behavior that are potentially dangerous are forbidden.

These four rules will ensure the mature parent that life can continue without total disruption while the teenager is swinging wildly from happiness to sorrow, delight to anger, affection to rejection, child to adult. Emotions *can* be controlled by a child.

## REBELLION

As the teenager grows into maturity, he has to reject much of what he believed in the past, reexamine life from various new perspectives, and come forward, at least temporarily, with a concept of life different from that of the parents. This process is known as rebellion.

Teenage rebellion extends from the emotional rejection of parental values, religious beliefs, standards, goals, and ambitions to actual physical distancing from the parent figure. While going through the personal hurts of their teens' rebellious behavior, it is difficult for most parents to believe that controlled adolescent rebellion is a necessary and healthy process through which every young person must pass before reaching adulthood.

As an older parent, you have rather fixed values tested over time. Your standards are not shaky and newly formed, but tempered by years of compromise and adjustment. Many of you will understand the pathways that can most easily lead your adolescent in positive directions. Instead, you are faced with rebellion, distancing, refusal to use your experience.

Try to understand where your teenager is coming from. Your youngster often feels even more strongly the competitive need to "get out from under" the implications of being the child of older, more experienced, and probably more successful parents, and to become *his own person*.

Allow rebellion, but do not permit self-destruction. Allow distancing, but do not accept a withdrawal. At no time can you disturb the inherent structure of your family life; the adolescent needs that knowledge of your consistent and fair discipline. It is the security of knowing that there is a safe family harbor into which he may return later that permits the teenager to take those frightening first steps into experimenting with the real world around him.

## TEMPTATION VERSUS VALUES

There is very little reason to suspect that our world will return to the more restrictive environment of the thirties and forties. Even a mild conservative swing will still leave us with a society that is both more permissive and more stressful than the one in which we matured. In the current society, our teens can get just about anything they want, including drugs, sex, and alcohol, by walking only short distances from home. Today's adolescents are confronted daily by the temptations that plague and worry us as parents. The adolescent of today has a different question to ask himself than we did when we were his age. Then we questioned: "If I wanted it, where and how could I get it?" This took thought, time, effort, and money. Today's youngster asks himself: "How can I refuse it when it is offered to me?" His is a very different perspective indeed.

The teenager of the more mature parent often lives in a home that is both more affluent and more permissive than that of the younger family. He has been reared by adults who are comfortable with their own value systems and have not pressured him into conformity, but have allowed their lifestyle to become part of the youngster's. Since the child from older parents is often an only child or has only one sibling, there is more money available to him/her. In addition, the older parent not infrequently introduces the youngster earlier to the sexual and social life scene through the choice of media and the books lying around the house. There tends to be a more relaxed, permissive, accepting ambience about the biological naturalness of life in the home of older parents. This is to be desired; it is the healthiest way of approaching intimate human relationships on all levels. However, the older parent must realize that this easy accessibility will often extend to an earlier surrender to external temptations. In other words, by rearing your youngster in a healthy, relaxed way, you may be subtly easing him or her into accepting the temptations that lurk in the world.

Teach your youngster a very simple but crucial message: "Whatever you do, remember that you have a responsibility to yourself and you have a responsibility to the other person." If every teenager would pause before giving in to one of the many temptations that exist in today's world and ask, "What does this mean to me as a person? What effect will it have on me? What consequences?", and at the same time ask himself, "Am I being fair to the other person? What will this mean to the other person? Am I responsible? Am I willing to carry my share of any consequences to the other person?", temptations would not be a worry. If you, as an older parent, have successfully taught this rational thinking to your adolescent, you can sit back and relax a bit more than you realize. You've gone about as far as you can go.

## ROLE MODELS

As adults we are mosaics, fragments of the significant people who have passed through our lives. Some impressed us and we copied a gesture, a philosophy, a way of speaking, thinking, or loving. Others caused us to shift, eliminate, reject, take opposite attitudes, postures, or beliefs because of their negative impact on us. Usually the most important time in our lives was during our teen years when we found these role models. Maybe it was the soccer coach, the drama teacher, the local priest, the father of a close friend, or a grandparent. But the two people who probably contributed the most to our character development were our parents. So often we listen to ourselves or watch ourselves react to a situation, and are astonished to recognize one of our parents in what we're doing or saying or thinking.

As "together" parents of a teenager, you may be "a tough act to follow." You are older, successful, and have obvious self-confidence and poise. You have an impressive vocabulary. Your problem-solving skills are keener. It's hard for your teenager to try to copy you at his age.

Let's look deeper into the role-modeling problem. Your musical tastes were born in a different era. Your tastes in clothes, movies, theater, sports have emerged from a childhood in another time and have been seasoned over a longer period than those of many younger parents.

What can you do? Nothing. Be yourself—don't try to be ten years younger or to shed the tastes that have been carefully nurtured over time. Both you and your teenager will quickly recognize that you are putting on an act. Give it time. Your youngster may emulate other, younger people initially as he tries to find out who and what he is becoming. Gradually you'll notice that bits and pieces of your identity have become incorporated into your older adolescent. Because you are older, it may take longer to be used as an important role model. But when your time comes, you will be presenting a much more fully realized person to be emulated and integrated into your child's personality.

## SELF-ACTUALIZATION

This is the final step of adolescence. It is the major stumbling block for far too many young people, who never really leave their adolescence because they have never actualized themselves. Self-actualization means being able to say to yourself: "You're Monica Smith. I know who you are, what you stand for, what you believe in, where you are going, and why you are who you are. I accept you and like you." This must happen for the teenager passing through the final steps that lead into adulthood.

You waited a long time to have your child. He existed in your mind years before his conception. After he was born, you planned quietly for the person he was to become. Because you had your child later in life, you've kept your family size smaller than younger parents might. So you've invested heavily in this teenager. You know exactly who and what you would like this special person to become at the end of his adolescent voyage.

Be careful. Tread gingerly over this mine-laden field of hopes and dreams, or your world may explode in your face. There are no guarantees that your teenager will become the person you have fantasized. Your child will become his own very special, very particular adult. And he will return to you to be accepted exactly as he is, despite the fact that he may be very different from what you had dreamed, hoped, and planned for. Be ready to greet with warmth, love, and dignity the new person who walks off that adolescent bridge and into your arms as an adult. Too many parents lose their child at this end stage by the subtle rejection of what that person has become as an adult—different from their dreams, less than they wanted.

This is a crossroads for you and your emerging young adult. Erase those previous expectations and accept the young person who will walk with you into your own twilight years.

These are suggestions for realistic ways that an older parent can deal with each of these periods successfully. Many of you with very small children will be thinking, "I'll cross that bridge when I come to it. Let me deal with what I have now." But you'll be there long before you realize it. Time moves on roller skates as you grow older. Be ready. Be aware and informed, and you'll be able to deal with your child's adolescence with equanimity and knowledge—two virtues that every adolescent needs from his parents.

# CHAPTER EIGHTEEN

# Preparing
# Your Adolescent
# for Life

It is vital for you, as an after-thirty parent, to look ahead into the future and prepare your child for an adolescence that may be somewhat different from that of his peers who have younger parents. When your child has reached sixteen, you may be approaching, or well past fifty years of age. This, of course, isn't old. But being near or over fifty is quite different from being thirty-five during your youngster's adolescence. In addition, because adolescence is the preparation for the decisive twenties that follow, a time when you will be of retirement age, you must consider the unique importance of your role as an older parent of an adolescent.

We have discussed, in the earlier chapter, realistic roles and actions that you can take as an older parent suddenly confronted by the earthquake of adolescence. Here are some of the actions you must take to prepare your youngster for his role as an adult. These real situations illustrate a few of the typical problems that parents face during the adolescence of their after-thirty child.

The Atwoods lived in New York City. Sylvia was fifty years old and had just been promoted to head a new publishing firm; fifty-four-year-old Philip was a senior executive on a large newspaper. Their only child, Margaret, was seventeen. The Atwoods were an extremely close family. Margaret did almost everything with her parents. She shopped with her mother; her father helped her with her homework. It was during her first year in college that the troubles began. Margaret adjusted poorly to being away from home. Although she was only ninety minutes from New York City, she felt unable to cope alone. First, she called home every night, but her parents were often not there to receive her calls. Then she would appear unexpectedly for several days, tearful and depressed. Sylvia and Philip tried juggling their heavy career responsibilities to meet the obvious needs of their very dependent daughter, but it was impossible. The family was in a state of crisis because the parents had not prepared Margaret for the real world before exposing her to life by herself. What was unique for this couple was that the crisis in their daughter's life caught them at the age when they themselves had reached the zenith of their careers. They were after-thirty parents who had left out one issue in preparing Margaret for adulthood: *independence*.

Because both of them were always busy with their jobs and community obligations, Sam and Ruthie Miller had always felt concerned and somewhat guilty about Mark's lack of time with them. They wanted his free time to be exciting and productive, so they kept him busy with expensive after-school activities when he was younger and bought him his own car when he reached sixteen. There was nothing Mark wanted that he could not have. Christmas and Easter vacations were spent in Florida or the Caribbean, often with a friend instead of his parents because they were deeply involved in their successful business. Mark learned to be independent. However, what he did not learn was *self-sufficiency*. When Mark was in his first year of college, the business took a nosedive and the Millers, then in their fifties, had to pour all of their resources into the business to keep it going; they could no longer afford Mark's expensive tastes. The result? Angry, bitter, hurtful arguments between Mark and his parents, and the final blow—Mark failed during his first year in college. What the Millers had overlooked was Mark's need for *realistic reward systems* and the use of *quality time* rather than material gifts to compensate for their busy life while he was growing up.

*      *      *

Bobby come from a pair of very successful parents. His mother stopped working when he was born during her thirty-second year and stayed home with him for the first five years. Then when Bobby started private school, Monica got involved in community activities, eventually becoming president of several local oragnizations. Stanley was the vice president of a local manufacturing firm when Bobby was born; he was thirty-six at the time. Three years later he bought into the firm and moved up the corporate ladder, so that by Bobby's junior high school days, Stanley was president of the company. Stanley transferred many of his personnel management skills to the rearing of his only son. He was fair; he listened well; he made the final decisions; and he never mixed business with pleasure. But Bobby got very little in the way of physical or emotional affection from his aloof yet concerned father. Monica was unaware of Bobby's needs. She was so preoccupied in coping with the demands of the community that she overlooked Bobby's gradual retreat into depression. It took an abortive and pathetic attempt at suicide with a few too many aspirin tablets for fifteen-year-old Bobby to signal his parents successfully that he was feeling rejected, alone, and seriously lacking in self-confidence. If someone had told Stanley that he didn't show his son *love* or teach him *self-confidence*, he would deny this vehemently. Hadn't his methods worked with his own staff?

These subtle dangerous parenting traps are not specific to after-thirty parents, but such issues are often far more prevalent among this vulnerable parenting group. You'll want to reflect on your answers to a few pertinent questions:

1. How do you communicate?
   a. Have you set aside a time when you and your child can talk together?
   b. Do you do the talking, or do you listen to your child as well?
   c. Do you set the agenda for discussions with your child?
   d. Are you willing to accept your child's silences as well as drop everything when he/she really needs to talk?
   e. Can you honestly say that your child can discuss *anything* with you? Have certain attitudes blocked off specific areas of communication?

f. Are you a sexist in communication? Does the wife talk only about certain things, while others are exclusively the father's area?

g. Can you accept your child's disagreement with you? His anger? His controversial views?

Stop for a long minute and then answer this last question: Do you think your child feels comfortable talking with you?

*Communication* is the essence of success as an adult. Preparing your adolescent for successful adult communication begins long before the teenage years. Time must be set aside during your busy days to talk with your small, growing children. Be very careful that you listen to your child, as well as teach him to be able to listen to others. Obviously, the child may not be ready to chat every time that you are; relax and accept those silences. Be ready to sit down during a very busy moment and listen when a child is obviously bursting to tell you something. If you don't, you may have lost an important opportunity. Be open in your conversation; don't limit a conversation just because *you* find the subject distasteful. If the subject of death upsets you, then with whom will your child be able to share his own concerns? If you cringe when homosexuality is brought up, what will your youngster do when the normal sexual questions arise in his mind during early adolescence?

There should be *no* "feminine" or "masculine" issues. Everything is fair game. Fathers should discuss the ability to cry, while mothers talk about feelings of aggression. Prepare your child for future relationships that permit total sharing.

Children will disagree with parents. Older parents, used to general agreement and acceptance of their ideas by their staffs, clients, patients, et al., will often find these differences of opinion unacceptable. This is dangerous and precedes withheld information, gradual distancing, and eventually broken or unsatisfying relationships.

Work hard so that you can answer easily, "Yes. My child feels comfortable sitting down and talking with me."

2. How do you encourage the development of personal identity?
    a. Does your youngster view himself as your child, or as a separate individual?

    b. How much and how often do you permit your youngster to do things by him/herself?

    c. How do you handle your child's differences of opinion, philosophy, values?

    d. How much personal responsibility do you give your child?

    e. How often do you answer questions addressed to your child?

Finally, pause and reflect before you answer this last question truthfully: Do you think of your child as a separate person who will leave your home in the future?

The older you are as a parent, the more definitive will be your own sense of identity. This can make the realization of a separate identity tougher for your youngster, who must cope with two strong parent figures overshadowing him. It is essential to prepare your youngster for life by encouraging his self-actualization—finding out who and what he is and liking himself. This can be accomplished by allowing your child more responsibility, more opportunity to experiment with ideas and actions of his own, and more acceptance of the differences between you and him. Realize that at no point in his life should you be the child's alter ego. You *do not* know the answers to questions asked him; you *do not* know what your child is thinking, feeling, or needing much of the time. He knows because he is experiencing these reactions—not you. See your child from the earliest days as a very separate and distinct individual so that you can strive to help him complete the search for himself successfully. By the end of his adolescence he should be prepared to enter the world without needing you to complete his image of himself.

3. How do you discipline and reward?

    a. Are you consistent in your discipline?

    b. Do you reason, punish, or physically discipline?

    c. Do the two of you disagree about the methods of discipline? In front of the child?

    d. Have you ever said, "I was wrong. I'm sorry"?

    e. Do you reward with emotional, cultural, or material things?

    f. Are these truly rewards or bribes?

    g. How much does your youngster need to do to earn a material reward?

h. Do the rewards take the place of attention, affection, and time spent with your child?

Answer this question after careful consideration: How much of an impact does your being busy, older, and less patient have on the consistency and rationality of your child's discipline and reward system?

The outside world is not waiting to excuse your child every time he or she errs. There may be a second chance, but that's all. You must prepare your child for this reaction. Also, he has to know that the real world rewards rarely. When rewards are given, they have been justly earned. One might consider a paycheck to be a reward. But your child will not understand this essential concept if everything is handed to him on a silver platter because you feel guilty about your age, your busy life, your crowded schedule. Stop feeling so sorry for your child—he's a very lucky kid! Two mature, successful parents can realign their priorities to find the time to play their proper roles as disciplinarians, rewarders, and parents. Then he'll be prepared for adulthood.

4. How do you give and receive love?
   a. Do you permit physical affection between yourself and your child?
   b. Does your child witness physical caring between the two of you?
   c. How often do you tell your youngster how much you care for him/her?
   d. Do you allow him/her to be affectionate with you—even after the child is thirteen years old?
   e. How do you demonstrate happiness with something your child has done?

Basically, the question is simple: Have you made the time to allow love into your home?

The busy, active, preoccupied older parent may not realize how programmed his life has become. A quick kiss before breakfast, a rare phone call during the day, an exhausted hug on arriving home, a quick cuddle at bedtime. Who gets this cursory treatment?

Not only the spouse, but the child as well. And yet we want our children to grow up believing that we love them. We may limit their emotional responses by failing to allow the youngster to open up fully as an emotional, caring, loving person. If the expression of love doesn't begin in the home, it won't emerge later.

No matter how much you think that you give your child affection and help him or her to feel secure in returning that feeling, consider carefully what affection you *do* allow, how often, to what extent, with whom. Do you shake hands with your fourteen-year-old son because you feel men shouldn't hug and kiss?

Give your adolescent sons the proper preparation for meaningful relationships in their future. Give them permission to love you, mother *or* father, in any manner with which they are comfortable. Help your daughters to know that sex, marriage, *and love* can be a workable blend. Show your youngsters those moments when the two of you touch each other or hold hands or hug or kiss in front of them. They may tease or laugh or turn away, but they'll never forget the sight.

The one crucial thing your adolescent needs from you is *your recognition of his successes.* Any minor victories warrant your praise. It is during adolescence that self-worth is wobbly. Sincere reassurance will go a long way toward bolstering the self-confidence needed to meet the outside world successfully. The older we get, the more miserly we can become with our praise. Don't allow this self-containment to dull your senses to your adolescent's need for your honest praise. He may shrug it off in your presence, but it will spur him on to try again.

5. How are you preparing your adolescent for life without you?
    a. Have you encouraged the youngster to seek an independent career?
    b. Have you allowed enough experimentation to build personal self-confidence?
    c. Have you prepared your child for separating from you?
    d. Have you encouraged warm and close relationships with others?
    e. Have you experimented with shifting roles? On occasion, have you allowed yourself to be dependent on your child and

given him/her the sense of what that will feel like in later life?

f. Have you prepared yourself for the expense of educating your youngster in today's world?

In essence, are you working so that your adolescent will be able to function in the outside world without your help?

You can't predict when you might have to turn to your child for help in a time of ill health or misfortune. As older parents, you must be aware that you may possibly need your youngster earlier than younger parents will. Prepare your adolescent for this possibility by permitting him or her to care for you at appropriate times. Allow her to nurse you through a bout of the flu, ask him to drive you around to carry Christmas bundles, encourage her to make dinner for the family once or twice a week. Develop a subtle "role reversal" and acceptance that will permit both you and your child to accept that day in the future when the shift in need might occur.

The most successful parent is the one who can look at his or her grown child and state honestly: "I'm still loved, but I'm no longer needed. My child can function by himself." This realization creates a wellspring of pain in many parents because of the time, love, and dedication given to their growing child. Was it all leading to this—no longer being needed? Yes, it was. You were helping in the formation of a totally independent, self-sufficient person who could stand alone successfully in the outside world. If you have done that with your adolescent, then you get rave reviews as a parent. You are a winner—in more ways than one.

Older parents often develop very close, binding ties with their growing children. Separation to go to college, to marry, or to leave the city and take a good job creates emotional crises for both parent and child. But you must encourage independence and close relationships with others during the child's entire growing phase— and particularly the adolescent period—so that your young adult can leave you without a sense of guilt or worry. Both you and your child must understand that you can and will function adequately without each other. It is essential that this goal be realized for several reasons, all equally important:

*At the same moment that independence is required from your child, you will be reaching the zenith of your own career and beginning to look toward a lessening of activities, a change in direction, or a new challenge.

*Your own parents will be growing older and needing more assistance in time and money.

*Your marriage may need that "shot in the arm" that follows the years of dedication to careers and parenting.

*You are becoming more susceptible, physically and emotionally, to the stresses of life.

*Retirement is within view. You may choose to continue working; but this may also be the time for a change in climate or job or home. You need the freedom from parenting to make these crucial moves.

You have a virtue that comes with your advanced age which younger parents do not have—the knowledge and experience to assist your adolescent in choosing a future career. Beware, however, of choosing his future for him. He may not want to be what you would like him to be. You must overcome the need to plan your adolescent's future, but you can be immeasurably useful in pointing out the pros and cons of your teenager's fields of interest. The best approach is a gentle offer of assistance, a waiting period without reminders, availability, sensitivity to know when you are being obliquely invited into his life, and careful and cautious counselling without judgment or command. This is a very significant part of preparing your adolescent for life in a world of complex opportunities and frequently changing messages.

When your youngster reaches the age of thirteen, take this quiz; then repeat it every year. You should score higher each time. By the time your adolescent has reached seventeen, you'll be ready to get 100 percent.

*Is Your Adolescent Ready for Life Without You?*
1. Can your child communicate easily with peers?
Yes     No
2. Can your child communicate comfortably with adults?
Yes     No

**3.** Does your child feel that he/she is a separate individual?
Yes      No
**4.** Does your child appear to like himself?      Yes      No
**5.** Is your youngster self-disciplined?      Yes      No
**6.** Does your youngster still expect you to set the rules?
Yes      No
**7.** Does your child expect rewards for all successes?
Yes      No
**8.** Does your child make all of his/her own decisions without asking for help?      Yes      No
**9.** Does your youngster play the dependent role all of the time?
Yes      No
**10.** Are you the most important people in your child's life?
Yes      No
**11.** Have you and your child talked about future careers?
Yes      No
**12.** Can your child show affection without embarrassment?
Yes      No
**13.** Has your youngster taken trips without you?      Yes      No
**14.** Have you saved money for your child's college education?
Yes      No
**15.** Has your child earned any money on his/her own?
Yes      No
**16.** Are you planning to remain where you are until you are sure that your child is a "success"?      Yes      No
**17.** Would you feel embarrassed to ask your child for physical, emotional, or financial help?      Yes      No
**18.** Does your child have very close friends?      Yes      No
**19.** Can both you and your child admit you have made a mistake?
Yes      No
**20.** Are you prepared to watch your child move out of your house?
Yes      No

What should you have answered? Numbers 1 through 5 should have received a firm Yes. Numbers 6 through 10 require an equally decisive No. Numbers 11 through 15 warrant Yes if your adolescent is ready for the world without your immediate support.

We hope that you could answer Numbers 16 and 17 with a strong No. Numbers 18 through 20 are best reacted to with a Yes. Keep trying to score 100 percent and your youngster will be well prepared to face life.

# IV

*Special Problems
of After-Thirty
Parents*

·

# CHAPTER NINETEEN

# Parenting Alone
# After Thirty

"August 5: A month! I've been a single, thirty-two-year-old parent for one month. One month that has been five years long. And I'm no better adjusted now than I was one month ago when it happened. Will I ever be? Of course I'll adjust! All the books say so. Statistics say so. My mother and priest say so. But they are not me. They don't have my deep feeling—what is it?—ANGER.

"Anger! Finally I've said it. I am angry. Mad as Hell. I feel inside like I want to hurt someone. My husband because he left me. My daughter because she needs me and can't help me. Myself because I feel so damned weak. I find myself helpless—a creature crying without tears, shouting without sound, hitting and throwing, and kicking without force. I actually hurt with all this anger bottled up inside me. I have begun to curse my life, so alone and unfulfilling. I want to run—run out of here, run away from people, run toward people, begging to belong, and then run back here again and hide. I want to strike out against the injustice of my aloneness. Against the expectations that it forced upon me, to be both mother and father to Wendy, to be a strong recovered widow to the world, to be the same optimistic, cheerful, energetic woman to my friends. I am imprisoned by my anger, because I cannot release it.

"But anger doesn't explain it all. What else paralyzes me? It's a fear. But of what? Not poverty, for I have a job. Not loneliness, for Wendy keeps me too busy for very much self-pity. Not fear of growing old alone, for I want no others—right now. What is its name?

"Independence. I think that is its name. With John I shared. I gave to him and took care of my life. But he also allowed me to be dependent at times. I miss the possibility of that dependency. I need to be dependent at times. I can sense it. And that frightens me. Can I ever be truly independent? Can I face making decisions for myself, for my daughter, for my future? How can I teach independence to Wendy when I'm running away from the thought as fast as I can?

"We need help, Wendy and I, to find the ability to live independent lives."

This is a personal journal entry shared by a sensitive woman, suddenly widowed by an automobile accident at thirty-two years of age, who was trying to get in touch with her feelings about being single and the consequences of adjusting to a single life. She was experiencing what so many suddenly single after-thirty parents feel—a very special mourning characterized by anger and frustration on the one hand and a debilitating loss of dependence on the other. The frustration of having to change drastically to a lifestyle that society looks on as inferior creates an intense, repressed anger. Losing another adult to share in decisions and responsibilities created a great sense of loss—as if part of her body and mind were missing. This occurs with any kind of loss, death or divorce.

Are there solutions to these intense emotions among single after-thirty people? No. The lifestyle changes are inevitable. Independence is a necessary consequence, relieved only partially by finding another caring adult. There is no escape, especially when children are involved. Society *does* discriminate against the single after-thirty parent, whether that parent is male or female. A single older parent *is* independent. She has to be independent; survival for both her child and herself demands it.

How can the single after-thirty person continue to be an effective parent? What can she do about these destructive feelings of rage and fear? What kind of new role must she assume to compensate to her child for the loss of the other parent?

*Compensation* is loosely defined as the selection of an alternative method of coping which corrects balances within yourself. The after-thirty parent has to compensate by redirecting the energy arising from anger into work and child raising. The loss of dependency must be channeled into new experiments in becoming independent.

Naturally, the process of healthy compensation isn't easy, but it is usually attainable. Hundreds of thousands of after-thirty single parents have done it—with varying degrees of success. None will tell you that they have totally conquered their anger and sense of dependence. But after working on redirecting their lives as single parents, many will report that they are feeling better about themselves, more successful, and more capable of finding gratification and reward in the progress and achievements of their children. Those people have made compensation work for them.

How can you prepare yourself for a new life, for healthy compensation? By starting to make important decisions. You must reassess your time, energy, and goals for yourself and for your children, and then you must plan new ways of using your time and energy to realize these goals. This means consciously changing your lifestyle to promote the most efficient methods of child raising. You have to decide to become aggressive and realistic about your time, and plan carefully how to use it. Taking inventory of all of the potential options in child rearing, you can select those which meet your goals and are worthy of your investment of time.

This won't be a futile exercise for you. You'll see clearly the "possibles" and the "impossibles" in your life. Taking inventory will help you see clearly what your lifestyle has been up to now and what changes are needed. Thus, the more serious and thoughtful your approach, the better your result. In fact, many people do this type of exercise yearly, to make sure they are budgeting their time effectively. They feel they owe it to themselves to tidy up their lives.

Jot down some of the activities available to you in the following areas:

*Career*—You are now the sole provider for yourself and your child. What can you do to insure your current job and begin working toward a necessary promotion? Would further schooling help? Should you take on extra assignments? Should you ask for a transfer, or do some unsolicited projects? Should you start over at another job? List *all* the options, and estimate as accurately as possible the money you need, the skills you possess, and the time you can afford. Then make a rational decision based on your role as career person and a mother.

*Social*—Who are the friends with whom you will be spending most of your time for the next six months? Who are the friends you and your child share in common? What other kinds of friends or relatives does your child need for adult models (grandparents, opposite sex figures, *et al.*)? What kinds of social opportunities are available that will allow you and your child to share both adult and child company? Do you have any friends with whom you can share parenting experiences? How can you satisfy your own personal needs for companionship?

*Recreational*—What do you and your child like to do together? What organized activities are available for your child? Which of these activities will bring the child into contact with good role models of the opposite sex? What are some options for your own personal recreation, both solitary and with other adults? What recreational opportunities are available that will bring you into social contact with other adults?

*Parenting*—What responsibilities do you have to your child that are above and beyond the household duties (like PTA, Scouts, etc.)? How can you participate in your child's life in ways that you *both* would enjoy? Have you looked at all possible situations of mutual interest with your child? How stable and mature is your child now? How well has he or she adjusted to the loss of the other parent? Will the demands placed on you to participate in your child's activities be increasing or decreasing in the next few years? How does that fit your general plans for your life?

This list will give you the available options for your plan of compensation. From it you'll see possibilities to provide some balance within your life. There should be activities for you, activities for the child, and activities that both of you can enjoy. Not too much of one or the other, although balancing may become difficult and unrealistic. For instance, you may have to spend a year of hard work preparing yourself to enter a new career that will ultimately prove financially and personally therapeutic. This may have to come first, shifting the balance for a temporary period. Afterwards it will be important to reestablish the child-oriented balance.

It's difficult to cut the deadwood out of your life. Use the list below to budget new options for yourself and for your child, but also budget *out* those people and activities no longer able to offer you and your child what you both need for the future. Be kind and tactful, but honest and uncompromising. You need all the time you can get. You owe a life housecleaning to your child at this crucial crossroads; you also owe it to yourself. Be sure to share your thoughts and proposed actions with your child (if he or she is old enough to understand) before and not after the fact.

Consider the following points in your decision:

1. Find one person who can be a "milestone recorder" for you. You need to know how you're doing as a person and as a parent as you progress in your new lifestyle. Who in your life can be candid, intelligent, and aware, and is someone whom you see infrequently enough so that he or she can assess your progress (or lack of it) objectively over time? If you don't know anyone like this, consider a professional counsellor. Many single parents go with their children to consult a mental health specialist once a year to obtain a clear, unbiased, expert opinion about their progress. Find or designate someone as your "milestone recorder," someone not related to you or interested in supporting your ego, someone who will tell you the truth—with tact, insight, and suggestions based on sound reasoning.

2. Look for and select activities that will place your child, and sometimes you, with other children. Your child also needs milestone recorders, counsellors, and supporters. Often children receive this information from other children in varied ways according to age, by acceptance or rejection in groups, off-hand remarks, or deep, serious conversations. Encourage your child to socialize, even if he is shy or timid. Select activities so that you can observe

your child with his peers. That observation will provide you with very significant comparisons.

**3.** Your child needs models of the missing parent. Find activities in which appropriate mature people interact with your child by coaching, teaching, leading, or otherwise setting themselves up as group leaders. Role models also should be comfortably introduced into your home. If you are invited for dinner at a home where a good role model will be present, ask if you can bring your child (occasionally). Always be on the lookout for warm, stable families and visit with your child so the "family concept" remains alive and well. Encourage activities that take him or her into other people's homes, such as Scouts, Brownies, etc. These also provide leadership models. Beware of using dating to provide a role model for your child. It's not wise to emphasize your dates as role models even subtly *at first*. Your child will be sufficiently confused about the possible role of this person in your and his current and future life, and may harbor some jealousy and resent the "intruder" initially. Allow time and contact to soften the hard edges, and permit a natural relationship to develop. Then the modeling can begin on the child's terms.

**4.** Investigate some of the organizations available for single parents. Parents Without Partners is a national organization that helps you to meet people and exchange ideas about child raising. The meetings are often held in members' homes to include the children at times. The group combines many positive features for you and your child: sharing, learning, socializing, and belonging. Many churches and synagogues also have single-parent groups. Remember also that because there are so many single parents in this country, almost any group of adults meeting together for any purpose will contain a significant number of single parents. Hiking and naturalist clubs and election campaigns rank high on the list of activities that encourage socialization, and as a result of mutual interests, permit an easier and more natural common meeting ground.

**5.** Help your child to deal with the loss of the other parent. Children of divorced or widowed parents suffer greatly from the loss, whether it be by death or separation. The child must also be helped to find a pattern of healthy compensation, but if that child is young, this adjustment to separation or death may seem almost impossible. The surviving parent may be so bereft from the loss that he or she can't be available to help the child; the parent must overcome his or her mourning before help can be given to the child. Children are great deniers. Don't think that mourning is complete until the child can talk openly about the loss.

To put life back together with remaining parent and child, the mourning must be complete and the undeniable loss faced with finality. In addition, the options for the future should be on the brink of realization. But neither parent nor child can reach this point until the shock and grief of the loss have been worked through thoroughly.

How can you overcome these problems? You *and* your child must talk about the loss to someone, indeed, to as many people as are willing to listen quietly. For your child, that listener may be you; but if it can't be you because of your own need to grieve, then the listener should be a professional—a minister, priest, or rabbi; a school counsellor; a coach or teacher; a psychologist or child psychiatrist—anyone who can listen, reflect, absorb, and understand the depth of a child's feelings. The child must be encouraged to speak about the loss—everything that he feels, everything that he wants to say—and to let loose all of his anger, frustration, and guilt. The listener will have to realize that the child will go through periods of hate and anger against the lost parent for desertion. The child will cry with longing one minute and kick the door in fury the next.

If you have your act together enough to be that listener, then be prepared for some rough going. You may be cursed for having let it happen. The youngster may condemn himself for not preventing the loss. For a while there will be no winners in either of your lives—only losers. But once the grief is out, a slow acceptance and mature realization will occur. The other parent is gone, but life remains. There are good memories along with the bad. There is still a future—and it can be reshaped. Together you can offer guidance to each other, not only by planning options for the future but by making the present a more tolerable place in which to live. You love each other, and that eventually becomes more important than the loss.

There are four important *negative rules* that are an integral part of being a single, after-thirty parent. These rules reflect ways in which you must change, since you cannot allow yourself to be the person you once were.

To be an effective after-thirty single parent, you *cannot*:

. . . expect to have many married-couple-with-children friends. You are single, available, and often a "fifth-wheel." You are also a constant reminder of marital and physical vulnerability. Only your most mature couple friends can survive this test.

. . . be passive about your activities. Nobody is going to make things happen *for* you.

. . . withdraw from social activities. Your child needs a sociable parent and you need a social life.

. . . become dependent without becoming independent. Dependency, at this stage in your life, means alienating friends, regressing, or demanding premature maturity from your child.

In order for you to become effective both as an adult and as a parent, you will have to be aggressive and assertive, change friends, and seek a new, more compatible life. No successful single after-thirty adult can escape the realization that some things must change; there are "can do's" and "cannot's" that have never been necessary before but are certainly integral to the life of the after-thirty single parent. Accept these life renovations and move forward.

Sketch out your life, your goals, your activities, your role as a parent. Mentally budget your time for the next few months and years, so you can care for your child and yourself. You are undergoing some self-therapy, plotting your own psychological compensation. You are taking your life, your destiny, and your child's future in your own hands.

But will compensation help with the anger and the pain? We borrow again from our friend, the woman who kept a journal to observe her own milestones:

"July 1: Almost a year, now. A decade of a year, it seems. I have grown. The year has been full, new projects, graduate school, a promotion, classroom mother for Wendy's school, book seller at the school carnival, and some pleasant evenings with male and female friends. I've grown. I can feel it. I have achievements. I have Wendy who is growing into a beautiful young adult. I have my own place in the world.

"I am tired. It's a full-time job being so many different people. I'm too busy to be angry. Too independent to be dependent. Too physically alive from everyday actiivties to be mentally dead.

"It has been a good year. My lists have included fun as well as purpose. I have laughed totally and forgotten that I was independent: I have loved totally and forgotten that I was angry. I have gotten angry for honest reasons, and forgotten the dishonest reasons. I have delighted in independency and forgotten that I wasn't supposed to. I have, thank God, even gotten to like the new me. Wendy has, too. We get along. We share. She's going to make it. That means a lot right now.

"I wouldn't have changed back then if I had been given the choice. But I had no choice. So I did it. And it's getting better.

"Hey, I am realizing—I did it!"

You can be a very successful after-thirty single parent. Thousands of people are. Let your maturity, experience, common sense, and good judgment conquer your fears, angers, and loneliness. Once that battle is won, you're on the way to one of the most important victories in your life.

·

# CHAPTER TWENTY

# Previous Families

One or both of you has a "past"—a "past" filled with a previous family. Now, suddenly, both of you are one family, but one family with more members than in the past. Even if the addition is only one child, if that youngster is from a previous family, the expansion will be significant. You'd like to have the happy, hilarious equivalent of the popular television show, *The Brady Bunch*, where children from both previous marriages were combined into a loving, caring, single family. The Brady Bunch lives happily ever after with few, if any, observable adjustments to each other or changes from previous family lifestyles. This is television, not real life. In reality, adjustments to previous families are rarely, if ever, cause for bellylaughs. It is a difficult and delicate problem.

To adjust to and enjoy blending someone else's family into one family takes lots of work. Because each previous family situation was different and unique, there is absolutely no way to describe the *typical* previous family situation as a framework for advice. There are no guaranteed happy endings for family blending.

But we can make the following assumptions:

1. You're more mature than the younger person coping with a previous family. This maturity and experience in dealing with di-

verse people may enable you to act more efficiently, tolerantly, and decisively.

2. Either you or your new spouse has already experienced a family. Either or both of you know the roles of family members very well. You know what worked and what didn't work in the dynamics of the previous family's life. One or both of you know the children well, what motivates them, what directs them, and what rewards and punishes them. Therefore, you have the advantage of being able to anticipate a particular child's viewpoint when making decisions about the newly constituted family.

3. You are old enough to see the past in perspective and young enough to hope for a more satisfying future. What is more important, though, is that you are mature enough to tell the difference between past and future, to know that the mistakes of the past need not be repeated. You have entered a new marriage, a new life, and therefore should anticipate a new future. In this future, you can "start fresh" with the children—you can't erase the past completely but you can add new perspectives for the future. Bringing the previous family into this new family allows for an honest and clear look at the kids. You can reorganize priorities, child-rearing methods, goals, disciplinary methods, and renegotiate the contract of daily living with the children. Apply the managerial skills that you have learned throughout the years at work to your new home situation. And take the opportunity to reassess and redirect this period of reorganization.

The key to blending the previous families into a cohesive unit lies in being able to chart the future collectively. Aiming toward common goals dispels most of the fear, jealousy, guilt, and suspicion inherent in bringing kids into a new family. Being over thirty, you have the advantage of being sufficiently secure and stable to attempt relevant "future planning." In other words, you and your spouse need to make decisions—many decisions—about what you want in your future, what is best for both of you *and* the children, and how you are going to blend all of those diverse feelings and goals into the structure of your new family. This blending of very divergent past histories, experiences, associations, relatives, and especially expectations must be the first family success if the newly formed group is to move together into future planning.

To do this, you and your new spouse are going to have to recognize and deal with potential problems that arise out of the union of two previously unrelated families. There are hidden and unexpected hurdles for every family that attempts to bring together already established lifestyles and make these differences in past experience fit a new shape. This blending can't occur without careful study and hard work. It will be necessary to study the family: where it has been, where it is now, and where you would like it to go in the future. Only then can you predict the areas of potential problems and begin working on prevention and compromise. Here are six of the key areas of conflict in blending previous families. How can the two of you deal with these conflicts? Your answers are vital in creating a stable, cohesive, comfortable environment in which the children in the new family can adjust and grow in a healthy, happy way.

You'll have to ask some very basic questions about where you are and have been, and where your family was, is, and will be. Discussing this list will help you make decisions. You *can* control the destinies of your new family. The list is merely a starting point. You can add or delete items, or make up your own list, if you prefer. But sit down together and work through this or a similar one.

*Family List*

|  | PAST | PRESENT | FUTURE |
|---|---|---|---|
| 1. Lifestyles |  |  |  |
| 2. Parenting philosophy |  |  |  |
| 3. Spouse's and ex-spouse's needs |  |  |  |
| 4. Careers |  |  |  |
| 5. Nuclear family |  |  |  |
| 6. Stepparenting issues |  |  |  |

Some real-life stories with which you may be able to identify will stimulate you to look at yourself and your family.

## LIFESTYLES

Helen sighed as she put down her fork and savored the last mouthful of dessert. She looked at Alan sitting across the table.

"Remember where we were on our anniversary last year?" she asked.

Alan's calm face registered a surprised, hurt expression. "Are you going to bring that up again?" He felt vulnerable to an attack. "You know I *had* to be there. You know it was important for the kid's sake."

"Alan," Helen spoke gently, "I'm only bringing up our last anniversary so we can feel good about how far we've come since then."

Helen was talking about the first item on the Family List, the item that compares lifestyles of the past and present with potential lifestyles for the future.

This couple's lifestyle was purposefully changing. Their last anniversary had brought the issue to a head. Alan had gone to a Girl Scouts parents' meeting with his daughter Susan, and, in his haste, had forgotten his anniversary. Helen had been hurt. Alan had reacted defensively, then both had become angry. They had talked, cried, accused, yelled, berated—and then forgiven and, finally, understood. Then they had talked again—about what should be, what was necessary, about who should parent, what the children's time should mean in their lives, about priorities and perspectives. Eventually, they understood the temporary nature of childhood schedules in the overall scope of a parent's life. They added up what would be lost and gained if they joined forces to become responsible parents to their two children (one from each previous marriage). It emerged clearly and comfortingly that becoming involved parents for both children would in no way diminish what they felt or could do for each other in the long run.

They entered the life of the suburban parent, with rounds of PTA meetings, Scouts, neighborhood groups, and countless other responsibilities—at times with reluctance, but always with humor and patience. They knew that they would be older than most of the other parents. They understood that each of the two children was from a previous family, but that there could not be an imbalance over which parent responded to which child. They began inviting other parents of similar age home for coffee after meetings and found several compatible couples. Helen and Alan were adjusting to a new lifestyle. Neither had been particularly child-oriented in their past families. But each was changing. They wanted their family to work successfully this time. This couple had considered important elements in their lives: the past, the present, and the future.

Stop and think if you are the parent in a family of previous marriages. What was your lifestyle in the past? What is it now? What do you want it to become?

## PARENTING PHILOSOPHY

Herb had always been a structured father. He set rules and he expected his children to obey them, which they did. He was not too rigid, however, to modify the rules when circumstances demanded change. Herb always asked for the opinion of his wife and kids before he made a major decision involving the children, but he was unquestionably the boss in his own home. The structure he gave to his family was a source of security to his children since he was always consistent and fair as a father.

But Herb's rules caused great conflict with his wife, Pat, who was caught up in the process of trying desperately to find a suitably rewarding image of herself in an attempt to overcome an extremely poor personal concept left over from her childhood. Pat was trying to find a self that she could like and live with at this late stage in her life. She needed to make the rules, not merely live by them. Herb could not tolerate her quiet rebellion, and as a result, Pat left him and the children.

During the period of mourning and anger that followed her departure, the rules gave comfort to Herb and the children. They provided what their lives needed most at that time: predictability, consistency, security—a sense of permanence.

Then Ellen entered Herb's life and things began to happen

to the family. Ellen had a child of her own, a young man two years older than Herb's oldest girl. Ellen's son was starting college, was a straight A student, and was handsome, popular, and well adjusted. But Ellen had used very few rules, very little structure in rearing him.

Ellen became involved with Herb and his children. She was not surprised when Herb proposed marriage one night several months after his divorce became final. But Herb was shocked speechless by Ellen's answer.

"Herb, I want to marry you. I want to be a mother to your children. But you have to know this. I did not and I cannot raise children by so many rules. I believe that each situation is different. I believe in changing standards. I believe in equal participation in decisions affecting two people. I raised my son that way and it worked. I would have to raise *our* children that way. And for that reason, I can't marry you until we settle this serious difference in the way we operate."

Herb was stunned. Where did his parenting philosophy fit in? What was wrong with his approach? His kids accepted it. Why couldn't Ellen accept his parenting rules for *his* children and use her own methods with her own son. Why was his parenting philosophy such a major obstacle? Should he change?

Herb and Ellen began to talk about their stalemate. They tried to be honest. They posed potential problem situations and tried to reach compromises on the "correct" parent response. When they disagreed, each would tell the other why a particular approach had been used. They soon found points on which they could agree. But they also reached points of deadlock, of seemingly intractible disagreement; and, at those times, they would leave each other full of anger and resentment. But they didn't stop. Herb and Ellen returned to the talks, sometimes with changed perspectives, sometimes with firmer resolve. They discovered each other during these talks. They learned about each other's childhood, fears, and weaknesses as well as strengths. They learned quickly that neither had *all* the answers to parenting—but both had answers.

Even after they were married, they continued their talks about parenting. They weren't always consistent, but they had learned how to agree and how to agree to disagree. They established a new family based on a mutual trust of each other as parents and a love for each other as individuals. They could discuss parenting openly with each other, and finally with their children as the youngsters grew older. Herb and Ellen moved sensibly from the past to the present, and then decisively and wisely into the future in their talks on parenting philosophy.

A parenting philosophy is one of the most important items on the list for new families.

## SPOUSE'S AND EX-SPOUSE'S NEEDS

Do you ever worry when your husband goes over to his ex-wife's house two nights every week to see the children? Sometimes he doesn't get home until eleven o'clock at night, and you know the children go to bed at nine.

Are you upset when your wife meets her ex-husband for lunch and tells you they were talking over the children's school problems? Most of you will deny vigorously having such thoughts. But these concerns do exist in remarriages where children are involved.

Such common fears can be damaging to the couple who have never put the treatment of the ex-spouse's needs on the Family List of issues for discussion. When two people unite to form a new family that contains children from previous families, the involvement of the ex-spouses will naturally be a factor. Make this involvement a positive experience for the reconstituted family by taking the time to consider what happened in the past to ruin the previous relationship and what effects this tension had on the children. Then look at the present situation for similar symptoms.

This question on the Family List is particularly relevant in contrasting the past, present, and future. No doubt those of you who have remarried have heard remarks like: "Don't make the same mistake twice," or, "Don't marry the same kind of person you did before," or, "Two mistakes will destroy your children's trust and faith in you forever."

It is indeed important that you don't make the same mistakes with your new mate (and new family) as you did in the past.

Share the following questions with your new spouse; each of you should answer honestly, if previously married:

*How did you treat your mate in the past?

*How did he/she respond to this treatment?

*During moments of anger, what did he/she tell you about your faults in relating to him/her?

*How much time did you give him/her?

*How much did you share family, job, and your private feelings?

*How much time did you spend in talking about parenting problems?

*What role did the other person play in your planning for career and family?

*How realistic about your strengths and weaknesses were each of you when you got married?

*How realistic were you later in the marriage?

*How well did you communicate?

*Did you view the other person as a good parent?

After both of you have answered the questions about the past and analyzed the mistakes, begin to work on the present. What is happening now? Then consider what you want for the future. How are you going to avoid those small hurts which can insidiously add up to unendurable marital pain? How, in effect, are you going to help each other become more relaxed people, more capable and assured parents, and better spouses?

There are, of course, no single answers to these questions. If you ask yourself, you'll find your own answers. This issue on the Family List offers you a chance to prevent problems in your marriage.


## CAREERS

Jane was reaching the peak time of her career when she met Henry. She had started in the firm after college. She climbed right through the ranks of middle management within the first ten years, becoming known for her creativity, her common sense, and her singularity of purpose. Now she was thirty-five, self-assured, independent and motivated.

Her social life matched her job. She was asked out frequently and always reinvited. She enjoyed exciting men and tolerated the rest. She was courted, flirted with, and propositioned so frequently that the idea of a serious relationship seemed elusive and unimportant—until she met Henry.

He was different. Brighter, older (forty-two), successful, and wise in a serene, quiet way. He offered Jane her romanticized ideal of a perfect husband. He became her counsellor, her friend, her lover, and to a degree, offered a new direction in her life. He was open and honest with her. She knew that he had been previously married and had custody of his three children, aged six, eight, and ten. She loved Henry. Yet she seemed genuinely surprised when he asked her to marry him.

In looking back, she still remembers thinking that their friendship should and could have lasted without marriage. She loved him and lived with him on occasion. It was a comfortable arrangement; it was enough. He loved her, she knew, but he also had three children. His love was tempered by his affection and his commitment to his family. Jane knew that she was not a mother. She was first of all a junior executive, and second, Henry's lover and best friend. Far, very far down the list, she sadly realized, was her desire to be Henry's children's stepmother.

But Henry persisted. They got married in June; by August, Jane was edgy about her stepmother role. She sought psychiatric help in October. Two days before Christmas, she fled from the east coast to a job in a branch office in her firm. Her career came first.

Many after-thirty couples who acquire previous families have faced similar though not as dramatic situations. All of a sudden their love has brought them not a new legal roommate but a houseful of children, a ready-made family. This can be an almost insurmountable responsibility, especially for someone trying to balance a budding career with sudden new commitments. Decisions need to be made about the allocation of time, the importance of jobs, the need for money, and the protection of self. Jane's career was her child; she had no room for other responsibilities. Most of you have that room—you just need to work through the past, the present, and the future of your careers when the dimension of a new family is added. When a marrying couple brings previous children into a new family, serious long-term vocational decisions are needed. Several assumptions should be kept in mind:

1. If both parties are earning salaries, child care can be purchased. If a family is reasonably healthy, it is *not* automatically best that there be a mother—or a father—at home to be a houseperson. The mental health of the parent (or stepparent) is the key to a healthy family.

2. Often a woman's career is severely jeopardized by staying away from the job for a few years to raise children. Consider a leave of absence or change of job for the father, if these options are feasible. Part-time employment for the father is also a possibility, as is working on different shifts at the job so that one person can be with the children at all times.

3. If a previous family will severely interfere with career opportunities, consider sharing the child care responsibilities with the ex-mates. This plan is not always as difficult as it may sound. If you talk through a philosophy of "together for them, separate for us" and take appropriate action (see the next chapter on Divorce and the After-Thirty Parent), careers often are still possible with joint custody and shared parenting.

4. What is best for you is often best for the child. This is particularly true if you are content and comfortable with being a parent, realize the needs of the children, place these needs in proper perspective and priority, make provisions that will meet the child's needs, and are relieved of constant worry about job and future. A big gulp of "if's." But the key words are: *You* . . . *child* . . . *perspective* . . . *priority* . . . *comfort* . . . and *career.*

You don't have to sacrifice your career when you become part of a previous family. Consult the Family List of past, present, and future. While discussing each phase, make very clear to your mate and the child (ahead of time if possible) the importance you place on your career as an integral part of your present and future life.

## Nuclear Family

Who is your family?

Is your family composed of those people who are related to you *and* those people who live in your house? Or is your family only those people who are related to you? Is your ex-mate part of your family? Are you part of your ex-mate's family? Are you a member of your children's total family? Are you included in your stepchildren's family and vice versa?

This is a central issue in the discussions of two parents who bring a previous family to their marriage. The only correct answer is the one that is of greatest benefit to you and your children. Each family and relationship is unique. But by being aware of your situation, you can determine the structure of your nuclear and extended family. Only you can define it.

Many fathers and mothers who do not have custody of the children find themselves drifting in an undefined space around the youngsters. They become a vague member of the nuclear family, dropping in and out of their children's lives like favorite aunts or uncles, feeling just about as related and having just about as much impact.

But other parents, even those living without custody of the children, form their own strong family units with their children. Many fathers, for instance, have developed a separate family with just their children. On weekends, the children become part of Dad's family in a home away from the mother; they are involved in activities quite different from their experiences during the week. The children grow up with an inheritance of two different and enriching families. These fathers—or mothers—can carve out for themselves and their children a new family lifestyle, one almost totally independent of the child's usual living arangement during the rest of the week.

But carving out a separate family after a divorce and/or remarriage takes great planning, effort, and emotional stability. It is a course of action that has to be undertaken carefully and sensitively, with the motivation arising out of a desire for the children's best interests, and not out of spite, revenge, or anger.

The after-thirty couple who find themselves inheriting a family from a previous marriage have the choice of defining the nuclear aspects as opposed to the extended aspects of that family. Should you and the children work toward a separate family identity on already existing family traditions? Should the new parent attempt to play an integral role in the nuclear family, or should that role be one of friend, counsellor, or just another adult living in the house? Should the nuclear family include other relatives?

Back to the Family List. The past is known. But what is happening now, and what do you want to happen tomorrow? Are changes and redefinitions in order? Other issues may come to mind as you go over the Family List.

*What do you think the children want and need?
*Ask them.*
*How comfortable are you with the family roles as now defined?
*Look inside yourself—hard.*
*How much of what is happening in the family is based on past bitterness and anger?
*Be honest. If it still hurts, say so, now.*
*What are the legal ramifications of your family roles?
*Ask, if you don't know.*
*Finally, is there any reason to change the status quo? Can the future look like the present?
*Don't mess with success.*

You can determine your family's identity and help your children know who belongs to which of their nuclear families.

## STEPPARENTING ISSUES

Do you remember how easy it was as a child to consider stepmothers wicked people? Certainly Cinderella's stepmother set back the art of stepparenting by several hundred years. Most children growing up under this stereotyping assume that a "second mother" has to be mean and overbearing, particularly since she is trying to replace their "real" mother in importance.

Unfortunately, fragments of this stereotype still exist in many people's mind. Stepmothers and stepfathers are seen as intruders, second-hand parents, or unwelcome child raisers. That this is absurd should be obvious when you remember the vast majority of stepparents who have and are doing a splendid job.

Being a stepparent is a difficult, sometimes thankless task if both parents don't accept the responsibility for defining the role and making things easier for the "second parent." The stepparent will find that he or she often is discriminated against by the courts, by business, and by the children themselves. Stepparents have problems buying airline tickets for their children with different last names; the airline companies, fearing kidnapping, require proof that you are legally responsible for the child. In some states, stepparents cannot sign emergency medical releases for their spouses' children because they are not "legally" related. Gaining access to inheritance monies for the care of minor children is still a major problem for both stepparents and stepchildren.

Thus the long- and short-term aspects of being a stepparent need to be discussed fully while filling out the Family List. A definition of role is the first order of business. A stepparent should either become a surrogate parent or should say that he or she wants a more peripheral role with the spouse's child. The child's future should be considered from the legal standpoint with an attorney, and both parents should agree on a course of action. Anything less is irresponsible.

Many adults look on stepparenting as a chance to adopt a new family. They want to become a new parent, to establish a new life and family with new children and new spouse. But all too often the attempt is too fast, too dramatic, too unexpected, and the child rebels, hurting the stepparent's feelings and damaging the relationship. Stepparenting must begin slowly, carefully, allowing the child to make his own moves, establish his own trust, decide his own involvement. The mature and wise stepparent works lovingly but tactfully, waiting for the child to decide what to call him, when to kiss him, and how to love him. The Family List will help. If the child knew the stepparent in the past, what were the problems in the relationship then? Why did they occur? Have they been overcome? Where is the relationship now? And where do you want it to go in the future? Knowing the child is the first step in knowing how to get there.

Successful stepparenting can be accomplished with patience, work, discussion, and understanding. Stepparents have much to offer. To offer yourself with sensitivity and dignity adds honor to all stepparents.

As you and your spouse discuss the Family List, important questions about parenting *specific children* in the new family will need to be resolved. These problems will often arise from discrepancies between the past and present for each child. Unless both of you are aware of these differences, you'll blunder into a morass of childhood anxieties and resentments. A practical solution to this blending of divergent personalities into a cohesive whole is to make lists for each child, describing what happened in the previous family, what is happening now, and what both of you want the young-

### List 1—Child up to 4 years old (preschool)

| | PAST | PRESENT | FUTURE |
|---|---|---|---|
| 1. Physical maturation | | | |
| 2. Emotional growth | | | |
| 3. Relationship to family members | | | |
| 4. Relationship to friends | | | |
| 5. Sense of belonging to new vs. old family | | | |
| 6. Contacts with old family members | | | |
| 7. Sense of the future | | | |
| 8. Recurring problems | | | |
| 9. Reactions to authority | | | |
| 10. Ability to communicate | | | |

*List 2—Child 5–11 years old (elementary school age)*

|  | PAST | PRESENT | FUTURE |
|---|---|---|---|
| 1. Maturation | | | |
| 2. School adjustment | | | |
| 3. Academic achievements | | | |
| 4. Close friendships | | | |
| 5. Self-discipline | | | |
| 6. Hobbies and interests | | | |
| 7. Recurring problems | | | |
| 8. Adjustment to new vs. old family | | | |
| 9. Contacts with old family members | | | |
| 10. Ability to communicate | | | |

ster you are discussing to be at specific ages. This will help the new parent recognize where the child has been, will give both of you insight as to where the child is now, and will help you plan rationally for the child's future as a member of your new family.

This new Child List is designed for each child in the new family, to pinpoint the differences in each child's past and present experiences and future orientation. Pick the list that fits the age of your child and move to the next list as your child grows older.

These ten important areas in each list must be filled out carefully with each child in the new family unit. After you have completed the task, you'll have a general idea of where the problem areas for each child and the family may occur in the future.

We have attempted to show you that raising a previous family can be done successfully if you discuss all child-related issues and share your thoughts and opinions. Speak with honesty and candor. The items on the Family List and the Child Lists are good starting points.

The lists contain those issues that cause the greatest diffi-

*List 3—Child 12–18 years old (adolescence)*

|  | PAST | PRESENT | FUTURE |
|---|---|---|---|
| 1. Maturation | | | |
| 2. School adjustment and achievement | | | |
| 3. Friendships | | | |
| 4. Dating | | | |
| 5. Reactions to authority | | | |
| 6. Sense of new vs. old family | | | |
| 7. Loyalty | | | |
| 8. Sense of planning for the future | | | |
| 9. Self-discipline | | | |
| 10. Ability to communicate | | | |

culties among parents of previous families; they also contain items that are often the most difficult to discuss. But as difficult, even painful, as these items are to talk about, conversations about them will pay off. The two of you will be able to agree on major family decisions rationally and consistently. You can provide a good home for your new family. With open feelings, with frequent discussions, with patience and love, that previous family will blend easily and smoothly into your new family.

·

# CHAPTER TWENTY-ONE

# Separation or
# Divorce of
# After-Thirty Parents

No family is immune to the ominous specter of divorce or separation. In 1978, there were 2.2 million marriages and 1.1 million divorces. An epidemic of divorce appears to be sweeping our country. The number of children involved in divorce rose from 361,000 in 1956 to 1,117,000 in 1976, with no lessening of the upward trend. An awesome estimate is that four out of every ten marriages will end if the current level of divorces persists.

The after-thirty marriage is by no means inviolate. Although the data suggest a much higher rate of divorce among younger couples, there are still a significant number of over-thirty marriages ending in divorce. In many of these marriages, young children—children born after their parents are thirty—are involved.

Let's focus on the aspects of *your* specific situation, what particular issues and problems an after-thirty couple might face in guiding their child through separation and divorce.

## IMMEDIATE FIRST AID

The time to begin applying emotional first aid to your child is during the early stages of the separation, when both of you are certain that a split is imminent, but actual arrangements have yet to be made. This preparation will allow the child to adapt to the situation. Obviously, each age of childhood will require a somewhat different approach.

It is not uncommon for your youngster to have adapted to your absences. Both of you may work, so that daily caretaking, nursery school, regular school, and so on, have been a natural and accepted part of your child's everyday existence. One or both of you frequently have to work late at the office or may actually be gone for extended periods of time on business trips out of town. Your family may differ significantly from a younger separating family in this regard. The risk in your situation is that your youngster may deny that a real separation is occurring and begin to fantasize that this "separation" is merely a more prolonged business absence. Don't allow yourself to fall into this fantasy. Be honest and realistic. Be sure that your child understands that there will be a *significant* change in the family's living arrangements—the two adults are no longer going to be living together.

The next step is also crucial. At this point the youngster will have the real sense that everyone is separating from him, that the parent moving out of the house is abandoning him rather than the other parent. It is essential that the child of any age understand that he is *not* being abandoned by either parent. It is the parents who are moving away *from each other*; not him. Only your actions will convince your child. Despite whatever tensions precede and accompany your split, both of you *must* be available and in frequent contact with the frightened child of divorce.

## Roots: Strengthening the Extended Family

Your extended family (grandparents, uncles, aunts, cousins) can help your child feel more secure. Contact with these people will reassure the youngster that although his parents are splitting, there is still a firm family structure supporting him. But you are older; therefore your parents are older. Some of you may have chronically ill parents or may have lost one or both parents before your separation. Looking to grandparents to support family stability may work for only some after-thirty parents.

In the rush of moving aggressively up the promotion ladder and from city to city, your *own* nuclear family may have suffered; your closeness with your own siblings and other relatives may have weakened. Are they available to you now, to help you demonstrate a deeply rooted family to the threatened child of divorce? It may require mending a few fences and reestablishing several relationships to find the true sense of family from which your child can derive that special sense of security during this time of disruption.

As you have matured, you have become aware of the differences between yourself and other members of your family. These differences may have tended to keep you apart, each person following his or her own path, intersecting briefly at holiday time or at such family events as births, weddings, or funerals. You are on the brink of another family event: your divorce. Attempt to find the intimacies that existed before you took those separate career and social pathways. Try to restructure a sense of family so that your youngster can develop the roots necessary to cling securely to his world during the earthquake of your divorce.

These problems are not uniquely those of the after-thirty parent; they may not be yours. But if, on reflection, these concerns strike a familiar chord, begin to rebuild a wider nest within which your child of divorce can feel protected. Roots are a good idea even if you're not separating.

## Controlling the Anger Level

Bitter anger can overwhelm parents' ability to consider the best interests of their child at the time of their divorce. Whatever precipitated the split, there is a normal period of personal loss, grief, and anger on the part of both separating adults. Lost in that morass of self-pity and bitterness is the child.

However, as older, more mature parents, you *should* be ahead of the game. You have experienced disappointments, setbacks, losses, and failures before in your mature life. This marriage dissolution is but another of your adaptations to life. Hopefully you will have the experience and maturity to recognize the need to continue "business as usual" despite the upset of the separation. "Business as usual" applies particularly to your child. Don't let your anger interfere with the thoughtful consideration of what your youngster needs and wants at this difficult period in his life.

## Maintaining the Parenting Job

Because both of you are busy people, with more responsibilities for your career and your own parents, you likely discovered early in your mutual parenting careers who performed which job of parenting best. Daddy may have done a better job of explaining the problems encountered in the outside world (fights with other kids, teacher problems, etc.), while Mother may have handled childhood illness more rationally. Or the opposite may have been true. Each of you gravitated toward specific tasks.

Despite the ruptured relationship, it's essential that each of you maintain these same specific interactions with your child during and after the divorce. Consistency and reliability will provide him with the sense that his life is moving forward despite the painful separation of his parents.

## The Arrangement

As you are aware, more liberal custody laws are being adopted throughout the nation. One of the reasons for the more flexible consideration of custody and the relaxation of strict visitation times appears to be the increase of late parenting and two-career families. In the past, there was little question in the vast majority of cases that the mother became the custodian. Now with both parents often having careers and no longer nurturing a sex-linked attribute, it is conceivable that both of you will have to consider which one has the best potential to be the custodian. It is in the best interests of your child to be with the parents who has the inclination, the time, and the emotional make-up to be the daily custodian. This may conceivably apply to both of you. If so, it is a reason for recent decisions regarding joint custody where parents separate but live in the same neighborhood, and each takes the youngster for six months out of the year. Other arrangements allow one parent all of the school-free time—weekends, holidays, vacations—while the other parent has school-time custody. For the older couple who have busy lives but equal nurturing potential, either arrangement will work. Children tend to be even more adaptable than their parents.

It is very important for each of you to consider what lies ahead in your career, work, or community plans before you commit yourself to custodial arrangements. You can't graft a child onto an already overcrowded schedule. What might have worked when you dashed in and out of the house while married may become a childhood nightmare when you are out on your own. A case in point: A forty-two-year-old father of an eight-year-old girl played music in a jazz band every Friday night at the local club. This was the only night during the week when he could have dinner with the youngster. Instead of adapting his schedule, he took the little girl to the club, where she sat in the corner until late at night bored, rejected, angry, and tired, listening to him play music. When she finally rebelled and refused to see him any more, he was confused as to what he had done wrong. It was obvious: he had tried to force an eight-year-old into the lifestyle of a mature man. That simply will not work.

Whether you are the custodial or separated older parent, make certain that your crowded life schedule has been readjusted so that your "quality time" with your child is dedicated to the two of you rather than being merely an adjunct to another activity.

## The Child-Rearing Dollars

It's terribly disheartening to hear an affluent couple bickering and fighting over the money needed to rear their child. Often both are earning good salaries. What is required is a sharing of financial responsibility, a realization that whether together or apart, they are both going to be financially responsible for the child they brought into the world.

Fights over money rarely have very much to do with reality.

Usually they are the punitive reactions of hurt and angry people. And who suffers in all of this financial foolishness? The child, of course. One youngster couldn't get her final grades at a private school because her wealthy father refused to pay her tuition. Why? Because he was paying his wife back for years of marital discord. Later, the mother paid the bill and, in retaliation, took the father to court and had his visitation rights rescinded. Again the child lost. This time the loss was even greater: she was being denied a father. The child suffered because of a sum of money easily affordable by one or both mature parents.

Don't play these vindictive money games over the emotions of your children. You're mature people. Work out your financial arrangements through competent lawyers and resume the important task of positive parenting.

## Making Visits Count

The noncustodial parent often feels a tremendous need to become a "camp counsellor" during evening and weekend visits. He or she will fill up every hour with games, activities, movies, visits, and so on. There is a tremendous need to please the child. The older parent with financial resources tends to err even more in this regard. The more mature father or mother who is separated can feel that the wider discrepancy in age works against the likelihood that the youngster will enjoy quiet times alone or sharing times or walks together or merely watching television. Nothing could be further from the truth. The age discrepancy is in the parent's mind; to the child, the parent's age is irrelevant.

What is relevant for the child is to have the sense that he is sharing a very real part of his noncustodial parent's life. If this time is spent rushing from one activity to another, the youngster can't identify a lifestyle with this parent. Gradually the fun times become boring. As the weeks turn into months, the noncustodial parent realizes with dismay that parent and child have become total strangers sitting next to each other in movies, restaurants, and ball games. It is difficult to share or get to know one another and communicate while involved in other activities. Making the visitation times count as "quality time" is the essence of good divorced parenting.

## THE TWO-FAMILY CHILD

It is essential that the child of divorce realize that he has changed from a one-family child to a two-family child. Each parent forms the nucleus of a new family. There is much that the noncustodial parent can do to help make this transition both comfortable and natural. Usually the separating parent will rent an apartment or home as soon after the separation as possible. The older child should be encouraged to help select this new home and, once selected, designate an area within the new home that will be exclusively his. Helping to decorate his part of the new home will subtly but clearly demonstrate the two-family home concept.

Because of the need to adjust to the new living area in strange surroundings, the youngster needs the time to absorb his new space by living in it. It's wise *not* to drag the child around to numerous friends' homes during this adjustment period. Spend your times together in your new environment until your youngster feels that he has become a part of his second home.

## PARENTAL FRIENDS AND LOVERS

Both of you are older and more likely to move within an active social/work situation than your younger counterparts. If there were not "other people" involved in the break-up prior to the separation, there probably will not be any lack of potential social/sexual relationships after the separation.

Bear in mind that your youngster has many emotional issues to adjust to—a separation of parents, new home, potential loss of security, and so on. If you attempt to introduce new faces into your lives too quickly after the break-up, you may be emotionally overloading your child to the point of rejection. Keep your social/sexual life out of the house for a time after the separation so that your child can see you as a separate, distinct individual. Once that concept has been assimilated and accepted, there should be little difficulty in being more open about your dating. One word of caution: Remember that the sexuality of parents, married or separated, should not be flaunted in children's faces. Consider this example for one moment: You are forty-five years old; your daughter is fifteen. She is going through the period of adolescence when the big question is "Should I be sexual?" What does your sudden open sexuality after divorce tell her? How can she adjust her values to those that you are waving so blatantly in her face. Can you honestly act as adviser and counsellor when she views you as just another groping adolescent in the throes of a middle-age crisis?

It is not uncommon for older divorcing parents to feel suddenly sexually released. There is a need to cram all the sexual behavior into a few years because age is creeping up and who knows when the potential will be out of reach. Middle-aged divorcing men and women are rarely rational in this particular area. We can't counsel you on the fallacy of the need to rush through sexual experimentation like a reborn adolescent. Our concern is the picture you're presenting to your child. How will a normal youngster respond to the sexually obvious behavior of a previously traditional parent figure? With dismay, anger, rejection, a sense of competition, and loss. Be rational in your sexual experimentation after divorce, and maintain a discrete privacy over your intimate sexual behavior during these critical years of adjustment.

## PHONE-REARING CHILDREN FROM A DISTANCE

It's quite possible that, some time after the divorce, one of you in the two-career family may have to move. Business moves are frequent in today's professional world. This move will place one parent a distance from his or her child, but you'll still want to have a hand in raising your child. Johnny is still your son, even though you have had to move to another city.

Don't try phone-rearing your child from a distance. The advice must be crammed into a few minutes, and therefore becomes general and glib. There is no physical contact or body language to punctuate the child's comments and your responses. You can learn more about how a child actually feels by watching his body positions than by listening to his words; as a long-distance parent, you'll be missing that essential element. It's also unfair to the custodial parent for you to give advice that requires constant follow-up and then hang up the phone leaving the responsibility for applying your advice to the other person (who may not even agree with what you have said).

If you are quite serious about your desire to continue rearing your child, you have two viable options. One is to invite the youngster to visit you for extended periods of time. This contact on your own territory is the very best way of influencing your child's growth. The second option is frequent visits to the city where your child is living, so you can see him on his own turf. It is the personal contact that is essential for parenting; otherwise you become a quickly forgotten disembodied voice over a telephone that fades soon after the receiver hits the cradle.

## THE CHILD AS MESSENGER

Both of you are busy. You've arranged your schedules so that your youngster will have the proper amount of "quality time." But the communication between the two of you to keep that rearing stable and uniform takes too much time out of your heavily scheduled day. So you both tell Cathy what you want each other to know. "Tell your father to send a little more next month for school supplies"; "Ask your mother if I can pick you up an hour later on Christmas Eve." You're forcing your youngster to act as your go-between. This is unfair to the child. Many times the message being transmitted puts the receiving parent in a bad light. And the words have to come out of the child's mouth. "Mommy says that you are two weeks late on her alimony this month." "Mommy said to apologize that your bill hasn't been paid. Daddy didn't have the money." This is unforgivable. "Mommy" can pick up the phone, call her former husband, and work out the details *without* involving her child as the messenger who must badmouth her father.

Many intelligent older couples slide into this message transmission via the child without even realizing that they are playing an insidious game. There is no malicious intent; it's just easier and more expedient. It is also *terrible* for your child. Don't ever use your child as a messenger between the two of you—no matter how busy your schedule or how insignificant the message. Nor should you use the child to get information about the other parent. Innocuous questions like "Where did Daddy go last Saturday night?" feel like an inquisition to the child of divorce. Make an ironclad rule against these often unintentional CIA tactics. If you want to know something about your ex-spouse, go to the source, not the child. Your intention may be innocent, but the child will feel like a tattler.

## WHEN IS ENOUGH?

Both of you feel rather guilty at having involved this later-in-life child in a divorce. You had waited until you thought everything was right for having the baby. But life crossed you up. Your marriage changed, and now the best-laid plans have gone awry—your beloved youngster is in the middle of a splitting older couple. How do you handle that sense of having done something terribly wrong to your child?

The easiest way to compensate for your feelings of guilt is to buy whatever the youngster wants: take her wherever she wants to go; spend every extra dollar in making him happy. *Stop. You are fooling yourself.* It is you who is being paid off—your sense of guilt is being bought and buried. Your child is actually being harmed by your excessive behavior.

When is enough? That is the question you must ask yourselves as mature divorced parents. Children feel extremely insecure without limitations in their lives; some actually feel unloved. A caring parent is a disciplining and denying parent.

Stop the excessive pampering and the unnecessary spending. Your child needs you to assuage your unnecessary feelings of guilt by dedicating yourself to good parenting. In no way can you be the "better" parent by spending a lot of money on your child. Since when did any child think Santa Claus was his daddy? Don't try to buy your child's love. Earn it. Keep it alive and well. You must know when enough is enough.

## SOME QUICK BITS OF ADVICE

**1.** Try to maintain the same roles connected with your youngster's school activities as you did before the separation. If both of you went to the PTA, continue going. If you can't go together, attend separately (and amicably).

**2.** The custodial parent must notify the other parent whenever the child is ill. This is essential not only for the other parent, but for the child. The support of both parents can be very important to a sick child.

**3.** Share the important events in your child's life, such as birthdays, Christmas, graduations, etc. Why can't you sit together at the class play? It doesn't mean you're still married. But think how meaningful it would be to your child to see you together for this important occasion in his or her life.

**4.** Religion often becomes the prerogative of one or the other parent. This can create problems. Solve these potential conflicts by acknowledging the fact that children can adapt to attending services of two different religions. The final decision of the child's religious beliefs will ultimately be the child's anyway.

**5.** Don't expect each of the two-family homes to have the same rules or methods of discipline. And stop worrying about what the other parent is doing. Just remember children are amazingly adaptable creatures. They can go to six different teachers in one day and know the do's and don'ts in each of these six classrooms.

These are but a few of the important issues that arise when two after-thirty parents decide to break up the marriage and the child stands, vulnerable and afraid, in the center of the split. No two divorce situations are the same; no two marriages are identical. But there are general principles of child care during divorce that can soften the terrible blow for the child and minimize the emotional rebound afterwards. The couple will often need outside counsel. But be careful. Few professionals have been trained to help you through your divorce while always bearing in mind the best interests of your child. The lawyer looks at the legal arrangements; the church often counsels the involved adults; your own parents are biased and often too upset to consider the impact of the divorce on their grandchild; and the pediatrician often has not been trained to do much more than offer his or her own (biased) opinion. So you might find yourself somewhat on your own regarding your child's dilemma.

But you have the maturity and the experience to work through such problems with your child. Use these guidelines and apply them to your own situation. In every event, consider the impact on your child. When you take that first responsible step, you're halfway down the path of solid parenting through the divorce period.

## BIBLIOGRAPHY

Anthony, E. James. "Children at Risk from Divorce: A Review," in E. J. Anthony and C. Koupernik, eds., *The Child in His Family: Children at Psychiatric Risk*, Vol. III, John Wiley & Sons, 1974.

Awad, G. A. "Basic Principles in Custody Assessments," *Can. Psychiatr. Assoc. J.*, 23:7, 441–447, November 1978.

Benedek, R. S. and Benedek, E. P. "Postdivorce Visitation. A Child's Right," *J. Am. Acad. Child Psychiatry*, 16:2, 256–271, Spring 1977.

Cherlin, A. "The Effect of Children on Marital Dissolution," *Demography*, 14:3, 265–72, August 1977.

Dell, P. F. and Appelbaum, A. S. "Trigenerational Enmeshment: Unresolved Ties of Single Parents to Family of Origin," *Am. J. Orthopsychiatry*, 47:1, 52–59, January 1977.

Derdeyn, A. P. "Children in Divorce: Intervention in the Phase of Separation," *Pediatrics*, 60:1, 20–27, July 1977.

Despect, J. L. *Children of Divorce*. Doubleday, 1962.

Drinan, R. F., "The Rights of Children in Modern American Family Law," *J. Family Law*, 2:101, 1962.

Duncan, J. W. "Medical, Psychologic, and Legal Aspects of Child Custody Disputes," *Mayo Clin. Proc.*, 53:7, 463–468, July 1978.

Gardner, R. A. "Social, Legal, and Therapeutic Changes That Should Lessen the Traumatic Effects of Divorce on Children," *J. Am. Acad. Psychoanal.*, 6:2, 231–247, April 1978.

Goldstein, J., Freud, A. and Solnit, A. J. *Beyond the Best Interests of the Child.* Free Press, 1973.

Kalter, N. "Children of Divorce in an Outpatient Psychiatric Population," *Am. J. Orthopsychiatry,* 47:1, 40–51, January 1977.

Kressel, K. and Deutsch, J. "Divorce Therapy: An In-Depth Survey of Therapists' Views," *Fam. Process,* 16:4, 413–443, December 1977.

Lambert, C. E., Jr. and Lambert, V. A. "Divorce: A Psychodynamic Development Involving Grief," *J. Psychiatr. Nurs.,* 15:1, 37–42, January 1977.

McDermott, John F., Jr. "Divorce and Its Psychiatric Sequelae in Children," *Arch. Gen. Psychiatry,* 23:421, November 1970.

Ransom, J. W., Schlesinger, S. and Derdeyn, A. P. "A Stepfamily in Formation," *Am. J. Orthopsychiatry,* 49:1, 36–43, January 1979.

Sorosky, Arthur D. "The Psychologilcal Effects of Divorce on Adolescents," *Adolescence,* 12:45, 123–136, Spring 1977.

Toomin, Marjorie K. "The Child of Divorce," in R. E. Hardy and J. G. Cull, eds., *Therapeutic Needs of the Family: Problems, Descriptions and Therapeutic Approaches.* Charles C. Thomas, 1974.

Wallerstein, Judith S. and Kelly, Joan B. *"The Effects of Parental Divorce: Experiences of the Preschool Child,"* J. Am. Acad. Child Psychiatry, 14:4, 600–616, Autumn 1975.

Wallerstein, Judith S. and Kelly, Joan B. "The Effects of Parental Divorce: Experiences of the Child in Later Latency," *Am. J. Orthopsychiatry,* 46:2, 256–269, April 1976.

Wallerstein, Judith S. and Kelly, Joan B. "The Effects of Parental Divorce: The Adolescent Experience," in Anthony and Koupernik, eds., *The Child in His Family: Children at Psychiatric Risk,* Vol. III. John Wiley & Sons, 1974.

# V

*Conclusion*

·

# CHAPTER TWENTY-TWO

# The Advantages
# and Joys
# of Mature Parenting

We have spent a great deal of time discussing mature parenting. You have been challenged to decide whether you are ready for child rearing after thirty. The issue of healthy babies and normal pregnancies at an older age has been explored. We have given advice in the crucial area of preventive parenting—methods and actions to assure that you will rear a healthy, well-adjusted youngster. We have attempted to answer questions frequently asked by more mature parents. Throughout this book, cautionary messages have been threaded about certain risks and dangers to be avoided during the process of after-thirty parenting. Don't think for one moment that we are pessimistic about the outcome of becoming pregnant or being a parent after you are thirty years of age. On the contrary, it is our belief that there are specific advantages and joys that are intrinsic to after-thirty parenthood. We encourage many of you who are considering postponing parenthood to minimize the impact of social, familial, and personal pressures, and give yourself permission to become an after-thirty parent. We advocate mature parenthood for many families as *the* most viable option.

Those are very strong words. We'll back them up with a dozen important reasons why mature parenting has inherent advantages and joys for many of you—advantages that you may or may not have considered.

## You've Had Your Freedom

When you have children and are relatively young, it's not uncommon to look back and wonder what you missed during the youthful years of marriage when both of you were consumed by starting a career, getting to know each other, and rearing children. There was very little time to "kick up your heels and live." The younger parent frequently wonders with reflective regret about the missed possibilities during those younger years of parenting.

You, as an after-thirty parent, don't have any of these feelings. You have had ample opportunity to explore the world around you as an individual and, together with your spouse, as a couple. You have been reckless; you have experimented and tested. You've traveled and you've played when and where you wanted. You have discovered yourself in many new and different ways. You should have little reason to live a life of regret because parenting has thwarted your chance to sample your share of life. You've had your freedom and, hopefully, have used it wisely, fully, and well enough to have prepared you to settle down into parenting without a list of unfulfilled dreams and excitements.

## You Know Who You Are

The full realization of who you are begins to crystallize during adolescence, but reaches fruition during the twenties when the total person has an opportunity for self-expression. When one commits oneself to parenting at this early age, there may be a delayed process of self-realization or a concurrent struggle between playing parent and searching for self. This can be disconcerting to both the young parent and the child. It is much healthier emotionally for a child to be brought up by parents who are certain of their own identities. The insecurity, inconsistency, and instability created by the younger parent who is grappling for self-identity during the twenties will often rub off onto the parenting process and adversely affect the child.

You know who you are—at least as much as you ever will. You have certainly had the time, opportunity, and freedom to search for yourself. Not only should you know who you are, but by thirty years of age, you should have established peace with the warring factions within your complex personality. In essence, you're reasonably satisfied and comfortable with who and what you are. Your dynamic life force is now resting in the hands of a mature person, fully cognizant of his/her own strengths and weaknesses.

Together, the two of you can honestly and clearly delineate who has the nurturing strength, who will be the better disciplinarian, who has more patience, and who has other particular parenting talents. Your realization of your total assets and liabilities allows for honest and healthy sharing in child rearing. Obviously your child will benefit from being brought up by relaxed, actualized, sharing parents who are not only comfortable with the child but also with each other, and with themselves as well.

## You Know Your Own Parents

During their twenties, most young adults begin struggling to free themselves from the more subtle influences of their parents. In adolescence, young people generally free themselves from the sense of being their parents' child and strive to become an individual in their own right. But it is during the twenties in dealing with parents that their impact, influence, and subliminal power reaches a peak of resolution. Only after these issues have been resolved and there is a comfortable, easy rapprochement between the person of over thirty and his parent can parenting the next generation proceed without getting mixed up and confused in the issues of the previous two generations. Having made peace with his own parents, the more mature parent can become a specific individual, creating his unique part as parent in his own family drama.

## YOUR CAREER IS ON AN EVEN KEEL

One of the primary reasons many of you did not decide to become a parent before thirty was that you wanted first to realize fully your education, your job opportunities, and your career. Too often the young person was forced to quit school, turn down the job in a distant city, or watch parenting take a back seat to a burgeoning career when family responsibilities added stress.

By thirty years of age, both of your careers should be stable. Certainly there will be changes, new directions, and perhaps continuing education; but you have probably reached the point where security and long-range stability give a sense of permanence to your lives and permit a steadier approach to parenting. As we discussed, there will have to be a good deal of juggling in the two-career family to make parenting a success. Rarely, however, will you have to relinquish an ambition permanently, turn down an opportunity, or quit school if you have waited until after thirty to begin parenting. As a result, your life continues at a steady forward pace. This is both a joy for the career family and an advantage to the emotional good health of the parent/child relationship.

## YOU HAVE MONEY

It costs a good deal of money to bear and rear a child in today's inflationary economy. By waiting until your careers are settled and your financial situation reasonably stable, you enter parenthood without having to sacrifice as much as younger parents.

You also have sufficient income to enjoy your child and to be a parent. The appropriate caretaker, the right schooling, the vacations, the bikes, the clothes, the cultural events are the advantages to both you and your child of waiting until you have sufficient income to rear a child comfortably in this expensive world.

## You Have Other Adult Friends

One of the major problems of early parenting is the sudden retreat of the couple into the family situation. Often this will occur before the twenties parents have had the opportunity to establish firm and lasting relationships with other adult friends. As a result, there are no escapes from the process of parenting. Or friends are often struggling with the same problems of early parenthood, so that finding mutual free time can become impossible. When young friends do get together, conversations drift back to child rearing; the younger parents often feel as if they never walked out of their front door.

When you wait until you are older to have your first child, it's highly likely that each of you will have established a number of close and meaningful relationships with individuals and couples which you may or may not share with your spouse. After the birth of your child, the nurturing of these friendships is essential, since it will provide you both with the balance needed in your life between being a mature adult and being a mature parent. You'll need time away from your child and your role as a parent. Having friends who are accessible, understanding, and who have been developed and treasured over time can provide the necessary equilibrium to make parenting a joy rather than a jail sentence.

## Your Marriage Is More Stable

Is that really true? Can you feel comfortable that you are bringing a baby into a home that has a better chance of standing solid against the rising tide of divorce? Statistics suggest that marriages among the young tend to break up more readily than those among the after-thirty. Possibly the combination of youth, inexperience, job struggles, lack of identity, financial hardship, *and* a baby is lethal to a youthful relationship.

Your more mature marriage has one of two advantages:

1. You have been married longer or lived together longer than a younger couple. You've weathered the career crises, the financial

blues, and the search for individual identity. You've come through whole and together. Adding a baby to this relationship, therefore, is not likely to undermine the foundation of your marriage.

2. If your marriage is relatively new, then you have brought a wider range of interpersonal experiences to it. You have selected a partner after careful and thoughtful consideration, knowing far better now than you would have ten or fifteen years earlier exactly who and what you wanted in a marriage. As a result, you have a better chance of making it work, not only because of your maturity but also because of your background experience. You'll probably be together as a couple at the end of the long marriage marathon.

## You Have Probably Planned This Pregnancy

Chances are good that this is a planned pregnancy. Most first pregnancies after thirty are carefully scheduled; there probably will be no resentment that this child was "accidental." If this is a second child, the spacing between children usually has been considered intelligently. You're ready to bring this child into the world—emotionally, physically, and financially. It is this sense of readiness—of planning—that offers your child the distinct advantage over unplanned twenties pregnancies that "just happen" during the first years of marriage. It is this readiness that will make the birth of your child an unlimited joy—without any strings of guilt or resentment attached.

## Your Baby Has Lowered Birth Defect Risks

What a wonderful era in which to contemplate having an after-thirty child! You know that even if you want to wait until your late thirties or early forties, you'll have the advantage of prenatal diagnosis and the right to choose termination if a defect is found in your fetus. If you accept the concept of termination of pregnancy—if a defect is found—you have *no greater risk* of birth defect in your child than younger mothers do. You now have the advantage of not being penalized for waiting to have a child.

## Your Life Has Consistency

As you've grown older, you've developed a system of responses and behaviors. During your twenties, you experimented with being several different people and finally selected the type of individual you see as yourself. You are definitively *you*. Some spontaneity still bubbles up, but much less than when you were younger, and it's a controlled, safe, relaxed spontaneity. Is this the cutting edge of creeping conservatism in your lives? Hardly. Just the start of mature, steady, predictable, intelligent behavior. It is this consistency that you, as after-thirty parents, will bring to the rearing of your child. The ability to pause before reacting, the sense of fairness, the consistency of your responses, the willingness to listen and relent, the predictability of your expectations—all these are qualities of the after-thirty adult and also of the intelligent, sensitive, successful parent.

## You Don't Need the Energy You Thought You Did

One of the great fears of the after-thirty parent is that "I won't have the energy to keep up with her. Just think how old I'll be when she's an adolescent." Be reassured. Few of us, whether we are twenty or forty years old, have the energy to keep up with an active, two-year-old. *Life* magazine once pitted a football player against an active two-and-a-half-year-old girl. The football player did everything the child did. By dinnertime, the strapping young man was falling on his face, dead tired, while the happy, active little girl was still raring to go. You will be tired out by your young child. But so are all parents. You might get a bit more tired, but not enough to cause the youngster to slow down. Remember that you don't have to be her playmate; you're her parent. Find playmates her own age and solve a lot of your energy problems.

What about being able to keep up the pace of an adolescent? What makes you think your adolescent will even invite you to keep pace with him? He will have his own friends, his own activities, his own world; you will *not* be a part of that world, nor should you be. You don't need energy to cope with the problems caused by adolescence—you need experience, understanding, balance, maturity, stability, and a calm acceptance that your child is his own person. Here again you have the advantage.


## You Are Going To Work and Live Longer

You've been worrying about having a child later in life because you're afraid that you'll take ill, or die, or lose your job and become dependent just at the crucial time when your child needs you—during adolescence or the college years. You're probably worrying unnecessarily. The mean age of survival by the time your youngster reaches adolescence will likely be in the mid-seventies or older for both men and women. In addition, retirement will probably not be mandatory before seventy. And if you want to retire, you will probably have a pension to support you. Illness is unpredictable, but it can happen to younger as well as older parents. Remember that worry only adds to the risk of deterioration, so don't fret needlessly about becoming a burden to your children.

Some creative action can prevent this:

1. Make certain you have an adequate retirement plan.
2. Keep sufficient insurance to protect your spouse in case of your death.
3. Make out a will so that there is no delay in supporting those left behind.
4. If possible, buy the home or apartment in which you live. This will keep a roof over your heads as you grow older.
5. Be sure both of you keep up your driving skills.
6. Continue regular physical check-ups.
7. Stop smoking.
8. Drink only in moderation.
9. Reduce stress—a major killer—as much as possible, despite your careers and ambitions. You'll never get that promotion if you're six feet under.
10. Teach your child independence as early as possible. Also teach him/her what it feels like to care for one of you when you are ill,

to prepare meals for the family, to take other responsibilities. Teach him/her that there may come a time when some shifting in support will be needed. Care emotionally for each other, but don't depend on each other after he/she grows into adulthood, unless it becomes absolutely essential.

These are some of the advantages of being an after-thirty parent. The joys are the same as for any parent—having a child to touch, hold, feed, nurture, rear, teach, guide, watch, love, and lead into the world as a fully realized adult. Your joy may be just a shade greater than a younger person's because you have waited longer; you have the security and the stability and the money to move freely and enjoy the experience; and you have planned for this child as carefully as you have prepared for anything else in your life.

It's never too late to fall in love—with a child, with being a parent, with having a family. Not only is it not too late; we feel that after thirty may, in actuality, be the very best time.

# Index

Abortion, elective, 67, 69
Accountant, 166
  selection of, 167
Adolescence, 253, 265–266
  communication in, 267–268
  and decision making, 258
  discipline and rewards in, 269–270
  friendships in, 255–257
  independence in, 271–275, 321
  mood swings in, 259–260
  parental love in, 270–271
  and parent image, 254–255
  permissiveness in, 261–262
  and personal identity, 268–269
  and privacy, 259
  rebellion in, 260–261
  and responsibility, 257–258
  role models in, 262–263
  self-actualization in, 263–264
  sex education in, 249
  sexuality in, 311
  signals in, 199, 203
Adolescents, 325–326
  as babysitters, 42
  and blending previous families,
    303

Adoption
  and age discrimination, 49–51,
    52–53, 58
  of different and handicapped
    children, 56–57
  mixing natural and adopted
    children, 111
  and "natural order" of families, 52
  of older children, 57–58
  reasons for, 54–55
  and sex of child, 110
  and sterility, 52
  telling children about, 55–56
Affection, shifting from husband to
    baby, 42–43
Age, and number and spacing of
    children, 108–109
  see also Maternal age, Maternal
    death, Paternal age
Age discrimination, and adoption,
    49–51, 52–53, 58
Aging, and parenting readiness, 19
Alpha feto protein, and nervous
    system defects, 72, 74
American Red Cross, 147

Amniocentesis, and early detection
    of birth defects, 71–73, 88
Arts (the), helping children
    appreciate, 239
Atwood family, 265–266

Babies, 224–231, 234–236, 238–239
    fat vs. skinny, 237
    see also Breast feeding, Premature
        babies
Baby
    getting ready for, 32–33
    position during delivery, 62–63
    as rival of husband, 138–139,
        155–158
    timing, in two-career family,
        116–117
Babysitters, 42, 233
    shared, 231–232
Baby talk, attitude toward, 236
Bacall, Lauren, 152
Bambi (movie), 179
Barbano, H., 70
Basic Handbook of Child Psychiatry
    (Nophitz), 208
Baths, during pregnancy, 91
Bedwetting, 199
Belonging, vs. ownership, 138
Between Parent and School
    (Kappelman/Ackerman), 251
Bicycles, for children, 168–169, 170
Bird, Caroline, 161
Birth defects, 324
    early detection of, 71–74
    fear of, 44–45
    and maternal age, 65–67
    see also Chromosomal defects,
        Structural defects
Birth expenses, medical, 106, 161
Birth rates, and mature parents, 4
Body changes, during pregnancy, 84
Body image, and motherhood, 154
Books, on child rearing, 148
Boston Children's Medical Center,
    184

Bowel defects, early detection of, 73
Bowling, during pregnancy, 83
Brady Bunch, The (TV show), 288
Breast care, during pregnancy, 88
Breast feeding, 88, 92, 226–227
    and career women, 118
    and lactating, 94
    and vaginal lubrication, 93–94
Budgeting, 162–163

Caesarean section, 63, 92
Caffeine, during pregnancy, 85
Calcium (in diet), during
    pregnancy, 84–85
Caplan, Frank, 235
Caplan, Theresa, 235
Capparell, H. V., 208
Career, 5, 44, 322
    and blending previous families,
        295–297
    and delayed marriage, 23
    and single parents, 282
    see also Two-career family,
        Working
Career man, programming time for,
    130–132
Career readiness, 23–27, 28
Career woman
    child care vs. work, 164
    interrupting work to have child,
        100–104
    and motherhood, 152–153
    programming time for, 129–130
    time off before and after
        delivery, 117–119
Caretakers, 39–40, 44, 118, 175,
    227, 230–231
    and discipline, 192
    and emergencies, 186–188
Carter, Rosalyn, 152
Central nervous system. See
    Nervous system defects
Chauffeuring school-age children,
    247–248
Cheating, during pregnancy, 34

Chewing gum, during pregnancy, 86
Childbearing, time off for, 26
Child care
  and blending previous families,
    297
  vs. career, 164
  cost of, 106, 161, 164
  options for, 164
  preparation for, 39–41
  *see also* Caretakers,
    Househusbandry
Child of divorce, 304
  and buying love, 313–314
  and extended family, 305–306
  as messenger, 312–313
  and parental sexuality, 310–311
  phone-rearing, 311–312
  and visits, 309–310
  *see also* Custody
Children
  adopted, 55–58
  cost of raising, 27–28, 161–162,
    167–169
  dependency needs of, 14
  expenses: needs vs. wants,
    168–169, 170
  illness of, 155, 185–190, 193–194,
    314
  mentally retarded, 86
  mixing natural and adopted, 111
  number of, 99–112
  orientation toward, 22
  physical and mental health of,
    185–195
  and quality of marriage, 17
  spacing of, 99–112
  *see also* Handicapped children,
    Only child, Preschool children,
    Preventive parenting, School-
    age children, Special children
Chromosomal defects, 77
  diagnosing, 69
  early detection of, 72
  and maternal age, 65–67, 68–69

Cigarette smoking, during
    pregnancy, 86–87
Clark, R. A., 208
Cleft lip, 70, 71
Cleft palate, 70
Closer Look (parents organization),
    247, 251
Clothes, for children, 168, 170
Coffee, during pregnancy, 85
College
  cost of, 161, 165
  saving for, 163
  *see also* Education
Communication, 194–195
  in adolescence, 267–268
  with school-age children, 250
  *see also* Signalling
Compensation, and single parents,
    281–283, 286–287
Consistency, 325
  in discipline, 191–192
Contraception (partial), and breast
    feeding, 94
Cost, of raising children, 27–28,
    161–162, 167–169
  *see also* Expenses, Financial
    factors
Crying, of babies, 226–227
Custody, and child of divorce,
    307–308
Cystic fibrosis, 70–71

Day care centers, 193
Decision making
  and adolescence, 258
  and only child, 211–212, 221
Dehydration, 190
Delivery
  baby's position during, 62–63
  high risk, 62
  and husband-wife relationship, 33
  *see also* Labor
Dependency needs
  of children, 14, 236
  and retirement age, 110

Developmental Disabilities Council,
    76
Diabetes, 70
Diet, during pregnancy, 84–85, 90,
    95
    see also Nutrition
Dieting, during pregnancy, 86
Directory of Medical Specialists, 235
Discipline, 176–177
    in adolescence, 269–270
    consistency in, 191–192
    and only child, 216–218
    and preschool children, 225
    after separation, 314
    see also Punishment
Disney, Walt (early movies), 179
Division of special education,
    251–252
Divorce, 5
    vs. marriage, 304
    see also Child of divorce
Doctor. See Obstetrician,
    Pediatrician
Douches, during pregnancy, 91
Down's Syndrome, 76–77, 109–110
    early detection of, 72
    and maternal age, 68–69
Drugs, for nausea and vomiting
    during pregnancy, 87
Dumbo (movie), 179

Eating problems, of preschool
    children, 229–230
Education, 24
    costs, 107
    for handicapped children,
        246–247
    of mature parents, 5
    see also College, Sex education
Educational expectations, and only
    child, 212–213
Emergencies, handling, 185–190
Emotional flexibility, and number
    and spacing of children,
    104–106

Emotional readiness, 11–20
Entertainment, during pregnancy, 41
Environments (different), and
    children's behavior, 192
"Estate planning," 165
Events (sharing), after separation,
    314
Exercises
    after birth, 93
    during pregnancy, 83, 90, 95
Expenses (children), needs vs.
    wants, 168–169, 170
    see also Birth expenses, Financial
    factors, Medical expenses
Experimentation, and only child,
    211, 221
Ex-spouses, 294–295, 297
Extended family, and child of
    divorce, 305–306
Extracurricular activities, and only
    child, 221

Failure, and only child, 212, 213
Familial abnormalities, inheritance
    of, 70–71, 77
Families, previous (blending),
    288–290
    and careers, 295–297
    and ex-spouses, 294–295, 297
    and lifestyles, 291–292
    and nuclear family, 298–299
    and parenting philosophy,
        292–294
    and stepparenting, 299–303
Fat diet (high), during pregnancy,
    85
Father
    and creative individualism,
        141–142
    friendships of, 140–141
    as husband, 136–139
    private time of, 139–140
    problems of, 143–145
    as role model, 142–143

as structured professional,
134–135
Fatherhood, 26
preparation for, 46–48
and "wife care," 44–45
see also Husband, Paternal age
Feeding baby, 226–227
see also Breast feeding
Feminism, and motherhood,
152–153
Fetal death, and maternal age, 64
Fetal detection, and birth defects,
65–67
Fetal movements, 92
and ultrasound, 74
Fetoscopy, 74
Financial factors, 159–170, 322
and child of divorce, 308–309
and number and spacing of
children, 106–107
see also Cost, Expenses
Financial readiness, 27–29
Financial readjustment, and birth of
baby, 43
Financial security, long-term
(child), 165–167
Flexible demand feeding, 226–227
Flexibility readiness, 16
Flu vaccine, during pregnancy, 91
Folic acid, during pregnancy, 85
Freedom, 320
and only child, 213–214
Friends, child's fantasy, 199
Friendships, 42
of adolescents, 255–257
of children, 176
of only child, 210, 212, 215–216
of parents, 36–38, 141–142,
153–154, 242–243, 323
of siblings, 109

Gall bladder disease, 85
Genetic counselling, and planning
pregnancy, 70–71, 77
German measles, see Rubella

"Goodness," of children, 239
Grandmother, role of, 150–152
Grandparents, 192, 260, 305–306
Green family, 196–200
Gregg, Elizabeth M., 184
Groups (children's), play vs.
illnesses, 193–194
Guidance (anticipatory), for child,
182–183
Guilt, and buying love, 313–314

Handicapped children, 45
adopting, 56–57
education for, 246–247
Harris, Julie, 221
Hay, S., 70
Hemophilia, 72
Hemorrhoids, during pregnancy, 84
High blood pressure, during
pregnancy, 84–85, 92
Holidays, and only child, 215–216
Hook, Ernest, 68
Horger, E. O., 3d., 70
Hormone levels, during pregnancy,
93
Househusbandry, 26, 120–122
Housing, for children's growth, 29,
33, 106
How to Start Your Own Preschool
Playgroup (Watts), 231
Humphrey, Hubert, 57
Husband
baby as rival of, 138–139, 155–158
and natural childbirth, 90
see also Father, Fatherhood,
Househusbandry
Husband/wife care, as preparation
for parenthood, 41–45
Husband-wife relationship, as
preparation for parenthood,
31–35

Identity (personal)
in adolescence, 268–269
and motherhood, 152

Illness (children), 155
  as emergency, 185–190
  and groups, 193–194
  parental support during, 314
Immaturity (prolonged), and only
    child, 210–211
Income (family), 5
Independence
  in adolescence, 271–275
  and children, 178–179
  and only child, 211–212
Infant mortality, and maternal age,
    64–65, 70
Infection, during pregnancy, 89
Inflation, 27
Inheritance, of familial
    abnormalities, 70–71, 77
Injury, as emergency, 185–190
Insurance broker, 165–166
  selection of, 167
Insurance planning, 165–166
Intelligence, of children, 238–239
Interactions (with children),
    finishing, 184
Intuition, 18–19
Investments, and accountant, 166
Iron (in diet), during pregnancy, 85

Jealousy, and spacing of children,
    109
Job performance, affected by
    parenthood, 24–26
Jogging, during pregnancy, 83
Johnson, Ladybird, 152
"Junk foods," during pregnancy, 85

Kane, Dr. Sidney, 62–64
Ketones (excretion of), during
    pregnancy, 86
Kidney defects, early detection of, 73
Kindergarten, 193

Labor, during delivery, 83, 90
Lactation, and breast feeding, 94
"Latency period," in childhood,
    241–242

Lawyer, 167
  and preparation of will, 165
Learning, children's progress in,
    178–179
La Leche League, 88
Leg lifts, straight, 93
Life insurance, decreasing, 166
Lifestyles, and blending previous
    families, 291–292
Loneliness, of only child, 214–216
Loss (of parent), 284
  and mourning, 285
Love, 155–158
  for baby, 226, 227
  showing children, 179–180, 183
  see also Affection
Lubrication, for sexual intercourse
    after delivery, 94

Macho maleness, 121
March of Dimes, 76
Marriage, 323–324
  average age of, 4–5
  children and quality of, 17
  vs. divorce, 304
  preparation for parenthood,
    31–35
  two-career, 23
Maternal age
  and baby's position during
    delivery, 62
  and birth defects, 65–67
  and Down's Syndrome, 68–69, 77
  and fetal death, 64
  and infant mortality, 64–65
  and nervous system defects, 74
  and premature babies, 63–64, 90
  and structural defects, 70
Maternal death (risk of), during
    pregnancy, 95–97
Mature parents, characteristics of,
    4–5
Maturity (forced), and only child,
    209–210

Mealtime atmosphere, and eating
    problems, 229–230
Meat (in diet), during pregnancy,
    84
Medical expenses, for children, 162
Medical insurance, 161
Men, average age of marriage for, 4
Meningitis, 190
Mental retardation, prevention of,
    86
Mental security (of child), during
    emergencies, 187–188
Milestone recorder
    of child's development, 237–238
    for single parents, 283, 286–287
Miller family, 266
Miscarriage, risk of, 87
Mongolism. *See* Down's Syndrome
Mood swings, in adolescence,
    259–260
Motherhood, 118, 146–148
    and body image, 154
    and career, 152–153
    energy for, 149–150
    and friends, 153–154
    and grandmother's role, 150–152
    and loss of orderliness, 154–155
    and love relationships, 155–158
    preparation for, 45–46
Mourning, and loss, 285
Movies, and exploration of values,
    179

National Institute of Child Health
    and Human Development,
    71–72
"Natural" action myth, 164
Natural childbirth, 88–89
    and husband, 90
"Natural order" of families reaction,
    52, 55
Nausea, during pregnancy, 87
Neatness, and young children, 155
Nervous system defects
    and alpha feto protein, 74

early detection of, 72, 73, 74
    and maternal age, 65–67
Nuclear family, and blending
    previous families, 298–299
Number of children, 99–103
    and emotional flexibility, 104–106
    and financial factors, 106–107
    myth vs. reality, 109–112
    and parental age, 108–109
Nursery, decorating, 236–237
Nursery schools, 193
Nutrition, during pregnancy, 84–85
    *see also* Diet

Obstetrician, selection of, 81
Only child, 110, 220, 222
    and decision making, 211–212,
        221
    and discipline, 216–218
    and educational expectations,
        212–213
    and experimentation, 211, 221
    and failure, 212, 213
    and freedom, 213–214
    friendships of, 210, 212, 215–216
    and independence, 211–212
    loneliness of, 214–216
    parental competition and,
        218–219
    parental role and, 212
    peer relationships and, 212, 215
    performance and, 221
    punishment and, 216–218
    relatives and, 215
    rewards for, 219
Orderliness, and young children,
    154–155
Organization, and young children,
    20–21
Orgasm, during pregnancy, 89
Overstimulation, and only child,
    219–221

Parental competition, and only
    child, 218–219

Parental love, for adolescents, 270–271
Parental role, and only child, 212
Parental sexuality, and child of divorce, 310–311
Parent Effectiveness Training, 234
Parenthood
  career readiness for, 23–27
  classes in, 234
  and divorce, 306–307
  emotional readiness for, 11–20
  financial readiness for, 27–29
  mature, 319–327
  philosophy, and blending previous families, 292–294
  and single parents, 282
  social readiness for, 20–23
  spontaneous, 10
  see also Preventive parenting, Shared parenting
Parenting Advisor, The (Caplan), 235
Paternal age, and Down's Syndrome, 69
Pediatrician, 106, 188, 191, 250
  selection of, 40, 148, 234–235
Peer relationships, and only child, 212, 215
Perception, of self as parent, 12
Performance, and only child, 221
Permissiveness, in adolescence, 261–262
Pets, 239–240
Phone-rearing, child of divorce, 311–312
Physical activity, and uterine contractions, 87–88
Pinocchio (movie), 179
Planned Parenthood, 81
Planning pregnancy, and financial factors, 161–170
Play, 236
  in groups, 193–194, 231–232
"Postpartum blues," 224

Pregnancy
  continuing or terminating, 75–77
  detection of birth defects during, 71–74
  financial factors in planning, 161–170
  and husband-wife relationship, 31–35
  questions and answers on, 81–97
  see also Abortion
Premature babies, and maternal age, 63–64, 90
Prenatal detection, and birth defects, 65–67
Preparation for parenthood
  and child care, 39–41
  and friends, 36–38
  and husband/wife care, 41–45
  and marriage, 31–35
  and relatives, 35–36
  and self care, 45–48
  and work colleagues, 38–39
Preschool, 232
Preschool children, 224, 231–233, 235–239
  and blending previous families, 301
  and discipline, 225
  eating problems of, 229–230
  racial prejudice and, 234
Preventive parenting, 173–184
Privacy (need for), during adolescence, 259
Protein diet (high), during pregnancy, 84
Psychological adjustment
  and labor, 90
  and pregnancy, 95
PTA meetings, 246
Punishment
  and only child, 216–218
  and rewards, 176–178
  for school-age children, 249
  see also Discipline
"Push-aways," 93

Quality time, 103, 118, 119–120,
179, 181
for anticipatory guidance,
182–183
for child care, 28, 40–41, 44
for child's internal world, 182
and communication, 194
for finishing interactions, 184
for love, 183
for responsibility, 15
and role model, 183
and rules, 183–184
for values, 183

Racial prejudice, and preschool
children, 234
Reading, and developing skills, 238
Rebellion, in adolescence, 260–261
Recreation, and single parents, 282
Rehearsing, and shared caretaking,
189–191
Relatives
and only child, 215
and preparation for parenthood,
35–36
Religion, conflict in, 314
Responsibility, 15
and adolescence, 257–258
and school-age children, 243
sharing, 34–35, 42, 139, 189–191
Rest, during pregnancy, 87, 90
Retirement, 273, 326
and dependency, 110
Rewards
in adolescence, 266, 269–270
for only child, 219
and punishments, 176–178
Rh blood incompatibility, 71
Role maintenance, during separation, 314
Role model, father as, 142–143
Role models
of missing parent, 284
parents as, 183, 244, 262–263
"Role reversal," 121, 272

Roles, 12–14
sex, 233–234
Romping, 150, 224
Rubella, 92, 95
Rules
for adolescents, 259–260
for children, 183–184
negative, for single parents, 286

Sacrifices, and raising children, 28
Salaries, 5
Savings, 29, 162–163
School
as environment, 175–176
and handicapped children,
246–247
progress in, 244–245
public vs. private, 245–246
and special children, 250–251
School-age children, 241–242,
244–246, 251–252
and blending previous families,
302
chauffeuring, 247–248
communication with, 250
punishment for, 249
responsibility and, 243
sex education and, 247, 248–249
School/parent organizations, 246
Self-actualization, 320–321
in adolescence, 263–264
Self care, preparation for, 45–48
Self-image, 154, 158
Self-sufficiency, during adolescence,
266
Separation, 304–305
fears and crying, 227
see also Child of divorce, Divorce
Sex
roles, 233–234
of unborn child, 110
understanding and trust during
pregnancy, 33–34
Sex education, and school-age
children, 247, 248–249

Sexism, in communication, 268
Sexual intercourse
    after delivery, 93–94
    during pregnancy, 89–90, 93
Shared parenting, in two-career
    family, 122–128
Sharing responsibilities, 34–35, 42,
    139, 189–191
Sibling rivalry, and spacing of
    children, 109, 112
Sickle cell disease, 71
Signalling, behavior as, 196–207
*Signals: What Your Child Is Really
    Telling You* (Kappelman/
    Ackerman), 198
Sills, Beverly, 152
Single parents, 279–281, 285, 287
    negative rules for, 286
    and recreation, 282
    and socializing, 283–284
Single persons, and deferral of
    marriage, 5
Skiing, during pregnancy, 83
Sleep, during pregnancy, 87
Smith, Cynthia, 156–158
Smoking, during pregnancy, 86–87
Social activities
    for parents, 21, 22
    and single parents, 282
Social drinking, during pregnancy, 86
Socializing
    of single parent, 284
    of single parent's child, 283–284
Social pressures, 21–22
Social readiness, 20–23
Socioeconomic conditions, and high
    blood pressure, 85
Space
    for baby, 33
    for children's growth, 29, 106, 111
Spacing of children, 99–103
    and emotional flexibility, 104–106
    and financial factors, 106–107
    myth vs. reality, 109–112
    and parental age, 108–109

Special children, help for, 250–252
Speech, as bridge to child, 194–195
Spending styles, and birth of baby,
    43
Spock, Dr. Benjamin, 148
Sports, during pregnancy, 83–84
Stepparenting, and blending
    previous families, 299–303
Sterility, acceptance of, 52
Stress, 326
    and consistency in discipline, 192
Structural defects, 67–68
    and maternal age, 70
Stuttering, 238
Survival, mean age of, 326
Swaddling, 226

Taxes, and accountant, 166
Teacher's authority, child's response
    to, 176
Television
    and adopted children, 56
    and exploration of values, 179
Thumb-sucking, 237
Time, 40–41
    for baby in two-career family,
        116–117
    and only child, 219
    to prepare for baby, 33
    private, 139–140
    programming, for contact with
        child, 174–175
    in two-career family, 128–132
    *see also* Quality time
Toilet training, 227–229
Toys, 168–169, 170, 235–236
Travel, during pregnancy, 91
Two-career family, 25, 34–35, 115,
    135
    child care in, 106
    and househusbandry, 120–122
    loss of income because of
        pregnancy in, 106
    and pre- and post-delivery period,
        117–119

programming time in, 128–132
and quality time, 119–120
and shared parenting, 122–128
and timing of baby, 116–117
*Two-Paycheck Marriage, The*
    (Bird), 161

Ultrasound, and early detection of
    birth defects, 73–74, 88
Understanding, of children, 182

Vacations, and only child, 215–216
Vaccinations, during pregnancy, 91
Vaginal lubrication, and breast
    feeding, 93–94
Vaginal stretching exercises, 90
Values, 247
    exploration of, 178–179, 183
Varicose veins, during pregnancy, 84
Vegetables, during pregnancy, 85
Vegetarian diet, during pregnancy,
    84
Victoria, Queen of England, 34
Viral illness, during pregnancy, 91

Vitamins, during pregnancy, 85
Vomiting, during pregnancy, 87

Watts, Harriet, 231
Weight gain, during pregnancy, 86
*What To Do When There's
    Nothing To Do* (Boston
    Children's Medical Center—
    Gregg), 184
"Wife care," and fathers, 44–45
Will, preparation of, 165
"Woman above" position, during
    pregnancy, 93
Women, average age of marriage, 4
    *see also* Career woman
Work colleagues, and preparation for
    parenthood, 38–39
Working, during pregnancy, 82–83
    *see also* Career, Career woman

X-ray, 73

"Youth cult." *See* Age
    discrimination